15
YEARS OF WAR

How the Longest War in U.S. History
Affected a Military Family in Love, Loss,
and the Cost of Service

Kristine Schellhaas

Savas Beatie

California

Originally published by Life Publishing in 2016 / Cover design: Colleen Cahill, with Ian Hughes.

Library of Congress Cataloging-in-Publication Data

Names: Schellhaas, Kristine, author.
Title: 15 years of war : how the longest war in U.S. history affected a
military family in love, loss, and the cost of service / by Kristine Schellhaas.
Other titles: How the longest war in U.S. history affected a military family
in love, loss, and the cost of service
Description: El Dorado Hills, California : Savas Beatie, [2017]
Identifiers: LCCN 2017019155| ISBN 9781611213485 (pbk) | ISBN 9781611213492 (ebk.)
Subjects: LCSH: Schellhaas, Kristine. | Marine Corps spouses--United
States--Biography. | United States. Marine Corps--Military life. | Iraq
War, 2003-2011--Personal narratives, American. | Afghan War,
2001--Personal narratives. | Officers' spouses--United States--Biography.
| United States. Marine Corps--Officers--Biography. | Deployment
(Strategy)--Psychological aspects. | Families of military
personnel--United States--Social conditions--21st century. | Camp
Pendleton (Calif.)--Biography.
Classification: LCC VE25 .S34 2017 | DDC 956.7044/3450922 [B] --dc23
LC record available at https://lccn.loc.gov/2017019155

First Savas Beatie edition, first printing
ISBN: 978-1-61121-348-5
eISBN: 978-1-61121-349-2

SB

Published by
Savas Beatie LLC
989 Governor Drive, Suite 102
El Dorado Hills, CA 95762

Phone: 916-941-6896
(E-mail) sales@savasbeatie.com

Savas Beatie titles are available at special discounts for bulk purchases in the United States by corporations, institutions, and other organizations. For more details, please contact Special Sales, P.O. Box 4527, El Dorado Hills, CA 95762, or you may e-mail us at sales@savasbeatie.com, or visit our website at www.savasbeatie.com for additional information.

Proudly published, printed, and warehoused in the United States of America.

This book is dedicated to the men and women in uniform who serve our great nation, particularly those who will never feel their homeland beneath their feet again; to the military spouses who serve in their own way by volunteering and keeping the home fires burning, and to our children drafted into this lifestyle.

"Your freedom is the most expensive thing you have.
Even if you're not the one who paid for it, use it well."

— Unknown

Table of Contents

Preface   7

PART ONE: Off to Great Places

Reality Check   9

Back to his Roots   11

Waiting is the Hardest Part   14

The Adventure Begins   20

Sun on My Face, Song in My Heart   26

He Put a Ring on It   36

The Hills Are Alive with the Sound of Marines   38

Going to the Chapel   56

Go Forth Boldly   59

PART TWO: If You Can't Be Safe, Be Deadly

This is War   67

Freedom Isn't Free   85

Down With the Sickness   91

Going Back to Cali   93

Keep Calm and Aloha On   104

Together is a Wonderful Place to Be   109

Creating a New Destiny   114

A Beautiful Gift   120

Into the Fire   127

Seeds of Friendship   136

Table of Contents (continued)

Weeds in the Garden   142

Calling in Reinforcements   145

Monster-in-Law   149

Darkest Before the Dawn   158

Happiness is Homemade   164

Pain is Baby Leaving the Body   167

Back to the Grind   174

Double the Diapers, Double the Fun   180

In a Van Down by the River   187

PART THREE: Discovering Rock Bottom

Stranded in the Desert   197

The Cost of Imperfection   207

Broken Crayons Still Color   214

No Distance is Too Far   218

War Torn Afghanistan and the Taliban   224

The Best Way Out is Through   234

War Pigs   242

Let Go or Be Dragged   252

Every Picture Tells a Story   267

"They Sicken of the Calm, Who Knew the Storm"   274

PART FOUR: Turning the Page

Girl: A Giggle with Glitter on It   281

Smile Because it Happened   283

Table of Contents (continued)

Grab a Straw—Because You Suck   292

Hey I Just Met You and This is Crazy.
But She's My Momma and I'm Your Baby   303

Be Brave Enough to Start a Conversation that Matters   306

Don't Look Back—You're Not Going That Way   310

Create the Thing That You Wish Existed   314

Let the Wild Rumpus Begin   317

Let's Meet in our Dreams   322

These Sweatpants are the Only Thing That Fit Me Now   329

The Girl Who Smiles When Her Heart is Broken   336

A Rainbow of Chaos   344

Run Wild My Child   349

PART FIVE: Hold the Vision, Trust the Process

The Secret to Getting Ahead is Getting Started   355

Courage, Dear Heart   360

Be the Voice for Those Who Cannot Speak   364

Purpose and a Plan   366

There's No Education like Adversity   371

Author's Note   375

Acknowledgments   378

Honor the Fallen   382

Preface

I have done my best to offer accurate accounts of the people, places, and conversations included in this book. The email correspondence between Ross and I is real, though much of it has been combined or condensed for brevity's sake.

This memoir tells our story, but I willingly acknowledge that there will be some people we've met along the way who, when asked, would disagree with our version of events as they occurred. I respect their opinion and have given these characters different names, identifying details, and characteristics to protect their privacy.

The Department of Defense has conducted a security review of this book and has approved it for release. We're indebted to the handful of military members who have given their time to review the stories shared within the text for accuracy. We have also worked with the families of the fallen, whose loved ones' lives were graciously given in defense of our great nation. We are grateful for their support in telling the stories of the sacrifices of these men.

Part One

Off to Great Places

"Where we love is home;
home that our feet may leave, but not
our hearts."

—Oliver Wendell Holmes, Sr.

1

Reality Check

★ ★ ★

The day I realized I'd fallen madly in love with a man in uniform, I never imagined that I'd find myself sitting at his side, hunkered down under a highway overpass, waiting and praying to escape the fury of the F4 tornadoes nearby.

We were somewhere between Chicago and Sioux Falls—halfway between Virginia and California on one of countless such relocations at the Marine Corps' behest. The car swayed side to side for hours while the storm raged around us. All we could do was keep our kids calm, and try to find the humor in our situation.

Eventually, I got to a point where I closed my eyes and considered just how exactly I'd gotten myself there. Love. It's a funny thing. It had taken me places I never thought I'd go; it let me do things I never thought I'd do.

I met Ross in 1996. I was a wild 19-year-old, living it up in the summer after my first year of college. Sergeant Ross Schellhaas moved home after his four-year enlistment and was certain the Corps was a memory he only wanted to see in his rearview mirror.

He took me to the Western Idaho Fair on a date, and somewhere between the funnel cakes and Ferris wheel, I began to fall in love. I have so many great memories from that time in our life. Ross was laid back, caring, and funny. His sarcastic wit fit well with mine, and being with him was just easy. Of course, his well-built six-foot frame didn't hurt his chances either.

But soon the nostalgia of the Corps began whispering to him like the siren she is. He joined the Marine Reserves while attending college and signed up for an officer training program. I had no idea what that meant. We were young, determined, and ready to see where life would take us.

Several years later, we graduated from college. I moved to Arizona for work, and Ross returned to life as an active duty Marine in 2001. Those five years together brought an engagement; he was the best man I knew, and to me, it would be worth any sacrifices and hardships to be with him.

I was working full time, waiting for him to graduate from a school in Quantico, Virginia. I didn't know it then—and I wouldn't have believed it anyway—but it was the first of countless days, weeks, and months I would spend waiting for my Marine.

It was also the first time I'd played the military waiting game, knowing we'd be moving soon, but not knowing where. In my mind, it could have been anywhere in the world. I woke up each day mentally checking off another box. I kept telling myself it wouldn't be much longer. Soon. Soon we would be together again.

2

Back to His Roots

All I had ever wanted was to become a Marine. I signed up and left for boot camp after high school graduation in 1992. Like so many things in life, the Corps didn't meet my expectations—I had chased the *image*. I expected to be training, shooting, and deploying—I was left wanting. Despite making friends I knew I'd keep for life, I was nothing but dissatisfied with my time on active duty; the biggest upset was not facing combat. I didn't realize that those crucial years were shaping me into the person I would become.

I said goodbye to the Corps in the summer of 1996 and moved home with every intention of following in my mom's footsteps to become a high school teacher and coach. I enrolled in college, and put my Montgomery GI Bill benefits to good use. I reconnected with old friends, and looked forward to settling into the regular routine of a college student. And that's where I met Kristine.

I have to admit my first impression wasn't a good one. Sure, she was hot, but I was convinced that she was a spoiled, high-maintenance chick because of where she grew up. Thank God I actually took the time to get to know her, because it didn't take long for me to realize that in addition to being exceptionally smart, Kristine was humble and down-to-earth. She was like no other girl I'd ever met, and it wasn't long before I was completely head over heels for her.

As good as my life at home was, after a while I started missing my life in the Marine Corps—mostly the closeness of the men I served with, and the very spartan life we lived. As time passed, I realized I wanted to go back and see, once and for all, if I could pass the test on the battlefield.

I joined the Marine Corps Reserves, a stepping-stone on the path back to active duty, and set my new goal of becoming an officer. Acceptance into the Platoon Leader's Course program meant I would attend the Officer Candidate School, OCS, my time split over the course of two summers during my last two years of college.

After I graduated, I could then either accept or deny the commission. There was no guarantee I'd be able to secure an infantry contract like when I had enlisted; I would have to compete for it. I could land somewhere in the Combat Arms MOS community, Military Occupational Specialty—a job assignment in the military, with artillery, combat engineers, infantry, tanks or tracks, but I could also get supply, communications or one of 30-plus other career fields. All I wanted was to go back to my infantry roots.

In June 2000, I accepted my Marine officer commission, read aloud before witnesses and administered by my father, a Naval Academy graduate and retired Navy commander.

Later that summer I returned to Quantico to complete officer training at The Basic School, TBS. I conducted an informal poll on the first day of class, asking how many ground contract men like me wanted infantry as their MOS. A little over half of the 25 eligible men in my platoon wanted it.

Many of them had a romantic view of what the infantry was like. I at least knew what to expect. Life in the field can be miserable, and it requires a particular set of attributes to be able to thrive in that kind of discomfort. It's not always the athletic guy, the smart

In the field at TBS, The Basic School at Quantico, Virginia

guy, the dumb guy or the strong guy who makes a good infantryman. It requires someone who is resilient and focuses outwardly when most tend to focus on their own misery.

Fortunately for me, we went through TBS in winter, and many who had their hearts set on joining the infantry quickly changed their minds after the first few field exercises. Going to the field is important for honing skills: conducting patrols, fire support methods, and offensive and defensive techniques.

For many of them, it was their first exposure to basic Marine Corps elements: lack of sleep, freezing weather, annoying ticks, and all the other unpleasant things that came with infantry life.

Upon graduation we all created an MOS wish list for our job. Our leaders would then slate us for positions, haggling and trading Marines to fill their quotas, similar to drafting sports teams. The higher we graduated in the class, the more likely it would be that we'd get our MOS. But just because we wanted it didn't mean we'd get it.

By the time we started filling out our wish lists, only six of the 25 men still wanted infantry. I was thrilled to be one of the three assigned; I hadn't rejoined the Corps to be anything other than a grunt officer.

I was selected by the staff platoon commanders in my company to act as the class commandant for Infantry Officer Course, IOC, the next phase of training for those who received infantry billets. I would be the conduit between the instructors and students at IOC. It was an administrative job of sorts. I would also be responsible for passing on information and making sure students were ready for instruction, that they were where they needed to be.

3

Waiting is the Hardest Part

Spring 2001
Quantico, Virginia
Phoenix, Arizona

*I*t was another day, and I was spending it as usual waiting for him when he called me.

"Hey, babe."

My heart sank; I could hear it in his voice: something was wrong.

"What's up? What's wrong?"

"Nothing major, just a small setback." As he paused my mind raced with a million possibilities.

"It's crazy, really. We were doing a moto-run and . . . "

"Moto-run?" While he had been in the Reserves throughout college, it was barely a blip on my radar. Our lives were hardly affected by his service, and he hadn't used that many acronyms.

"Motivational run: moto-run. We're getting close to graduation, so it's a way for us to do something together before we get split up for our specialty training."

"Okay," I said still waiting for the boom to drop. "So you were on a moto-run and . . . ?"

"Well, I stepped in a pothole, sprained my ankle. Damn thing is swollen to the size of my calf, and my whole foot is purple; I'm going to be on crutches for a while."

He paused again, and I knew it wasn't the injury that had him upset.

"They're not going to let me move on to infantry training. I have to wait and rehab my leg."

And there it was. I imagined Ross in pain, unable to continue training. I knew secretly it was killing him. I wished that I could be there to hold him and tell him everything was going to be okay.

"So which one is it, the right or the left?"

"The right one, of course."

We both laughed. Since we'd been together he'd suffered any number of minor injuries, but they only ever seemed to happen to the right side of his body.

"That right side," I said smiling into the phone. "I thought we talked about this. While you're training, you're supposed to expose the other side from time to time." I paused a beat. "So, I guess the real question is—how long?"

"Twelve weeks," he said with a heavy sigh. "I have to wait for the next IOC class to pick up. It sucks—but it is what it is. They've got me in rehab twice daily with stem and therapy exercises. When I'm not doing that, I'll be answering phones and reading books."

"It'll turn out the way it's meant to be," I said, not believing my own words. I didn't want him to sense my disappointment. I had already turned in the paperwork to notify the apartment complex manager of my impending move. I didn't have the money for the substantially higher month-to-month fee for three more months. This was a disaster that I had to figure out on my own.

"Don't worry, babe; it'll go by fast, and we'll be together before you know it. I've gotta run. I can't wait to see you at graduation next week. I love you."

"I love you too, babe." I stayed on the line until I heard it click, then for a bit longer, listening to the lingering silence. I couldn't make him heal any faster, and the Marine Corps wasn't going to give him a pass and let him advance in his training. There wasn't a thing I could do to change what was happening, but I sure as hell didn't have to like it.

"Looking good in your blues, baby," I said, taking in his tall frame, decked out in his dress blue uniform. A row of ribbons hung on his jacket. I had no clue what any of them meant. We were just hours away from his Basic School graduation.

"Not lookin' too bad yourself." He nuzzled my neck, then kissed me.

"Don't be thinking too many wicked thoughts. We've got somewhere to be," I said.

"I can think whatever I want to think, but I'll behave. Besides, Dad and Charlotte just texted me. They're waiting in the car downstairs."

I looked in the mirror and adjusted my floor-length dress. The graduation ceremony was scheduled for the late morning, and after all the pomp and circumstance was over, Ross would spend 12 weeks rehabbing, then hopefully pick up with the next company for training.

He looked over my shoulder at my reflection. "You are so beautiful." He tucked a strand of my hair behind my ear. "Hey, before we go, there are a couple of things I want to make sure you're aware of. I'm in uniform now, so there are absolutely no public displays of affection. No handholding, no hugging, no kissing, nothing."

I nodded while trying to absorb the first of what I was sure would be a million rules.

He must have seen the look of apprehension on my face. "And just so you know," he continued, "not only are you off limits when I'm in uniform, but I can't chew gum, I can't walk while eating, drinking or talking on the phone. I'm not even allowed to carry an umbrella."

I sighed and gave him a smile. "Anything you are allowed to do?"

"Salute," he chuckled. "And this." He took my arm and wrapped it around his as we walked to the door.

I guess I'm going to have to get used to at least one of us being told what to do.

After arriving at the theater, I was separated from my beloved once again. I sat with his father, Rick, and stepmom Charlotte, both of whom beamed with pride for their son. Rick looked like an older version of Ross with the same broad-shouldered football-player build. He had sea-blue eyes and a salt and pepper beard.

"I'm a proud papa today, Kristine. It's neat to see my boy down there."

"He is quite the looker in those blues," Charlotte winked at me. "But then I'm a sucker for a man in uniform."

Charlotte was born and raised in Arkansas, and she had just a touch of a southern twang in her voice. She was a classic beauty who looked like a young Betty White. She possessed that unique Southern presence that exuded hospitality and kindness pretty much all the time.

The lights went down. The chatter-filled hall of over two hundred people went quiet. On stage, a senior ranking Marine officer addressed the audience, his words stressing the importance of being a Marine.

"The Marine Corps is the only branch of the US Armed Forces that recruits people specifically to fight. Our motto *Semper Fidelis* means 'always faithful.' That means no matter the enemy, how deadly a battle, or how tough a situation, we will remain steadfast with honor, courage, and commitment," he declared stoically.

Finally, the graduating Marines came onto the stage to receive individual acknowledgement. I felt such pride looking at him, the man to whom I had promised my hand in marriage. Whatever crisis, move or crazy military situation we were going to face, it was true; we did have each other. I also had my amazing family, and now I had Rick and Charlotte to lean on too. In that moment I truly felt lucky to be his.

When the ceremony was over, the room filled with a chorus of whoops and hollers. Ross was now ready to start his journey again in the fleet as one of the few, the proud; the elite warriors known as the US Marines.

I just hoped I could live up to the challenge of being this warrior's other half.

The Basic School Graduation in Quantico, Virginia

It was a long slow recovery from a severe 3rd degree sprain—an injury that would stay with me the rest of my life. The physical therapy I underwent helped with a speedy recovery, and I picked up with the next IOC class.

Getting hurt ended up being a bit of a gift. The students in the next IOC class were as hard as woodpecker lips. They were good dudes; not a complainer in the bunch. With few exceptions these guys all wanted to be there, and were doing their best to spread the load.

IOC was no joke. It offered 12 weeks of some of the most realistic and challenging training there is. Everyone was given a chance to fill a leadership billet. We rotated roles for each mission or live fire evolution. It was nonstop. We usually had class on Mondays, then headed out into the field from Tuesday until Saturday morning. While the Combat Endurance Test was challenging, it did not even make the top five most difficult events of IOC, which we've been ordered not to disclose. There wasn't a single day when my body didn't hurt, or when I wasn't tired or hungry. But there also wasn't a single second when I wasn't exactly where I wanted to be.

—— ⊙ ——

I crashed with a friend in Arizona while I waited for Ross to graduate. One morning I awoke to banging at the door that wouldn't stop. It was early—way too early. I rolled off the couch and slowly made my way to the door.

Our neighbor Lisa barged in, pushing me aside. "Turn on the TV. Someone has attacked the twin towers in New York!"

"What?" My thoughts immediately turned to Ross. *He's on the East Coast. Is he going to be called up?* We fumbled for the remote to turn the TV on. Neither of us said a word as we watched in disbelief. Then the second plane hit.

Lisa began rocking back and forth, crying. As the second building erupted in flames, we had our confirmation. It was no accident. We had been attacked. Then we learned a plane had crashed into the Pentagon. All I could think was, *is Quantico next?*

I sat down on the couch, unable to tear my eyes from the screen, barely breathing. When the towers collapsed, my gut told me everything had changed, that Ross would be sent off to war in the very near future.

Later that night I finally heard from him.

"Things have been nuts here. They shut down training; they have us patrolling the base."

"I'm so glad to hear from you! I've been worried about you all day."

"Don't worry about me. I'll always be fine. Right now they've got us tasked out doing patrols and wasting time. It seems like the guys who are stationed here should do this, and let us focus on learning what we need to learn in order to go to war."

I couldn't believe he'd come out and said it. War. My heart sank. I'd known this was a possibility, but up until that moment it had only been abstract—some chance happening at some point in the future. From the sound of Ross's voice he was not only unperturbed, he was looking forward to it.

"So," I said, "war, huh?"

"Don't worry, it won't be for a while. We have to go through unit training, so even if Congress declared war today, I wouldn't deploy for a while."

The voice in my head started screaming. *I don't want you to fight in a war.* When Ross had said he wanted to return to active duty service, I hadn't known precisely what to expect. Now here we were, miles and miles apart, our only connection hanging on by a phone line. I was scared; he was hungry for war. And the whole world was in uncharted waters.

4

The Adventure Begins

Fall 2001
Quantico, Virginia to Camp Pendleton, California

Ross was days away from leaving Quantico for good. I was buckled into a window seat on a six-hour flight en route to Virginia and my new life with my fiancé. Our first adventure: the cross-country road trip from Virginia to California and his first duty assignment.

I'd been counting down the days until we could be together again, but I had also been more than a little preoccupied with my job. I was working as a project manager for a large telecommunications company, and was responsible for managing multi-million dollar projects for fiber-optic installations; basically the high speed internet rings between private businesses or government buildings for data flow. I worked with everyone from construction crews to vice presidents of major corporations to ensure the job got done, both correctly and on time. It wasn't my dream job by any means, but I liked the people I worked with, and I was advancing in my career. I just hoped my new life with Ross wouldn't mean having to give up everything I had worked for.

As I grabbed my carry-on and made my way out into the concourse, I tried to imagine what Camp Pendleton would look like. All I knew was that it was smack dab between Los Angeles and San Diego.

My heart leapt when I saw him. "Ross!"

"You're a sight for sore eyes."

He picked me up and twirled me around. He set me down, looked at me hungrily, and kissed me. He grinned and whispered, "You're my everything—let's get out of here so I can have you all to myself."

I immediately blushed. I had been able to fly out once a month to see him for weekend visits. Our chemistry was still as fiery as ever.

He took my carry-on and I slipped my hand into his. "That sounds amazing. First though, I could use some good food. I'm starving."

He laughed. I'd missed that sound.

"Okay, you're worth waiting for."

He wrapped his arm around my waist and we walked towards the car.

Ross had always found a way to spoil me, even in college when neither of us had any money. He would carve out a few bucks or take an extra lifeguard shift so he could take me out somewhere special. True to form, we ended up in a fancy steakhouse with cherry wood paneling and glowing chandeliers. I couldn't help but wonder how much it would cost to eat at a place like this, but Ross just smiled at me.

We were seated, and I immediately slid over next to him, holding him close. Over the course of the last six years, we had shared the ups and downs of trying to figure out how to do life together. We knew each other's best and worst, and we were ready to commit to the good and the bad for the rest of our lives.

I was more than a little nervous about military life. My parents still lived in the same house I'd grown up in. I didn't have the first clue about this enigmatic life that I was venturing into.

"I'm scared, babe," I stammered. "With everything that's happened in the world, I can't help but worry. About war . . . about everything."

He turned and looked gently into my eyes. "I don't know what's to come. What I do know is that together, we can make it through anything."

I considered what future wars might look like. I thought about Desert Storm. Would it be like that? A short blast of firepower with little loss of life?

"Look," he continued. "I know we've been through a lot. I know you're taking a chance following me into this, but I don't want to do it with anyone else. I know anywhere you go, you're going to make it happen. That's the one thing that will get you through."

Our wedding was planned for the following May. I had no doubts he was the one for me—what I had doubts about was whether I could weather the Marine Corps.

"At least I have you. And you'll help me fill in blanks with how on-base life works, right?"

"Of course. You can always ask me anything and I'll do my best to explain it. Except if it's classified, then I'll have to kill you." He gave me a snarky smile and dragged his finger across his throat.

That man could always make me laugh.

Two days later, we were westward bound.

The long drive gave me time to ask a million questions, and Ross had time to share some of his experiences with me.

"So, is Officer Candidate School the same thing as boot camp for enlisted Marines? And why don't all Marines go to the same place?"

Ross shook his head. "No, they're completely different because there are different expectations.

"Enlisted boot camp doesn't really look to weed out anyone, and generally speaking, the recruits have no real responsibilities. The Drill Instructors—DIs—tell you what to do and when to do it, every waking minute. Of course some recruits are selected for leadership positions, but they don't exercise true authority. They're just there to ensure the DI's intent is being followed.

"The whole idea of enlisted boot camp is about breaking each recruit down, both emotionally and psychologically, so that they can then be built back up as a team of disciplined Marines who will, when their training is complete, become technical experts in their field.

"The officer's version of boot camp is more of a screening process. They're trying to assess if you're *fit to lead*. When they're weeding out candidates it's not too rigorous a process; but if someone can't hack it they don't keep recycling recruits to get them to pass like they do in boot camp. There's a measure of leadership you are expected to demonstrate in OCS. It's about being able to make good leadership decisions under duress."

"So it's kind of like corporate management?" I asked trying to connect pieces of his life to things I understood.

"Yeah, kind of. Take me, as an infantry officer. I know how to employ machine guns, mortars, and anti-tank weapons in conjunction with an infantry assault. I'm not going to be the best machine gunner. Instead, my job is knowing how to take the men under my command and put them and their skills to best use in order to accomplish the objective."

Things were beginning to make more sense to me. "Okay, I think

I get that. It's just that everything seems so much more complicated because of all the acronyms."

He laughed. "There's that, too. The longer you're in the Corps, you'll figure it out."

"In the Corps, huh?"

"You bet. You won't just be some spouse who is married to a Marine. You're issued a military ID; you're listed on military orders. You're going to be greatly affected by the decisions made by the military institution, and that means you're part of the Marine Corps family."

I liked the idea of belonging to a big family. "So what were you doing in The Basic School?"

"It's the first professional school that new active duty Marine officers go through. I was training to be a provisional rifle platoon commander. TBS is the beginning of everything for an officer. How each Marine performs in TBS will follow them around for the rest of their career. Promotions and selections are predicated on how well one does there. Marines go on a lot of humps—remember me telling you what a hump is?"

"Yes, it's a long hike with a pack and gear."

"Exactly. Some humps are longer and more arduous than others. We usually carry anywhere between fifty and seventy-five pounds, including our flak jacket, Kevlar, weapon, and water—walking at least three miles an hour. And all the Marines study tactics and basic infantry principles, even if they're going to be a pilot or lawyer. Every officer is a provisional rifle platoon commander."

The first night's stop took us to Tennessee, and on a tight budget we picked a no-name motel just off the interstate. The room's most memorable feature was a vibrating magic fingers bed.

Thirteen driving hours later found us in a small town in Texas called Shamrock.

"Well, at least this one doesn't look like the Bates Motel—what do you think, babe?"

He peered through the windshield at a neon-pink Vacancy sign. "We could keep going if you feel like it, but I'm pretty tired. I need to take a break from driving."

"This looks like as good a place as any."

We unloaded the car and considered taking a swim in the indoor pool, but decided to shower and get a pizza delivered instead. Even though we'd been sitting all day, it was nice to stretch out. Ross cuddled up next to me and we discussed what kind of place we'd want to rent in California. I wanted to buy a home, but he didn't know how long we'd be stationed there, and thought renting would be easier. Any home we looked at would have to take dogs—our black lab, Charlie, was waiting patiently for us with a friend until we got settled.

The next morning we ate a big Texas breakfast and hit the road heading towards Phoenix, Arizona. We had plans to crash with my friend Stephanie, but something unexpected came up for her. By the time we arrived, we couldn't stomach spending the money on another cheap hotel, so we opted to drive all the way through to California, 19 hours straight.

We were greeted with a glorious sunny day. We were over-whelmed by Southern California's beauty in the morning. We began exploring Leucadia and Encinitas, taking in the views of the Pacific Ocean. I stared at the miles of pristine beaches and watched hordes of surfers fight for a wave to ride while boats danced behind them in the water. As I looked at the dozens of beautiful homes overlooking the water I wondered if it was possible for anyone to get tired of that view.

We found a local diner for breakfast, and immediately jumped into setting up shop on the West Coast by beginning our house-hunting jaunt.

I checked the classifieds. "Looks like there's a condo right between Grandview Beach and Beacon's Beach off the 101 Coast Highway. It's in our price range. Want to go check it out?"

"Sure. Let's add that one to the list. Hopefully they take dogs."

"It doesn't say they don't, so that's a plus, right?"

After breakfast and checking out a couple of condos, we drove a little less than a mile up the coast. After a few quick turns we pulled into a quaint little cul-de-sac. I could smell the ocean air and feel the breeze on my face as soon as I opened the door. "It has such a cute little front yard. I could plant a little flower garden here."

"Yeah, it doesn't look too bad." There was a sign on the door indicating that it was an open house and that the agent would be back in about 30 minutes.

Ross held the door for me and I stepped inside. "It's nice and open." The doorway led to the family room with a wall of windows looking into the backyard. It was big enough to have people over without feeling cramped. We turned the corner and discovered the kitchen; it was on the smaller side, but certainly enough space to entertain.

Ross stepped through the sliding glass door to the patio.

"How's the backyard?" I asked.

"It'd be perfect for Charlie," he said. "It's fenced and big enough for him to roam around."

We walked upstairs, where there was a large bedroom with a balcony facing the cul-de-sac. "Bummer," Ross said. "I thought we'd be able to see the ocean from here. Too bad those big houses are blocking the view."

"Well I guess it's good we can't see it, because then it wouldn't be in our price range," I said, laughing.

"There's another room down the hall," he said.

We walked down the hallway and discovered a loft overlooking the living area. "It could easily be a bedroom. It even has its own bathroom. What do you think?"

"Look up, Kristine—someone used this as a nursery." He pointed to a cluster of glow-in-the-dark stars on the ceiling. "So . . . "

I looked at him. "Oh, no. Not yet, buddy."

"You know . . . I'd like to be a dad by the time I'm thirty."

"Let's just work on getting married first. Besides, we still need to announce our engagement to the world and finalize all our wedding plans."

He wrapped his arms around my waist and smiled. "So, seriously. When do you think we can have a baby?"

All I could do was roll my eyes and laugh. "Ugh, you're impossible sometimes."

A voice called out from downstairs. The realtor was back.

"So what do you think?" I whispered as we made our way back to the main level. "Is this the place?"

Ross nodded. "Yep, I think so."

It was our first home together. The first of many.

5

Sun on My Face, Song in My Heart

November 2001
Camp Pendleton, California

I reported to 2nd Battalion, 1st Marines (2/1) at Camp Horno, located on north end of Camp Pendleton, on my 28th birthday. The Marine Corps couldn't have given me a better present. I was nervous about the opportunity to lead Marines as an infantry platoon commander, but I was ready and excited. I would be responsible for a platoon of three rifle squads and any potential attachments for operations. Mostly I'd interact with my squad leaders, usually sergeants as well as the platoon sergeant, typically a staff sergeant.

My new boss, Captain Dale Burns, looked the part of a typical Marine commander. He sported a perfect high and tight haircut and a well-pressed camouflage utility uniform, lovingly known as "cammies." When I reported to his office he stood and shook my hand. He pointed to a seat opposite his desk, then scanned through my personnel file before leaning back in his chair.

He asked me the typical questions: where I was from, family makeup and history, my experiences as an enlisted man. He then began to tell me a little about the platoon I would be leading.

I asked questions about him, the future training cycle, and time-lines. He answered them in a direct, straightforward manner. My takeaway from our meeting was that he was a good Marine, and I left with a pretty good impression of him.

Lt Rich Maidens was assigned as the Weapons Platoon commander in my company. He and I had been in TBS together, and it was good to see him again. Maidens was very down to earth and funny, with a lot of self-deprecating humor; good spirited. He really cared about his Marines and about being a good infantryman. I looked forward to working with him.

His platoon sergeant was a Marine whom I knew from my

enlisted time. He was a great Marine as well. If first impressions meant anything, I had the feeling I'd landed in a top-notch unit. I couldn't wait to dig in and be a part of it.

*T*he cost of the haircuts was starting to add up.

Every Sunday, Ross had to stop whatever we were doing to go get one. Ten dollars each week, plus never being able to plan a weekend without the barber, inspired me to take matters into my own hands. Surely I could save us time and money by doing it myself. We owned clippers. I'd given haircuts before. How hard could it be?

"Are you sure you know what you're doing?" Even if I hadn't heard the concern in his voice, it was plastered all over his face in the mirror.

"Relax, I got this," I said.

It all started well enough. I got the top short enough, thanks to the clipper's attachments, and the bottom looked good since all I had to do was remove the attachment. Now I had to figure out the fade.

"Babe, please don't mess it up."

"Your confidence in me is overwhelming, you know. Can't tell you how much that helps."

"You know I love you, but it's been about 30 minutes since you started." He glared at me in the mirror. "Are you sure you're doing it right?"

I ignored his concerns and instead focused my attention on the back of his head. I tried every technique I could think of, but something still didn't look right.

Ross could see my face in the mirror. "Oh God, please tell me you didn't mess it up."

I squinted. "Well I wouldn't say I messed it up, exactly."

"Kristine, let me see." He stood up and snatched up a hand-held mirror from the bathroom counter. "No! I can't go to work looking like this . . . " He turned from side to side, examining the damage.

"Okay, so it wasn't as easy as I thought it would be, but it's not that bad." I did my best to stifle a giggle. I had finally figured out how to blend the longer hair on the top with the shorter hair at the back, but it wasn't even. The back of Ross's head looked like the zigzag that ran across the front of Charlie Brown's shirt.

Our eyes met in the mirror. "Barber," we said together.

We were both more than happy to put behind us the idea of cutting hair at home.

A couple of weeks after the haircutting incident, Ross brought a key volunteer network flier home from battalion. "This is about as good an idea as you cutting my hair," Ross said. "But you said you wanted to volunteer."

I scanned through the details. It was an invitation to a meeting of the battalion's key volunteers. Ross explained that they were the women who supported the family members of the unit.

I glanced at him. "You think it will be that bad?"

He shrugged. "I'll admit it probably is the best way for you to learn about the Marine Corps. It will give you an opportunity to meet some of the wives and girlfriends, but I want you to know—I've heard nothing but bad things about these meetings."

"Bad things?" I made a face at him. "What—do they make us do push-ups and eat expired MREs?" I had learned early on about Meals Ready to Eat, and their many pet names:

- *Meals; Rarely Edible*
- *Meals Rejected by the Enemy*
- *Meals Resistant to Exit*
- *Meals Requiring Enemas*, particularly because Marines became constipated after eating them for too many days in a row.

Ross shook his head and smiled. "Drama. Lots and lots of drama. Are you sure you're up for it?"

I looked back down at the paper. He was right; it was a great way for me to learn more about what it meant to be a part of the Marine Corps family, and I was eager to do what I could to find my place in our new community. "It's a little overwhelming, but I'd like to go. Maybe see what it's about."

Ross kissed my cheek. "We can drive down there together, since you don't know your way around. I'll do some work at the office and we can leave when you're done."

Two days later, dressed in my favorite pair of jeans and wearing the necklace Ross gave me for my birthday, I loaded the car along with Ross and headed to Camp Horno for the meeting. Truth be told, I was a little nervous. I must have checked my hair and makeup about a dozen times on the 35-minute drive. "You look great. What's going on with you?" Ross looked a little concerned. "We can turn around, go home."

"No," I said. "I want to go, it's just I have no idea what to expect. I want to make a good impression, you know?"

"They're going to love you, just like I do." He squeezed my hand. "And if they don't, you can tell them to kiss your ass."

I laughed as I felt the nervous energy drain out of my system. We walked hand in hand into the meeting. Ross introduced me to a couple of people, then kissed me goodbye as I took my seat.

A woman named Theresa introduced herself to us and thanked us all for being there. She was a married to a senior Marine and seemed very comfortable with the military lifestyle. We all sat around a briefing table in the battalion conference room without much else going for it. The Marine Corps infantry didn't exactly pride itself on having nice furniture or equipment. Knowing what I knew of Ross, I suspected they all secretly loathed being in an office environment.

The first half of the meeting was spent discussing the newsletter creation and what kinds of things should be included. Did we want to include wedding and birth announcements? Who could help with the content for each company's sections?

Key volunteers had to be able to handle anything that was thrown at them. Their connection to the unit was made primarily by phone, and from there they acted as a source of official information to married Marines' families. The KV would also act as the primary contact for everything from questions about the hospital or our medical insurance Tricare, to recommendations about base life, and dealing with personal problems in family life.

Eventually the talk moved on to instructions on how to deal with stressful situations and phone calls. Sometimes spouses would call in a panic because something major had happened. We discussed how some of those situations, while stressful, were pretty normal for the volunteer role.

The next topic was unit protocol if a Marine were to be killed in the battalion. Just the mention of Marines dying made my stomach drop. The whole conversation made me anxious. Once an official notification had been made to the family of a fallen Marine, the KV members were required to call all the other wives to let them know the family had been notified. I wasn't officially even a part of the Marine Corps family and they were already discussing death. What had I gotten myself into?

I was thankful when we moved on to the upcoming deployment and the amount of responsibility we would hold. The whole idea of being someone's emergency contact was a bit scary. Sure, I understood that they didn't want a thousand families calling the unit for every little thing, but when they discussed a few extreme examples of family problems, it was unsettling to say the least.

Finally, Theresa slid her chair back and raised the final topic on the agenda.

"Before we go, we need to discuss the call rosters. We are going to need at least thirty volunteers to help keep the call load to a manageable number. We need to decide who should be included on the call list."

A dark-haired woman in her late thirties seated near the front of the room stood up, visibly upset and angry. "There ain't no way some girlfriend of a Marine is gonna get information on my husband that's gonna get him killed! Some hussy who some kid happens to be dating doesn't deserve any information of any kind. No girlfriends. No fiancées. They don't matter until they're a wife, period. Wives are first and that's that."

My jaw dropped. This woman had just thrown every Marine girlfriend under the bus. The words were out of my mouth before I even had a chance to think about it: "Hey. I'm a girlfriend—a fiancée, actually. And I think I deserve to be on that list." I looked directly at the woman. "My Marine and I have been together for six years. That's longer than some marriages last—and for the record, I'm not a hussy."

The room fell silent. After a long pause, the key volunteer coordinator spoke up. "I think we can all agree that a piece of paper does not make a successful relationship, okay? Every woman who is brought into this organization is a valued member."

The outspoken woman rolled her eyes and sat down. I sensed

that she had more to say. I couldn't wait to get out of there and talk to Ross about it. He was right. Drama. If this was what it was going to be like, maybe I shouldn't waste my time.

After the meeting adjourned, Theresa—the meeting leader—followed me out into the hallway. "I'm so sorry about what happened tonight. I want you to know that none of the rest of us feel that way, and would really love it if you stayed on board with us."

"Thanks," I said. It was a kind gesture, and she sounded sincere. I decided to reserve judgment until I saw how the next few meetings panned out. "Don't worry, I won't let only one person ruin this for me."

"Good. I'm glad to hear it."

I said goodbye and headed outside to meet Ross. Despite the drama at the end of the meeting, I had actually learned a few things. A small part of me was excited about a chance to be part of this group. I was determined to make it work.

The alarm went off at 0530. I hit snooze, rolled over, and put my arms around Kristine.

"When are you going to get a day off again?" she asked, half awake.

"Not for another couple of days. At least I get to come home a few times a week for sleep."

After 9/11, the Marine Corps implemented an Air Contingency Force, ACF, which meant Marines were constantly on standby, just in case the country was attacked again. This tripled normal duty for Marines and since we were the new guys—also the lowest ranking officers in the unit—lieutenants, like Maidens and me, carried the brunt of the extra duty. 1stLt Johnson had even been roped in. We didn't have a lot of available bodies on deck.

Kristine's eyes opened into weary slits. "Yeah, but I'd like to actually get to talk to you at some point." She snuggled back into the covers. "How about I bring you dinner at work tonight? I'm beginning to forget what you look like when you're vertical."

"That would be awesome. I'll draw you a map and leave it on the counter. Can you come by around six? And can you bring a pizza? How about pepperoni and extra cheese."

"Six. Pepperoni. Extra cheese. Got it." She was still half asleep.

I practiced my super-silent ninja skills as I got dressed. I headed to work without making a sound.

The hours flew by. I was a platoon commander, so in essence I was responsible for everything 1st Platoon did or failed to do. That responsibility included accomplishing any mission assigned by my company commander, and ensuring the welfare of my Marines, which encompassed combat and equipment readiness. It also included making sure my Marines knew how to conduct fire and movement, became proficient with their weapons, and were ready to operate in any environment.

I was also responsible for knowing how to combine the effects of supporting arms, which would include the company's machine guns, mortars, and rockets. I was required to be able to maneuver my platoon effectively against an enemy in offensive or defensive operations.

After work I checked in for duty. The clock on the wall read 1945—7:45 p.m. for Kristine. I was reaching for the phone to call home when I heard the sound of high heels on the linoleum hallway floor of our command post.

I peeked my head out of the evening duty office.

"Hey babe, what took you so long? You okay?"

"Here's your pizza." She practically threw it at me, turned, and stomped back the way she had come.

I tossed the pizza on the desk and hurried after her. "Hey, wait up! What's wrong? What are you so upset about?"

She crossed her arms and glared at me. "I dunno. For starters, your dumbass map. You didn't draw a T in the road. You drew an L, which means I should have turned left where a right wasn't possible—which it was!

"So I spent about twenty minutes driving around another camp looking for Camp Horno. I found a Marine to ask, and he didn't even know where he was. It's completely dark outside with no lights, and every road is blockaded with razor wire. Our stupid cell phones don't work inside the base so I couldn't call you, and oh yeah, I almost died because I drove right through the middle of a bombing range! I guess that about wraps things up." She spun back around and made a beeline for the door.

I caught up to her in a few steps and hugged her.

"I'm sorry I drew such a crappy map. Bombing range, huh?" It was all I could do not to laugh. I didn't want to tell her that she probably just drove by a live-fire range; nothing like a bombing range, and that she was never in danger.

I could tell she wasn't happy, but I knew even she had to see the humor in everything that had happened. I kissed the top of her head and pulled her close. "Stay and have a slice with me and the guys. I don't want you to go."

"I can't stay. I'm too upset. I just want to go home and go to bed. I'll see you tomorrow."

I followed her out to the car and waited for her to get in, then leaned in to kiss her goodnight. "You know I love you, right, babe?"

"I love you too, but we need to talk about your seriously terrible map-drawing skills." But she smiled and kissed me back.

I waited until I couldn't see her taillights, then headed back inside.

The pizza was already half gone. "Damn, Schellhaas, remind me to never ask you for directions. Might get my ass blown up or something."

I stood there and took the ribbing like a good Marine. I didn't think my map was bad, but I could hardly blame Kristine for not wanting to stay. I promised myself I'd make it up to her.

After dinner it was back to officer of the day duty: barracks and housing patrols, answering phone calls, checking the chow hall to make sure the food was being served to standards, and essentially making sure that chaos didn't ensue. There was a lot of time to get to know my fellow lieutenants. It was a good time to talk about our lives, but more importantly, it was a time to anticipate what would happen, hoping we wouldn't be left out of the fight.

—— ⌀ ——

I circled the day on the calendar with a bright red marker. Our big day was set for Memorial Day weekend, 2002.

I liked the idea of a spring wedding, but the real reason we'd chosen the date was because it was the only weekend the Marine Corps would give Ross time off from work.

The Marine Expeditionary Unit was no joke. Ross' battalion was assigned to the next MEU rotation and linked up with air, ground, artillery, and other assets able to sustain a 2,500-man unit in a crisis situation—basically waiting in the wings just in case shit hit the fan. They could respond to natural disasters or humanitarian crises, evacuate an embassy or invade a country at a moment's notice. The tip of the spear, as they say. And he was forever off somewhere training—aboard a ship, in the godforsaken desert, in the high Sierra Mountains—tons of training to prepare for deployment.

All that training for war, combined with the constant duty of ACF, meant we didn't have many nights or weekends together. But on the rare occasions he was home, we talked often about our plans for the wedding. I kept records of all of the deposits we'd paid and made detailed plans, clearly marked and coordinated in an Excel spreadsheet; my favorite tool.

"Do we have a budget for everything yet?" Ross asked, looking over my shoulder at the spreadsheet that held the latest running total of wedding costs.

"Almost. I swear, everywhere I look I keep seeing one thousand dollar bills. There's the pictures, the video, flowers, tuxedos—don't get me started on the food cost per person. Thank God both of us are working right now."

"I always wanted to marry a sugar momma," he said, laughing.

"Yeah, well, I'm pretty sure this job isn't going to last forever." I had been able to transfer my position at work, telecommuting to the Phoenix office each week. But the company hadn't been doing well since the merge. Layoffs were imminent. "I can't imagine they're going to keep me on much longer. Then I'll either have to find another job or be the stay-at-home wifey."

"I think I should be the stay-at-home hubby. Then I can go to the gym, take care of the kids, and go hunting."

I laughed. "Oh sure, babe. I can see it now. I'd come home and the house would be a disaster. You'd be just coming back from the skeet range after teaching the baby to launch clay pigeons for you."

He crossed his arms in feigned indignation. "Whatever. It could be great. I'd cook and . . . "

"Oh yum, Campbell's Bean with Bacon soup, and cheese squares every night."

"I could learn, you know." He nuzzled my neck, but I pushed him back to arm's length, stood up and smiled.

"You're so right, and now's the perfect time to start. You can help me make dinner tonight."

He made a face. "Eh, or I could go do something else right now, and learn later." He laughed and smacked my behind before grabbing a cold beer and escaping into the living room. After a few seconds, I heard the sound of college football blaring from the TV.

Twenty minutes later, our dinner in the oven, I plopped down on the couch beside him.

"You should call your mom this weekend. When was the last time you talked to her?"

I got an I-don't-know shrug followed by silence.

"You know she misses you."

He took a sip of his beer.

"She's your mom. You have to call her."

"I'll call her next weekend. Besides, we still need to finalize our plans before we tell her about the wedding."

You got that right, I thought.

His mother, Trina, was the whole reason we had waited to announce our wedding. She was generous with her time and energy when it came to helping others, but those times where her help wasn't wanted or needed, came at a cost. Once she had her mind set on seeing something through, she expended all of her energy to make it so.

We wanted to have our wedding plans set in place so we could focus her boundless efforts of lending a helping hand where there was little room left for suggestion.

We were heading home to Boise for Christmas in a week, which would provide the opportunity for us to get one final look at all the venues we wanted to see. I was excited to go home and see everyone, but it was also difficult because we couldn't be everywhere at once. We couldn't make it to every get-together or Christmas party with friends; we couldn't be at all the family celebrations. It was just the beginning of how our lives would be impacted by the Marine Corps.

6

He Put a Ring on It

January 2002
Camp Pendleton, California

The server led us to a table overlooking the water. Ross ordered a bottle of champagne. "Are we celebrating something I don't know about?" I asked as I took my seat.

"I just wanted to have a special night out with you before I leave for Bridgeport."

"Gah! Don't remind me. I hate that you're leaving me for so long." I knew how excited he was about training in the Sierra Nevada Mountains, but it meant he'd be gone for four months.

"I hate to say get used to it, babe, but this is just the beginning. I will be gone regularly for long periods of time. Besides, while I'm at Bridgeport you'll be busy planning our wedding and making new friends. Think about all the beach time you can have."

"Yeah—it's pretty tempting having the beach right out our back door. But I'll still miss you—a lot."

"I'll miss you too, but I'll be there and back before you know it. I promise."

We watched the waves lapping along the quiet beach just yards from our table, taking in all the people seated around us. My eyes settled on an older couple seated two tables over. It looked like they'd been happily married for years. Part of me wanted to ask them their secret or see if they had any advice for us.

Over dinner we reminisced about our lives, about growing up and what we wanted out of our family life. We imagined what it would be like to watch our kids play sports and take them camping. To watch them grow into the best versions of themselves.

Ross took my hand, leading me down the length of the walkway that overlooked the ocean, then onto the beach cove in La Jolla. "It's such a great night out; maybe we'll see some seals," he said. We played around on the beach for a while. I combed the shore for seashells. When I looked over at him he just smiled a big 'ol goofy smile. "What?" I asked.

"Nothing. I just love you," he replied, beaming.

After a while we climbed back up the stairs to the walkway, where he stopped and pulled me close. "Kristine, you're the love of my life. You are my best friend. I am the luckiest man on the planet to have found such a beautiful, strong, courageous woman to love. You make me a better man every day. I only hope I can live up to being the man you deserve. I can't wait to spend the rest of my life with you." He spun me around so that I was looking down at the beach. In the sand he had scrawled with his feet *WILL YOU MARRY ME?*

He got down on one knee, and produced the biggest diamond ring I had ever seen. He looked up with the gentlest of tear-filled eyes and asked, "Kristine, will you do me the honor of becoming my wife?" He slid the ring onto my finger.

"Yes!" Everything went blurry for me. I stammered out, "But you already asked me to marry you."

"True," he smiled. "But I decided we needed to make it official, something to celebrate the announcement of our wedding date. And now of course I'm able to give you the ring I've always wanted to give you."

I held out my hand, admiring the ring. It was gorgeous; a simple classic cut diamond in a platinum band. "How big *is* this?"

"A couple of carats," he replied, like it was no big deal.

"Who did you rob or kill in order to get this?" I joked.

"I drove your favorite beater truck for a year longer than I originally planned to. Instead of a truck payment I made a little ring payment." He took my hand and kissed the back of my fingers. "I wanted you to have the perfect ring forever and always. I didn't want us to feel like we ever needed to replace it ten years down the road. I like the idea that you'll always have this ring on your finger, whether you're twenty-five or seventy-five."

"It's beautiful, Ross. But I'm the lucky one. Lucky that God brought you into my life; lucky I can marry a man I admire, trust and love with every inch of my body."

"Hmmm . . . " he said. How about we head home so you can show me all those inches?"

I laughed and led my Marine towards the car.

7

The Hills Are Alive with the Sound of Marines

January 2002
Bridgeport, California

Kristine stood in the doorway of the guest room. "You think you have everything?" she asked. "I thought you said it was only going to be a couple of months. You've got enough gear here for years." The entire room was filled with olive drab, black, and desert tan.

"This is business, not pleasure," I said, cinching down a pack strap.

She laughed. "And men give women a ration of crap about how much we pack. Remind me again why they're sending you to Mountain Leader School in the middle of winter? How could this possibly relate to Afghanistan or Iraq?"

"Survival skills, babe. We're going to learn how to operate in a cold weather environment. It gets pretty cold in the mountains. They do have mountains in Afghanistan, you know."

"Well I hope you have a good time up there on that cold mountain . . . eating MREs and cuddling up with other hairy men in small tents."

"A gentleman never kisses and tells," I said, and winked at her.

Later, as we loaded up in the car, she asked, "How long do you think it will take us to get to Bridgeport?"

"I'm thinking about five hours or so. It's up there between Tahoe and Mammoth. There may be some snow on the road; it may slow us down."

We always loved a good road trip.

We rolled up to the Bridgeport drop-off point a little after 0300. In our six years together, we'd made a lot of effort to never be apart for more than a month, even when I was at school in Quantico. I could tell she was nervous.

"I'm going to miss you, sugar," she said, sliding her arms inside my coat and hugging me tightly. "Four months is a long time."

"I'm going to miss you, too," I said, "but know it's just for a little while. Hopefully we can carve out a couple of weekends for you to drive up. Maybe we can have a long weekend in Tahoe or something."

"I'd love that."

I kissed her, breathed in the scent of her hair, and smiled. "As much as I love having you in my arms, you need to get going. The weather is supposed to turn, and you need to find someplace to get chains put on the car before they close the road." She nodded, reluctantly let go of me, and crawled back in the car.

"Be safe. Make sure you call me when you get out of the snow so I know you're okay."

"Alright, love. Talk to you in a few hours."

"I love you." I watched her go, then grabbed my gear and focused on what lay ahead.

The Sierra Nevada Mountains were nothing if not picturesque. The Marine Corps Mountain Warfare Training Center, MCMWTC, was developed after the Korean War so that the Corps could train units to operate effectively in a cold weather and mountainous environment. Just being able to exist in cold weather and high altitude is a battle; individuals and collective units must master the disciplines of survival so that we can remain tactically effective and lethal when a real, thinking, breathing adversary is thrown into play.

Mountain Leader's Course was not a "Gentleman's Course" where we spent all our time sitting in a classroom. It was an ass-kicking, test-what-you're-made-of kind of school.

One of the other platoon commanders, Lt Greg Johnson, came with me. Johnson had been a platoon commander on the last deployment, and stayed in the company. He had played strong safety and special teams for the University of Tennessee. After college, he worked for FEMA before becoming a Marine. That meant we were closer in age than the others. We became good friends, sharing duty together on Air Contingency Force and during our time at Bridgeport. One thing I knew for sure: he was not a fan of Burns—our company commander—by any stretch.

The first day of training was interesting. It was already freezing at base camp, and it was still early afternoon. The class was almost completely comprised of lieutenants and sergeants, along with a handful of staff sergeants.

The first week consisted of gear issue (a shit-ton of it) and a lot of classroom time. We participated in what was called "backyard training" with our new equipment, and some gradual yet challenging physical training, PT. The primary goal during the first week was really to give us time to acclimatize to the new altitude.

The start of the second week began with a two thousand-foot ascent, with all the gear we'd need to last us one week strapped to our backs. We carried 70 lbs. of gear—including skis and snowshoes—up a plowed trail to the top of a small summit. This hike was a graded event; only half the class made it within the maximum allotted time, for a max (perfect) score.

Our living quarters for the week were squad arctic tents with small heating stoves. Daytime hours brought ski lessons and snow-shoeing on the relatively flat terrain. We started off with small day-packs and gradually added gear, carrying full packs the following week. Evenings consisted of prepping for the next day's events, cleaning weapons, melting snow for water, and packing and repacking our gear in order to take only the essentials.

Near the end of the week, we had our first opportunity for libbo, liberty; off time duty. Johnson and I planned on going to Gardnerville, where there would be a thick, juicy steak and a warm hotel room with my name on it.

Late on Friday afternoon, we had to complete one final event before we could go. We gathered in an enormous snow-covered meadow and broke up into small groups for instruction on various skiing and mountaineering techniques. The Mountain Leader Chief Instructor blew a whistle, the signal for us to consolidate at his position and head back to base camp. Before we left, our station instructor called for a friendly ski race down the very small hill.

We lined up and took off. Halfway down the very gradual slope I executed a wedge, a technique often taught to new skiers that allows them to slow their descent. I was doing fine until I wedged straight onto a snow-covered stump in the middle of this supposedly open meadow.

The force of the impact split my skis.

I heard my knee pop.

I lay in the snow looking like a cartoon, my skis crossed vertically. I had rotated face down in the snow. The pain was excruciating. I could already feel my knee beginning to swell. The worst part was that I knew no one would come to help me. They'd all assume I'd just fallen, not that I was seriously injured. It took me several minutes to find my feet. I finally managed to extricate myself and hobble slowly down to the holding area where we loaded onto vehicles and drove back to our camp.

Our instructor was a Navy chief, which is rare at any Marine Corps school. He had been with Force Recon and he was impressive to watch on skis. He looked at the swelling and manipulated my knee. "That hurt?"

"Like I got hit by a truck."

He looked at me matter-of-factly and asked, "So what do you want to do?"

I felt like I was being called out. The course chief had joined us, and he shook his head when he looked at my knee—it was now three sizes larger than the other. It was an out. I don't think anyone would have faulted me for not continuing, but I knew I wouldn't get another chance like this.

"Hell with it. It's only a knee, right?" It was just another in a series of injuries that required me to gut it out. TBS, jacked up knee; IOC, jacked up ankle; MLC, same jacked up right knee.

"You can miss two days of the course without being dropped," the course chief reminded me. "Do what you can to get back in the fight. That means ice it, take Motrin, elevate it and stay off it—we'll see what it looks like on Wednesday."

That gave me four days to heal up, which would have to be enough. I spent the entire weekend icing my knee, which was miserable because it was already so cold out. I slept like crap because every time I moved, I woke up in pain.

The next week really sucked; we were skiing at a resort near Tahoe so that we could master downhill skiing, only Marine Corps style. That meant we were trying to downhill ski on government-issued skis, which were essentially designed for backcountry touring, not downhilling, plus they were made by the lowest bidder. Just walking felt like someone was knifing my kneecap, but there weren't any other options for me. I wouldn't go back and face my Marines without having completed this course.

I spent Monday and Tuesday sitting in the same place I usually only slept—the window seat of our six-man resort condo, into which we squeezed 13 guys, with a bag of ice perpetually on my knee. Wednesday morning rolled around. I had to go out and try to ski or be dropped from the course.

A couple of the instructors, and some fellow students, took the time to go one-on-one with me. I was grateful for the assistance, but I was two days behind. It showed.

With every turn I made, my knee screamed. I could feel it starting to swell, but at least the pain subsided the more I used it. The next morning was a completely different story. I couldn't even bend my knee—it took me an hour before I could walk straight. Despite all this, I felt I was getting the hang of things, and I was determined to suck it up and get through it.

The next morning was the day of the test. It was another make or break moment for me in the course. We had three chances to pass. Failure on the third run would see me dropped from the course.

The instructors told us to prepare for a pretest so that they could judge our form. I was happy to hear that—I had missed so much of the instruction already. The test was on various ski techniques—stopping, doing flip turns, sliding sideways on skis, and more. At the end of the pretest, I'd done better than I thought I would. They told me I would have passed—barely.

That was good enough for me, considering how far behind I was. I asked the instructors if I could go first in the actual test, before my knee started to give me problems. I could feel it swelling again, and I thought if I failed, at least I could watch everyone else's techniques so that I could implement them and maybe improve my result in the next one. As it was I knew I wasn't alone; a handful of others were struggling to reattempt the techniques in their own pretest.

Our instructors huddled off to the side, writing our scores on clipboards. I prayed they'd call my name in the first group to test.

The chief instructor circled his fist in the air. "Okay ladies. Free-ski time."

We all looked at each other, confused.

"Don't just stand there—get moving. There was no practice test. That was the test." He shifted and looked directly at me. "Some of you have some tightening up to do, but everyone passed. Now go enjoy the slopes, on the Marine Corps' dime. You won't get another chance like this, not ever."

I'd never been so relieved. I turned and gave the hill the finger. I'd passed. Then—against my better judgment—I rode a chair lift up so that I could take advantage of the ski time.

We loaded up that night to head back to base camp. I was looking forward to another weekend to rest my knee.

———— 💍 ————

Three weeks after I'd left him at the top of that mountain, my phone rang. "Hey there, stranger! I'm so happy to hear from you!"

"Hey babe, he said. "I've missed you, you have no idea. How are you?"

"I'm doing good. Missing you, but good. What have you been doing?"

"Freezing my ass off. No kidding, I can't remember the last time I felt this cold for this long. But we're having fun. I finally learned how to ski," he laughed.

"I can't believe it took the entire Marine Corps to get you to finally learn how to ski. All those years I asked you to come with me and you refused—but now you're doing it."

"Well it wasn't as much fun as it probably would have been with you. They made us downhill ski on mountaineering skis with a sixty pound pack."

"That sounds like a whole lot of suck. Did they at least give you some lessons on the bunny hill?"

"We practiced on a flat area, then on a little hill. I was one of the few guys who had never even tried skiing before, but I'm getting the hang of it."

Then he told me about his knee. "Let me guess, it was your right?"

"Yeah, of course it was. Still hurts bad, but I'll make it work. I think the worst of it is over."

I groaned. "Just be careful, okay? I'm planning on dancing with you at our wedding."

"Yeah, yeah. You just show up and wear a pretty dress. I'll be there with my dancing shoes on."

We laughed. It was good to laugh with him.

"What have you been doing while I'm up here conquering this winter wonderland?"

"Working, reading, trying to make friends. Remember that girl Mia I met at the platoon party before you left?"

"Yeah, the blonde—the one dating Cpl Spinner? She seemed nice."

"Well I met her for dinner and drinks a couple times. I really like her, but it's so hard to get to know people, you know? We're only twenty minutes from the base, but all the same it's hard not to feel isolated. Mia lives all the way up in San Clemente. Getting together with her isn't easy—it's a good forty minute drive."

"You'll make more friends, babe. Just keep putting yourself out there and getting to know people."

"I know, don't mind me. I'm just lonely when you're gone. It feels a little bit like I've been abandoned in SoCal. And on top of that, Mia brought me a bunch of scary Patricia Cornwell novels."

"I don't know why you do that to yourself. You know you get all worked up with creepy books and movies."

"Yeah, but they're so good! I just can't help myself. I end up reading until one or two in the morning, then freaking myself out. I sleep with Charlie at the foot of the bed and your loaded shotgun leaning against the nightstand."

He chuckled. "And that doesn't raise any red flags for you?"

"Well, it doesn't help that there's drunks and meth-heads walking around all hours of the night. I don't like leaving the bedroom window open, but you know there's no AC. It gets so hot at night."

"Well, think of me freezing alone up here every time you think it's too hot down there. I'd kill to be lying in bed next to you right now."

I missed him more than I could say. I wanted to tell him that it wasn't so much the books as it was the empty bed that made it hard to sleep, but I knew he needed to focus. I didn't want him to think I was one of those girls who couldn't manage while her man was away.

"We'll be together before you know it," he said. "Just focus on the good, okay? I've gotta go. I love you, babe."

I hung up the phone and fished another book from the stack Mia gave me, flipping to page one.

Each week of Mountain Leader's Course had a theme. Towards the end it was time for survival week. We lived in snow caves for four nights and practiced building emergency fires, land navigation, avalanche assessments and various other elements of field craft.

At one point during the week, we were tasked with making field expedient snowshoes out of willow branches and 550-cord (parachute cord, a ubiquitous military-grade line, like heavy shoelaces). The instructor harped at us to take our time fashioning them correctly, saying we'd never know when we might need something like this in the future. I did my best to focus on the task at hand but we were all so tired, cold and hungry that none of us had the mental energy to spend time tying and wrapping endless lengths of cord on sticks. We had to do a patrol that night, so orders had to be written and gear needed to be prepped. Snowshoe making was last on our list of things we wanted to be doing.

Survival week included much more interesting classes like ski marching and learning how to skijor. Skijoring traditionally involves someone on skis being pulled by a horse, but instead of using horses, we tied a rope to the hitch of a lightly armored personnel vehicle called a BV. We tied the other end of the rope to our ski poles and formed two lines of six in a V formation behind the BV.

It's fun.

Until the guy in front of you wrecks.

If you're lucky, you're furthest from the vehicle, so you can let go before you crash into anyone else. But being last in line has its drawbacks as well; it's like playing crack the whip.

Eventually we learned to put the least experienced skiers closest to the vehicle. After about five weeks of learning to live on skis, I was doing pretty well. I was able to get where I needed to go, and I was building on the skills I'd learned during the previous weeks, able to cover varying distances over different terrain.

The end was in sight; survival week was almost done. We had been cold for weeks on end, spending every night in a snow cave or tent, where the high temperature barely reached 30°. It was literally freezing all the time. Inside our snow caves, we were able to keep the temperature right around freezing. Outside, the lows were around -10°. I was entirely grateful for the 40° difference in temperature, but I never slept soundly inside the snow cave.

I don't think I had ever been so happy to make it to another Friday. It was late in the afternoon, and we were all looking forward to being warm again. As we began our descent off the mountain, the instructors stopped us with orders to immediately go to ground and dig ourselves a coffin, a hole in the snow the size of our bodies. The coffin provided a place for us to get out of the wind when we couldn't see in whiteout conditions. It's an immediate action drill for when we're caught in a strong snowstorm and at risk of getting separated because we can't see a foot in front of us.

But apparently, Friday as I'd come to know and love it meant nothing during survival week.

We were given five minutes to dig our holes and get in our bags. My mountain buddy Sgt Walker and I devised a plan to break out our ponchos, snap them together and make an overhead cover to try to retain some body heat. Even getting our shelter 5° warmer would make a huge difference. The instructors came over and stood over our coffin, watching as we fumbled around, and began to count down aloud. By the time they reached zero we were expected to be zipped up in our sleeping bags.

But our plan wasn't working. Our cold hands did nothing but fumble with the ponchos; we were running out of time. We had to jump into our bags with all of our gear on—including boots, gaiters and our Gore-Tex parka and pants. We were supposed to take the gear off and place it all into a waterproof bag inside our sleeping bags for the night.

The last night of survival week was the most miserable of my life to that date. I'd hardly slept at all when I was tapped to pull night watch. I spent the rest of the evening outside in ski-march boots in -12° cold. A previous surgery had put two metal pins into my two big toes, and I could feel those pins as the temperature plummeted. I rummaged for an empty MRE bag to stand on, just to provide some insulation from standing on the ground, however slight. When the sun broke over the horizon everybody got up, and we continued our ski march back to base camp.

"Don't get too comfortable, gentlemen. Take your gear to your squad bay and suit up in your long johns and PT shoes. Be back here in fifteen minutes with your gear."

"Our long johns and PT shoes?" Sgt Walker asked as we hurried to the bay. "What the hell?"

I shook my head. "I have no idea." Saturday morning usually meant waking up in a warm bed, but we were still in the throes of survival week. I wasn't looking forward to what was coming next.

Twenty minutes later, we loaded up and they drove us across the valley to a small lake. Our instructors took a moment to remind us about the class on frozen lakes, which gave us instructions on what to do if we ever fell into the water.

SSgt Cabrillo, our chief instructor for the course, emerged from one of the transport vehicles and donned a long white parka, similar to the dusters cowboys used to wear. It came down about mid-calf. This ridiculous ensemble was made complete with running shoes. One of the other instructors was standing over a six-by-six-foot hole in the ice they had cut with a chainsaw, shoveling out slush to keep it from freezing over.

"Alright, gents. This course is about working under adversity and uncertainty." He stepped onto the ice, stopping short of the hole. "Whatever you do—don't act like a bitch." With that he whipped off his parka. Underneath he was sporting a lacey, black and red thong. With a smile, he dropped into the hole and the icy water.

One by one the rest of the instructors followed suit, though no one else sported lingerie. Each one of them followed the same procedures we were required to follow. They recited their name, rank, and unit before climbing out of the water.

All the officers went first. When it was my turn, the moment I hit the water, it took my breath away. It was so cold it was all I could do to remember my name and social security number, and when I tried to say them out loud it was barely recognizable. It came out more like, "jjjjsjjsjsjjjj RRRRRRRoooooooosss."

An exchange Royal Marine colour sergeant instructor knelt at the edge of the hole in the ice and gave the go-ahead for us to climb out. I waited for his thumbs up, but he made the officers answer additional questions to force us to stay in the water longer. In the end, we officers generally stayed in the water twice as long as our enlisted counterparts. We were held to a higher standard because we're expected to lead under greater adversity.

Once out of the water I rolled onto the snow, a technique intended to help us dry off. We were then ordered to take a shot. There, next to the hole in the lake, they had set up a table festooned with shot glasses. When the Brits complete it they have whiskey, but since we are such a risk-averse institution, the Marines had punch instead. We celebrated our rite of passage with a toast. The Brits raised a glass to their queen and the Marines toasted the president, George W. Bush, although we should have probably toasted the constitution. Frozen balls and a mouthful of punch marked the end of our survival week.

All that now stood between graduation and us was the final exercise, which consisted of a series of very long movements. We would be tasked with missions designed to test everything we'd learned over the entire Mountain Leader's course.

The simulation exercise included both an enemy and our higher headquarters component, both played by instructor cadre. The first three days consisted of making long movements with the equipment we'd need to operate for the rest of the week. The fourth night in, higher headquarters tasked us with the establishment of an ambush site nearly two ridges over from our then-current position. We'd be losing and gaining a total of about four thousand feet with this movement, a considerable feat even without a 60-pound pack on your back.

Each night the instructors selected a new training leader from among the students; this movement would see one of the sergeants at the helm. The lieutenants offered help too, as did the Recon SSgt—a few guys looked at the route the sergeant had selected and gave it the thumbs up.

It took us several hours to ski down one of the ridges. We reached the bottom just before 0100 hours. The other side was rather low, but its steep slope looked climbable. It would provide the opportunity for us to make up some time.

What we didn't account for was that this slope was south-facing. That meant it melted slightly from direct sunlight, then quickly froze—it was hard as rock, and difficult to scale. But we were at the point of no return. The only way to keep our time obligation with the instructors was to keep going.

The five hundred-foot ascent took us almost seven hours. We really needed a pickax, which was about the only piece of gear we didn't have in our packs. We'd take one step forward and two steps back because of our heavy packs, and the fact that we were constantly falling. Once someone got a pack moved six inches, they would have to dig another foothold with their boots, skis, and poles, and do it over and over again. Frustration was the word of the day.

Most of the lieutenants, and a couple of sergeants, finally made their way to the top. Many of them ended up going back down without skis and packs to help carry other people's packs up.

When it was all said and done, two sergeants—one infantry, one non-infantry, but both drill instructors—said that they were "hyping out," which meant that they had hypothermia. I just think they threw in the towel because they didn't want to stand watch with the rest of us after everything we had just been through. Personally, I don't see how anyone could claim hypothermia issues after that climb. I was finally warm, for the first time in weeks, from that climb.

Because we were in a leadership course, we were only allowed one cold or heat injury. If a student gets two injuries, they're out. It means they didn't do the proper preparation. Those who suffered as cold casualties were usually dehydrated, or they suffered because they didn't apply the discipline to keep from being a casualty. It was a matter of leadership and professionalism. If you can't take care of yourself, how can you take care of your Marines?

The two sergeants who hyped out knew it was their second time. Because they hyped out, we were forced to build an emergency tent, which wasn't part of our original plan. We had planned on sleeping in cold coffins.

I was tasked with setting up the emergency tent and babysitting this pair of quitters all night long. I boiled snow, forcing them to drink fluids all night to ensure rehydration. I was angry, exhausted, and beyond pissed. They faked being disoriented and went to sleep while I stayed up all night to keep an eye on them. I ended up with no sleep instead of the four hours everyone else received; all to ensure these two asshats *lived* through the night.

Morning came. We packed up so that the pretend helicopters could pick us up (the helicopters being the BVs). We skied down a steep hill and met the BVs in the open. We were cold and exhausted. Relief and happiness rolled through me. We had reached the end of our exercise. We loaded ourselves into the vehicles.

I immediately fell asleep, but when I woke up a short time later we were nowhere near base camp. One of our instructors ordered us out of the vehicle into a meadow that I didn't recognize. It was then that we learned our pretend helicopters had "crashed."

We were told to take out a poncho and lay it on the snow, placing every piece of gear from our packs on top. Then, the instructors walked around randomly confiscating various items.

They moved up and down the line saying, "I'm taking your stove," or, "I'm taking your black bag." When they got to me, they took my skis, poles, and stove. I was relieved that they left me my sleeping system. One of the instructors suddenly disappeared into one of the BVs, coming back to formation with all the field-expedient (homemade) snowshoes we'd half-assed a couple of weeks before.

Shit.

All of us whose skis had been taken were made to wear our poorly built snowshoes. We were given four hours to melt snow into water, build warming fires to dry our socks out, eat some food, and get a little sleep before we stepped off.

We got our gear together, made a route, and went over immediate action drills should we come into contact with "the enemy." This was not a mission in which we were to seek out the enemy; we were simply evading them after our "helicopter crash." The biggest challenge was in not knowing exactly where we were.

Within the first five hundred meters, all of us burdened with homemade snowshoes gave up on wearing them any longer. Time was as much an enemy as any other and we didn't have time to repair them. The guys on skis broke trails for us so that we wouldn't sink up to our crotches in snow with every step. However, it was still exhausting. I used my broken snowshoes as walking sticks. Every step was a harsh reminder to never half-ass anything again.

We pushed all day. I didn't think it was possible to feel any colder, but the lack of sleep, plus the added strain of marching through miles of four-foot snow, had taken its toll. As evening set in, we decided to spend the night. This was also in part because the instructors passed the word that it would take us three days to get back.

After several sleepless hours, we abandoned the idea of sleep. We discussed our situation as a team. The instructors who remained with us encouraged us to sleep, but ultimately they left the decision up to us. We decided we weren't going to stop for sleep again. We stepped off at three o'clock a.m.

It took us 16 hours to get back. I couldn't have told you the distances we covered because we were so slow, but we made it back a full day early.

Sleep is a crutch.

We were happy to have completed the exercise, and we relished the fact that we were cleaning our gear for the last time. Because we got back early, we had time to get a meal from the chow hall, along with a decent night's rest. That evening we all took part in an informal graduation ceremony, complete with everyone making fun of one other.

It had been two and one-half months since I'd left sunny San Diego for the freezing cold of Bridgeport. Now that we were done, the rest of 2/1 was to join us for field training.

Burns graciously offered to let Johnson and me go home for a week before the rest of the battalion started training there; otherwise it would have been five more weeks before I could have seen Kristine again. And while Johnson and I were gone, the entire unit would get their acclimatization period, classes on survival, and ski lessons.

When I returned, the battalion participated in a substantially abbreviated version of the training I had just completed. We had a shell of a company due to a large number of transitions; our company consisted of about twenty-five Marines instead of the normal full complement of 168. My platoon had two squad leaders and two team leaders. This would be a good opportunity for me to see my NCO's, non-commissioned officers, in action and find out what they were made of.

Company commanders were encouraged by the instructor staff to refer first to those Marines who had just passed the Mountain Leaders Course as far as decision making, route planning and more, as we were considered subject matter experts in the environment. Our function now was to be a resource for the commanders conducting operations in the cold weather environment.

Captain Burns wanted me to tent with him to help with the planning process for company operations. Johnson got out of it mostly because he'd been around longer. He really disliked Burns. I drew the short straw.

Looking back, I think the real reason Burns wanted a mountain leader in his tent was so that somebody could do everything for him. That included all of the individual preparations that were required in the mountain environment. It's a never-ending cycle of prepping gear, melting snow, cleaning gear, drying gear, and on and on.

As a mountain leader, part of my responsibility was to ensure our Marines stayed hydrated. We designated a piss tree, where one of us could inspect the color of everyone's urine to make sure it was clear. Squat buckets were used for taking a dump. Normally, we'd bury or burn our shit, but this wasn't allowed inside a National Forest. Instead, we all made our daily contributions, one load on top of the next, until the five-gallon shitters were full. Once they were full we'd put in a request to have someone pick up these sealed paint bucket cans, and someone at the bottom would have to wash them out. I've had to burn shitters before. It's completely disgusting.

I soon began to understand why Johnson despised Burns. The man participated in nothing. I believe he fabricated the requirement for him to be—all the time—at the battalion's command post, essentially big tents with wood burning stoves, so that he could get out of the cold. He'd leave the company XO and me to melt snow for water and all the other daily requirements.

Truth be told, as much as I hated having to do everything for him, it turned out to be a mixed blessing because the only time he tried to melt snow, he almost burned the tent down. Before lighting the stove, it must be primed by pumping a small plunger, which pulls fuel into the lighting chamber. Burns forgot this important step. When he pressed the igniter, flames shot up to the top of the tent. What was worse, this experienced Marine leader screamed like a little kid. I calmly reached over and turned it down.

"Relax, sir."

"I sounded like a little girl there, didn't I?"

"Yes sir, you did," I replied. I couldn't tell if the look on his face signified genuine embarrassment or if he realized my respect for him was beginning to falter.

Bridgeport winter trainings had a way of bringing out the weaknesses in people. Guys who appeared to be the hardest of the hard at sea level were completely different when the cold set in. There was nothing like a little snow and ice to reveal a person's true colors. It showed who the real leaders were.

Burns made a lot of decisions that began to really cause me to question not only his decision-making, but also his leadership. Almost every decision he made was comfort-based, especially when tactical scenarios were involved. To make matters worse, he refused to take advice from Johnson or me. At the end of the unit training period, we received a poor evaluation from the instructors. It was because of Burns and his poor decisions. We were dinged for taking the easy way out on most of our tasks. By the time our training in Bridgeport was over, I had lost all respect for him.

*R*oss returned from Bridgeport sunburned and sore, but ready for mountain warfare. He also came bearing gifts—including a bottle of my favorite wine.

I couldn't even begin to imagine all the hard work he'd put in while he was up there, but I could tell from the way he shared stories about everything that he'd loved it. He had the time of his life up there.

"This was what I was looking forward to the most, you know," he said a couple of days later, polishing off an egg sandwich. "There's nothing better in life than kicking back with my girl and my dog."

We were sitting at the kitchen table sharing a bit of breakfast. He'd been home for exactly 48 hours, and was already back in uniform. It was back to regular duty at Camp Pendleton before he left for Bridgeport again shortly.

"How are the wedding plans coming along? Anything new?" he asked.

"Well your Mom is trying to take control of the rehearsal dinner, but I don't know if that constitutes anything new . . . we knew this would happen," I said.

Trina—Ross's mother—and I were already having disagreements. Clichés are cliché mostly because they're true. Trina and I lived out in our relationship that old saw of the adversarial mother-in-law. It didn't help that he was an only child.

"I don't understand why she has to make such a big deal about this. She keeps saying that it's her *right* to make the rehearsal dinner what she wants it to be—the where, the when, and the how. She even insists that our location will reflect poorly on her."

"She can think whatever she wants," Ross said, "but we're making reservations where we want to make them. We already told everyone not to feel obligated to contribute. Even though she's offered, we still need to budget everything to pay for it ourselves. Then, of course, if family contributes in the end awesome. But I don't want to count on that—she doesn't even understand why we want to have it downtown."

"She doesn't care," I said, my frustration level rising just thinking about her. "She wants it to be close to her home for convenience. She doesn't think the restaurant we picked is nice enough."

"Seriously? Did you tell her they have good food? And more importantly, that the cost per person best fits our budget for the number of people we need to feed?

"I told her, but you know how she is. I know she's excited about the wedding, but she has to be realistic when it comes to what she wants versus what we want. After all, she's had two weddings of her own in which to do whatever she wants."

"Honestly, I don't know what to do about her." Ross sighed and stared up at the ceiling. I could tell he was as frustrated as I was. He kissed the back of my hand. "I know you've been gentle when dealing with her. I'll give it a go this time."

It was already a struggle for us trying to meet her expectations, and we weren't even married yet. Hopefully, she would step back and realize she needed to listen to what was important to us.

He stood and pulled me to my feet. He wrapped his arms around my waist and kissed me. "I love you. Try not to worry about it too much. I'll get her to see reason."

Some women daydream about finding their Superman. For me it wasn't phone booths and capes, it was cammies and boots. Ten minutes later my hero was out the door, and I was alone in the house again. I sighed. *I love that man. God, keep him safe.*

8

Going to the Chapel

Memorial Day Weekend, May 2002
Boise, Idaho

I'd never been much of a morning person, but when the alarm went off that morning, I jumped out of bed like it was on fire. We'd come home to Boise, Idaho to get married. It felt good to be home, to be surrounded by friends and family.

The day had finally arrived. I was hours away from becoming Mrs. Kristine Schellhaas.

Ross and I had been through a lot in our six years together: growth, pain, love, separation, and joy. All those experiences had led us to this day. We would make our vows with our loved ones as witnesses, pledging our lives to each other.

In the months leading up to the ceremony, I'd tried on multiple occasions to write my vows, to put down on paper how I felt about our union and my love for Ross, but I could never seem to find words to express the magnitude of my feelings for him. Now I had less than 24 hours until I would stand in front of God and our family and tell him what he meant to me—and I couldn't get more than a couple of words down before crumpling up the paper. It was just so much bigger than I was, bigger than any moment I had ever lived through up to that point.

I resolved to simply hang on and enjoy the ride. I hoped that when the moment arrived, I'd know exactly what to say. I looked over the wedding dress my mom and I had designed and sewed, at the bridesmaid dresses my mom had lovingly made. All these beautiful things were made especially for a moment that was almost here. I set aside a few little things I needed for the wedding. My dad shared the story of how Ross had asked him for my hand in marriage.

"I told him yes," he said, "but only if he promised to make sure he took great care with you, to which he said, 'Of course I will take care of Kristine, and take care of her needs above my own.'"

My dad started laughing. I told him, "No, *you* need to make sure you take care of yourself and don't let Kristine call all the shots!"

They both knew me. I had a propensity for planning things. I was glad they could laugh about it together.

Both the ceremony and the reception were held at the Shakespeare Theater, nestled in a grove of pine and cottonwood trees along the winding Boise River. The trees were lush and green, birds serenaded the wedding party, and the earthy scents of river rock and weeping willow filled the air. A few deer even hazarded a glance at us during the reception.

Before I walked down the aisle, my dad looked over at me. He smiled at me as tears welled in his eyes. "I'm so proud of you. This'll be the only time I get to walk my little girl down the aisle."

I was undone. I was already standing with my finger in the dam, doing all I could to hold back a whole reservoir of emotion. He'd set loose a stream of tears flowing down my face. "I love you, Daddy."

My father walked me down the aisle, towards my destiny and my Marine.

The officiating ministers were two of my cousins. We gave them carte blanche on preparing the words for our ceremony. They provided the perfect blend of sincerity, thought-provoking insight, and humor.

The time came for our vows. After that moment I knew life would never be the same. I had long ago reconciled my heart with the fact that this day signified I was accepting a whole life with Ross—and everything that would come with it.

There was going to be war.

There would be heartache.

Ross would surely at some point be half a world away from me, in harm's way, and I would have to deal with it as best I could. That was what you got when you married a military man.

After a few shared moments together we were pronounced man and wife.

It was official: I was his wife. He kissed me, and for a moment it was just him and me, and the world was ours to conquer. Our friends and family applauded as the music started for our walk back up the aisle. Now it was lined with Marines, swords drawn and raised high. I thought I was prepared for the usual tradition—a Marine sword whacking my butt as I passed by, but I was surprised when the sword was brought down in front of me. Ross' friend, Lt Johnson, announced that passage could only be granted by a kiss!

I was not expecting this.

I stole a glance at Ross, then leaned over and planted a kiss on Johnson's cheek. He laughed. "No ma'am, I meant kiss your new husband!"

I could feel the color bloom in my cheeks, but I laughed along with him, then turned and planted a sweet kiss on Ross's cheek.

Seconds later I received my official welcome into the Marine Corps when that blade slapped my ass.

Wedding photo captured alongside the river at the Idaho Shakespeare Theater

9

Go Forth Boldly

★ ★ ★

January 2003
Camp Pendleton to Destination Classified
Boise, Idaho

*I*t didn't take long to learn as a military spouse that I could no longer count on kissing my husband goodnight most of the time. I had to get used to eating alone, sleeping alone, and managing pretty much everything without him. Ross was away more than I had ever expected he would be. I was doing my best to keep things light and as close to normal as I could for when he returned.

I learned that the bliss of normalcy only lasts so long in our world. We evolve and drift in a sea of ever-changing currents, tides, and depths. Change can only be embraced. Those who don't accept it or walk willingly into it will leave their happiness behind.

We knew this day was coming. We'd done our best to prepare for it but I still wasn't ready for him to leave. Deployment—and—war—were imminent. He'd be gone for at least six months. I could only hope and pray that Ross would come home to me safe.

My growing apprehension was only exacerbated by the fact that I had recently lost my job due to downsizing. With no job, few friends, and Ross heading into harm's way, the loneliness in California was too much for me.

I decided to move home.

I loved my parents; they'd always supported me, they'd been my biggest cheerleaders, but how was I going to live under their roof with no job and nothing to do?

Then there was the fact that I would be living in the same town as Ross's mother Trina. She moved to Boise after retiring from teaching high school in Oregon during the time we were attending college. Every encounter was a gamble, I was hopeful for the times when she was pleasant and lovely, but rued the others when she scrutinized or interrogated me for information.

Ross hadn't even left yet, and already I was feeling like he couldn't get back fast enough. I resigned myself to the idea that I would figure it out when I got to Boise, hoping for the best.

I spent weeks boxing up our home. I hired movers to load it onto the truck for delivery to our storage unit while Ross was busy working. The last of our money was spent in-between that and the wedding.

I packed up the final boxes, our black lab Charlie, and my new wedding gift—a black cocker spaniel puppy named Zazu—and settled into a hotel a few days before Ross was to deploy.

For the first time in my adult life I was in a state of limbo. How long would it be before I began to feel normal, before I could enjoy some kind of stability or routine again? How long was I going to have to just sit and wait?

Ross was due to sail out of San Diego on the USS *Duluth* (LPD-6) with the 15th MEU, sailing with the USS *Tarawa* (LHA-1) and USS *Rushmore* (LSD-47) to destination: classified.

Navy protocols allow family aboard the ship just prior to departure to say goodbye.

There were a lot of uniforms, a lot of tears, and a lot of gear being jostled about.

Ross leaned over and squeezed my shoulder to try to reassure me.

I smiled.

"You know, babe, this is all going to get worked out diplomatically. They're never going to declare war."

"You think so?" I asked, trying to keep my voice from cracking.

An early morning photo captured before the Duluth pulled out to sea, headed for Iraq.

"Yeah. It's going to be okay."

I nodded, but something in my gut told me that wasn't going to be the case.

It only took a week for the cold reality of his absence to set in. I missed everything about him. I missed his smell, his scratchy face kissing me softly, our after-dinner walks, and cuddling up on the couch.

I know I can make it.

I could feel that there was something right around the corner, but I didn't know whether it was a threat or a promise. It churned in my stomach and soured there.

I imagined him in his tiny little berth, speeding steadily towards the Middle East, sharing 20 square feet with three other guys. A shared desk. No bathroom. No nothing.

But then I remembered that he loved it.

He knew what he was getting into. But did I?

People said it all the time: *You married a service member. You knew what you signed up for.* But that wasn't exactly true. I'd signed up for love. Love was supposed to be bigger than that. It was supposed to conquer all, wasn't it?

I'd known there were going to be sacrifices along the way, but no two couples ever experience the same thing. Just as every relationship was different, every deployment was different and every experience was different.

Would he be coming home alive and well—or with the Stars and Stripes draped over his coffin? Every time the thought entered my mind, my breath caught in my throat. I couldn't think about it. I didn't want to think about it. I needed something to distract me, something to focus my attention on. I needed it desperately.

From: Ross
Day: January 10, 2003 5:32am
To: Kristine

> I already miss you so much. It's hard to believe this day is here. How was the move to your folks' place? Believe it or not, I'd like to be there to massage your feet. Bet you never thought you'd hear that.

I've been in contact with a friend of mine over in the sandbox. He said things are pretty slow. So that's good news.

My days are pretty routine, so I don't have a lot to talk about, other than how much I'm missing you. I can't talk about when we're going or where; that's how email privileges get jerked away from everyone. I won't be going to our first stop, and our second one, which was mentioned before we left, is iffy.

I was out on the upper deck tonight, and you wouldn't believe how clear it was. You could see a ton of stars. I saw Orion's belt, and hoped that maybe you'd see it too while you waited for Zazu to poop in typical wake-you-up-in-the-middle-of-the-night fashion.

I miss you more than I can say. I can't wait until we're together again. I really need you to talk about your days, no matter if they're good or bad. It brings me comfort having a little piece of home. I won't have a lot of time to email because bandwidth is limited, but know that I love you, and that you mean everything to me.

And there it was. He couldn't tell me where he was or where he was going. I didn't need all the sexy details but to go on without a clue? I sighed. I knew my plight wasn't unique among all of the loved ones in the world who were waiting for their special someone. But it was clear: Trying to figure out the rhythm and rhyme of whatever was going on in Ross's life while he was deployed was going to be more difficult than I'd previously thought.

How am I ever going to get used to this?

Being on a MEU with email was a huge improvement from the last time I had been on float. Hell, we'd had neither email nor internet nor cell phones when I'd been an enlisted man.

Thankfully, I'd learned from my previous two deployments that I couldn't just fill every Marine's daytime hours with classes; all it does is raise tensions and contribute to fights. Just because we didn't have anywhere else to be, didn't mean I should make my Marines sit through eight hours of classes a day—it's just too much.

I limited our classroom training to just two sessions a day: one between breakfast and lunch, and the other between lunch and dinner. SSgt Lerma and I would go over breaching scenarios, conducting ambushes, establishing a defensive position, operating in chemical suits—then tack on martial arts training for the mornings and combat lifesaver for afternoons. Getting into a routine would make our days bearable.

My full focus was on getting us ready for a war that I truly believed was never going to happen. Still, I had to make sure our Marines were fully trained. Most of us on ship agreed that everything would be worked out diplomatically—that we would just show up in the Middle East and the enemy would wilt before us. Saddam would surely open up for the inspectors in short order after that.

But no one knew anything for certain. All we knew was, after 48 hours of liberty in Singapore, we were bound for the Persian Gulf.

> From: Ross
> Date: January 17, 2003 4:44 PM
> To: Kristine
>
> We have a change of pace this week. We've had three live fires (we lay on the flight deck and shoot towards the sea), which is good for the whole company and a great way to break up the monotony.
>
> I'm continually thinking about war and what we're potentially embarking upon here. As I stand on the eve of probable combat, I wonder: what do my Marines think of me? Save you, there is no one in the world I care more about.
>
> I've always been confident in my ability to handle fear, but as we prepare for arrival, these thoughts have been pervasive in my mind this past week. Everyone thinks I'm this great leader. But am I? Will I do everything I have to do to keep these guys alive in combat? I know some things are out of my hands. Have we done our best to get them ready? How will I face their families if I lose even one of them?
>
> I'm worried because it isn't a matter of *hoping* I do well; I *have* to do well because I've got to bring as many men back as I possibly can.
>
> And I have to come back to you.
>
> I wish I could be there with you even now.

*T*he first month of living with my parents went better than expected. The dogs enjoyed the large backyard. Zazu's sweet puppy
face masked her cunning ways as a master escape artist. I'd lost track
of the number of times she managed a way to Superman over the
chain-link fence or how many times my dad forgot to close a gate
because he wasn't used to having dogs around.

Life at home wasn't what it used to be. Maybe I thought I'd have
a bit of my old life back, but it turned out everyone had moved on
with their lives; they worked day jobs or were occupied with taking
care of their kids.

And there I was, just waiting to get on with my life. It was
frustrating at times to not have anywhere to be. I had the entire
day to do what I wanted, and I was living rent-free, but I was
miserable. The house I'd grown up in was starting to feel like a
prison. Without something or someone to contribute to, I
struggled with my own self-worth.

I made a diligent effort to get together with Ross's family on a
weekly basis. I went out to lunch with his mom, Trina, about once
a week. I spent time with his grandparents. I even taught his
grandfather how to use his computer and email.

But no matter my efforts, I didn't feel like I'd managed to make
a difference in the way Trina felt about me. Her disapproval only
added to my feelings of despair.

Part Two

If You Can't Be Safe, Be Deadly

"Civilized men sleep soundly because rough men stand ready to do violence on their behalf."

—*George Orwell*

10

This Is War

February 2003
Kuwait and Invasion into Iraq
Boise, Idaho

Some of our battalion loaded on to CH-53 Super Stallions, better known to Marines as Shitters because of the smoke that streams out the back of the helicopter. The rest of us climbed into CH-46 Sea Knights, known affectionately as Phrogs because well, they look like frogs.

We loaded up about 12 at a time, weapons in hand, eventually landing just outside the Kuwaiti Army's 6th Brigade base in Camp Bullrush. They had created a crude compound by piling up an earthen berm around the camp's perimeter in the middle of the wide open desert.

If we ended up invading Iraq, we were going to need all the help we could get taking our gear in with us. Camp Bullrush became the 15th MEU's new headquarters. General Conway, the MEF commander, Marine Expeditionary Force, was waiting to address the US troops and Royal Marines.

Once the MEF Commander was done with us and we were let go, our scavenger hunt began. Because we were short one cargo trailer, the company gunny grabbed me; he knew I had friends at Camp Commando, and we started looking for a trailer for our Humvee to help carry our ammo and other mission-essential equipment.

Each day we discussed the invasion with one another, talking about what our roles might be. We worked on rehearsals, conducting as much realistic PT as we could in conjunction with fire, movement, and demolition classes. We crafted our orders so that we would be prepared for anything we could possibly imagine. All that was left to do after that was wait for orders to move out.

———— 💍 ————

I celebrated my 26th birthday without Ross. I'd hit my first relatively major life event without my Marine. I knew it would be the
first of many missed holidays, birthdays and anniversaries, but it was
frustrating not being able to at least talk with him.

I invited my family to go out to dinner, along with Ross' stepdad
Frank, and Trina. I chose a place that I knew would meet my in-laws'
dietary requirements, which wasn't exactly the kind of place I would
have normally chosen to go for a special night out. It was one of those
barbeque chains, complete with wagon wheels and cattle brands on
the walls.

I drove there with my parents, putting on a happy face about
the evening. I missed Ross. Mostly what I hoped for that night was
simply that it would go well with both families.

I sat between my sister-in-law Cindy and my mother-in-law
Trina. "What are you going to have for dinner?" Trina asked me.

"Oh, I've been craving some ribs, so I think I'll order those. And
maybe even some French fries, since it's my birthday."

"You shouldn't have the fries," she said. "They're not good for
your figure."

My forced smile melted right off my face. At first I thought she
was kidding. I played it off by saying, "Well, calories don't count on
my birthday, right?"

Wrong.

"Do what you will, but you know the rule: one minute on the
lips, a lifetime on the hips."

My jaw hit the floor. I had been working out a lot, trying to get
leaner, but I certainly wasn't fat by any means. Trina kept on going,
though, like an attack dog working over a stuffed dummy. She talked
on and on about "calories in, calories out," and any other diet phrase
she could think of.

My sister-in-law leaned over and whispered, "Order the fries—it
is your birthday, after all." She looked at Trina and shook her head.

Why does Trina hate me? Nothing was ever good enough for her.

I smiled at my sister-in-law.

Then I ordered those damn fries.

The transition to move from Camp Bullrush to Camp Viking had begun. Then the news that we had been expecting to come since our departure from California finally came. It was news that would forever change our generation of the Marine Corps: we were invading Iraq.

We had orders to secure the port of Umm Qasr. My platoon would provide the blocking position in the south to facilitate the company's attack into the port. Umm Qasr sat where two ancient rivers, the Tigris and the Euphrates, flowed into the ocean. It was a small town; almost all of the people who lived there worked at the port.

SSgt Lerma guided the platoon through detainee procedures so that we'd be prepared if and when the Iraqis surrendered. We rehearsed the building of a field-expedient containment area with metal stakes and several strands of concertina wire. We anticipated we might have as many as 50 enemy POWs initially.

It was almost time to execute those orders.

We were as ready as we were going to get.

I looked out across the flat desert, trying to imagine what would come. Units adjacent to us were also tasked in the invasion. Our 15th MEU was attached to the British 3rd Commando Brigade, Royal Marines. Battalions from the Commando Brigade were assigned to seize the Al Faw Peninsula. Our battalion, 2/1, was responsible for securing both the new and the old ports of Umm Qasr.

Four days passed without word one from Ross. I could only imagine that he was preparing to invade, because what else would precipitate that kind of isolation?

Invasion.

I had no way to define what that really meant. I knew he was in Kuwait training with his men. Holding on to any kind of hope for a diplomatic resolution to the conflict was becoming less and less realistic. My gut told me they were getting ready for the inevitable.

Riots and unrest in the area were in the news constantly; conflicts were breaking out all across the world.

I knew Ross was looking forward to being tested on the battlefield with his fellow Marines. They had the tactics and the training—this was, after all, what they'd signed on the dotted line to do. But it was the last thing I wanted him to do, and I was scared.

On March 17, 2003, President George W. Bush gave Saddam Hussein 48 hours to step down as dictator of Iraq or risk a military invasion.

I hadn't slept well a single night since having to say goodbye to my husband in San Diego; sleep had become entirely evasive. The two days that followed progressed in a haze; I fought the urge to cry often.

I was lying in bed staring at the ceiling wondering how long I could go without sleep when the phone rang. *Please let it be Ross.* "Hello?"

"Hey, babe."

"Ross! Hi!"

"Look, I don't have a lot of time, so I need to keep this short. Just know that I love you. Marrying you has been the best decision I've ever made and I'm so proud to call you my wife. I'll call you as soon as I can, all right? I have to go."

"Okay, Ross," I said through my tears. "I love you. Don't be a hero."

He laughed and replied simply, "I love you."

Then the familiar sound of silence—my new nemesis—took hold of me. I realized his call could only mean one thing . . .

The invasion had begun.

News and images of the action flooded the networks. Several embedded reporters reported via live feeds from Iraq. There was a lot of speculation. Could it really be true that this invasion would end just as quickly as the last one had? I hoped and prayed that the pattern we'd established in Desert Storm would continue; a short excursion for our troops in-country, very few injuries, and even fewer fatalities.

Words couldn't express the depth of the fear I held in my heart for our military men and women. I prayed that God would give them all strength throughout their endeavor, and bring them home safe.

In the days that followed, I found myself glued to the TV. Every news station showed both live and recorded footage of the war. They announced that the 15th MEU was attacking the port city of Umm Qasr, Iraq. I was in shock when I read the ticker tape along the bottom highlighting Ross's company from the MEU. A British reporter gave the play-by-play as bullets flew right outside an Iraqi stronghold.

I sat watching a freaking *war* unfold *on television,* knowing that Ross was right in the mix. I could no longer pretend none of this would have a direct impact on my life.

Moments later I heard someone in the background call out, "Gas, gas, gas!" The camera panned and zoomed. There was an ominous white cloud on the horizon—all I could think was that now there were weapons of mass destruction at play. *Is this something that's going to forever change the physiology of my husband's body? Will we be able to have kids?*

Before he left, Ross and I had discussed storing his semen at a medical facility just in case something happened. We ultimately decided against it because it was completely outside the limits of our budget. We knew some of the costs of war—there were too many reports of men permanently injured by chemical agents introduced during Vietnam and Desert Storm. We weren't naïve; we knew there was always a chance that he could become terribly damaged from whatever he was going to face in Iraq.

The next scene on the newscast showed the Marines in Ross's platoon donning gas masks. Then something that looked like a bazooka was fired. The impact downrange blew up a large portion of the enemy's buildings. The reporter called the weapon a Javelin, and said that the Marines from his platoon were the first to use it in battle.

Later that evening, I learned the pivotal role the port of Umm Qasr played strategically; it was crucial for bringing humanitarian supplies in and shipping oil out. While the Marines were busy fighting on land, it was reported that Navy SEALS and Special Forces were busy clearing mines and securing oil platforms and infrastructure that was endangered in the waterways so that humanitarian aid could be expedited. The Polish Special Forces and Marine Security Forces stationed in Bahrain seized some of the oil platforms outside the port as well.

The day after the invasion something unexpected happened.

Phone calls and emails poured in expressing concern for me and for Ross. Everyone wanted to know where he was and if he was safe. The truth was I didn't know anything beyond what anyone else knew. We all saw the same newscasts. I was just as much in the dark as they were, but they all felt better having talked to me. I indulged their need for comfort out of love, and by the end of the day I felt as if I had taken on the burden of everyone else's stress and anxiety on top of my own.

I didn't realize it until later, but I had really messed up by isolating myself from my military community. I hadn't built a network. I hadn't invested enough in the community of my military friends. Instead, I ran home to my civilian sanctuary, the one I'd grown up in, the one I knew, the one I was comfortable with. But this community had no idea what I was going through, and further—had no mechanism to help me cope.

Sure, I was volunteering with the KV network from afar. But I was still isolated. It wasn't difficult maintaining rosters, creating newsletters, and taking part in the phone tree—but I lost out on the *relationships,* walking alongside a friend, discussing what we'd seen on TV. Most importantly, I didn't have anyone to talk to about the emotions we all felt. I mean if anybody *got it,* then they were people who were living the same life I was.

This was the first of many revelations in the new reality Ross and I faced. We were watching a war unfold on the news—live. In past wars there was a constant underlying fear of what terrors might be taking place, but no one knew anything for sure. In the past we got by on the "no news is good news" mentality. Now, we watched the horrors of war unfold live on TV. Each time a plane crashed or a tank blew up or a service member was killed on the battlefield, we would wonder if he was ours. And we imagined the knock on the door each and every time.

Had I known then what I know now, I would have never moved home.

Saddam Hussein didn't have a great fighting force. We knew that if he felt desperate enough, he'd use any means he had to stay in power—which meant using WMDs on us. To that end, we were prepared for a chemical attack.

Before the invasion took place, Burns stood in front of the company at Camp Bullrush, trying to get us motivated for war. He referred to the Marines as pawns and to himself as the chess master. His condescension was appalling. I'd met plenty of tools in my life, but as some of the enlisted Marines whispered, Burns was the whole damn toolbox. While he delivered what I was sure he thought was a momentous speech, a SCUD missile was launched. We received early warning of the enemy launch over the radio (later, it was reported the missile had been directed at Camp Commando in Kuwait).

We were assigned to work with the Brits. They needed access to some of our assets in order to complete their mission, so we loaned them helicopters, artillery, and other material. In exchange, we could call on the British artillery and engineers to support us from the ground as we drove forward into Iraq.

In the hours before dawn, more SCUD missiles were launched. When the sun broke over the horizon, we headed out. It wasn't very exciting for us at first: all we could hear was the sound of our helicopters and vehicles. I kept thinking something was going to happen; command was going to stop us just short of the border, announce a diplomatic decision, and tell us to go home.

We had driven, chemsuits donned, half a mile into Iraq when the Iraqis engaged Lt Johnson's Combined Anti-Armor and Heavy Machine Gun platoon (CAAT). They were attacked by an enemy observation post consisting of about three or four guys. The CAAT platoon was wasting valuable time waiting for Burns to make a decision about what to do.

Burns called in a request for aircraft support. I thought it was a waste of time and resources. I thought we should keep moving. Now, an entire reinforced rifle company was being halted by a small observation post. In the meantime, Lt Maidens was working on a quick-fire plan to get our mortars firing on the Iraqis' position.

Then we began receiving a massive barrage of fire. It was either artillery or mortars. I directed my Marines to dismount, to find cover away from the column of vehicles, as the enemy was likely targeting the trucks and would adjust their fire onto our position. Our vehicles began to turn around, moving five hundred meters towards a covered position in the southwest. Once they were ready to go, I ordered all the Marines to mount up again. They jumped in or clung on to any part of the vehicle they could. We looked like the Clampetts on their way to Beverly Hills. Second Platoon's five-ton had already gone down, so those Marines executed the bump plan, wherein they dispersed themselves throughout the rest of our vehicles so that we could continue the mission.

A second barrage of artillery sounded off in the distance. There was an explosion and a cloud of dust, into which the whole column suddenly disappeared. Our vehicles had no real protection against the enemy—just a layer of sandbags, most of which had been thrown out because the vehicles were already overburdened. This was true for Johnson's CAAT Platoon, Burns' vehicle with Maidens and the rest of the fire support team, the vehicle with all our ammo in it, and even the company executive officer, and gunny. The first thing I thought after the explosion was that we had lost all of them.

I ordered my Marines to dismount, and began making my way on foot to the impact area. Before I could get one hundred meters, I could see that the vehicles were backing out of the dust and smoke. There was so much powdered dust streaming off the vehicles as they moved, they looked like they had donned smoke dispensers—like what you'd see on an aerobatic plane at an air show. Burns' vehicle was heading straight towards me, and Maidens was clinging to the hood of the vehicle, getting bounced all over the place.

They met me in the open desert. Maidens' hand was bleeding, and there was shrapnel in the vehicle. Burns got out of the truck completely covered in dust. He slapped the map on the hood and yelled, "Rich, I want you to tell me how you just almost killed me!" Burns thought Lt Maidens had called those rounds on their position, that they'd fallen victim to friendly fire.

Maidens responded, "Sir, I hadn't even sent in our grid."

Burns looked to be on the verge of panic. He kept repeating himself and staring at the map.

By now, all the lieutenants had reached our position, and began looking at each other as if to say *what do we do now?*

I said what the other lieutenants were thinking. "Uh . . . sir?

Why don't we worry about who called in what later, and get out of this position."

Burns stopped for a moment, seeming to realize what was happening—the expressions of anxiety on our faces. In training, if something is really dorked-up, we stop in the middle of everything and call everyone in to un-ass ourselves. We called it a training timeout. That's what Burns seemed to be doing here, only we weren't training anymore. This was the real deal. We needed to actually do something.

He ordered us back to the vehicles.

Cobras arrived shortly thereafter and blew the shit out of the Iraqi observation post, even though it had likely been abandoned 15 minutes earlier. We started moving forward again, soon reaching the paved road that would take us to our objective.

Along the way we encountered a full Iraqi Battalion—hundreds of men, including the Iraqi Battalion XO—walking towards us unarmed and waving white flags of surrender. Second Platoon received them as prisoners, while my platoon continued towards the old port.

As we drew close to the port and its buildings, two civilian vehicles raced towards our formation. We had been briefed about the possibility that suicide bombers would attack our positions. These two vehicles fit the bill.

Johnson's platoon fired warning shots, hoping to get the vehicles to stop, but it was to no avail. Then our heavy and medium machine guns engaged the vehicles. Nothing. The vehicles still continued towards us, albeit much slower. Moments later they stopped—a man jumped out and began running towards the tanks. A sniper put five rounds in his chest. He took a few steps and fell dead.

We gave the damaged vehicles a wide berth, continuing our forward movement. As we passed, we saw the wounded inside one the cars. We could tell now that it had been driven by a desperate family trying to flee the port area. No one felt good about the situation, but as bad as we felt, we knew their actions had left us little choice. When a car speeds towards a convoy at a high rate of speed, it gives us little time to react; we must assume it's hostile.

Navy corpsmen—our combat medics—immediately began treating the wounded in the car. If the Iraqis had just pulled over and stepped out onto the side of the road, all this could have been avoided. We would have quickly searched the car and the men, then let them continue on their way.

We learned that one of the cars belonged to a family from Ethiopia, a husband and wife traveling with their two daughters. The other carried four men. All of the men in the vehicles were killed during the engagement, including the man from Ethiopia. The women sustained minor wounds, which were treated. What happened after that, we don't know.

They were the first casualties we saw in the war. I knew this was part of my job. I remember Norman Schwarzkopf said something to the effect that "Combat is awesome; war is awful." War encompasses everything: physical harm of the innocent, mental and physical trauma sustained by the noncombatants. Combat can be defined as opposing forces on the battlefield, each attempting to impose its will on the other. Ideally that situation would exclude the innocent.

We continued to push forward to our objective and secure the new port of Umm Qasr. As we drove to the blocking position our vehicle began to take fire. I could hear the snap of bullets over my head through the five-ton's open roof.

A squad leader yelled something at me, but I couldn't hear it. I opened the door, grabbed an assist handle near the top of the cab, and swung out so that I was standing on the step side of the truck, facing towards the rear. I looked at the squad leader. "Say again?"

He answered, "We're taking fire from what looks like trenches." I looked over, saw movement, and heard a few more snaps over the vehicle. Moments later, a mortar round impacted about three hundred meters short of our position. The squad leader looked to me for guidance.

We had been told we couldn't fire in the housing areas— we didn't want civilians getting hurt—but we hadn't reached the housing area yet. We were still in open space.

I directed him to fire back. The whole back of the truck unleashed on the enemy's position. I was still standing outside the vehicle on the steps when the .50 cal machine gunner above me opened up. The concussion of the gun hit my body like lightning; I realized I couldn't hear much of anything. I sat back in the cab, plugged one ear, and radioed to report the contact.

I provided Burns with the enemy's position—it was about five hundred meters from us—and told him we were maintaining contact. I asked him if he wanted me to clear the trenches. He said no, that we should continue moving forward to our blocking position.

The enemy stopped firing at us as we gained fire superiority. We didn't see further movement, so I figured they had either hunkered down or left the trenches.

I still couldn't hear much of anything. The Marines were redistributing ammo. Everyone had huge smiles on their faces. As we neared a set of buildings, I scanned the continuous second-story windows of those buildings standing closest to the road. I saw movement inside. I made out two figures running down the hall, heading in the same direction we were traveling, carrying something long and cylindrical.

"RPG, three o'clock," I yelled.

I fired at the two enemy combatants, which pinpointed their position for the rest of my men. The enemy went down quick, but I didn't know if they were dead or just hiding. I reported the contact to Burns and asked if we should clear the building. Once again I was told to continue to the blocking position.

We reached a choke point, where the buildings on both sides of the road reached a narrow spot. We were in real danger of an Iraqi ambush here. The convoy slowed down, and we proceeded with caution as gunfire crackled in the distance.

Eventually we arrived at our position and established security. One of the squad leaders quickly set up the marshaling position for enemy prisoners while we worked towards establishing communication, but I couldn't get hold of anyone. We needed to let command know about the potential ambush that could be waiting for our other forces, which were already en route.

I managed to get a hold of another platoon commander and asked him to relay that our blocking position was established.

While we were waiting, I directed my Marines to clear the small outbuilding in the immediate area. We dug some small trenches (called skirmisher's trenches) so we could have a little cover if we were attacked. I took two squads to reconnoiter the old port, about three hundred meters away from our blocking position.

Once there, I recognized a possible landing zone, LZ, for a sister company whose mission was to secure the new port. We scoped out the area and gained a foothold in the old port so that they could land their helicopters, allowing them to bypass both the open ground and potential ambush sites. It would also save them the five- or six-mile hike with all their gear on their backs; it was cleared and ready for the company to land.

But this message was never relayed to their company commander. The helos landed over six miles away by the old port, and the company had to hike with enormous packs in the middle of the day in 80° weather. They pushed through, and made enemy contact at the same place we did. Fortunately they didn't take any casualties from the enemy fire, but by the time they arrived there were more than a few heat casualties. We sent our vehicle out to pick them up.

I met up with the company commander who was responsible for security at the new port, and talked with him about the LZ we had cleared for them. He said he'd never got the word about it. Later one of the other lieutenants said that Burns never got out of his vehicle and never made any plans to enter the port with his Marines. It wasn't until one of our Marines, who was injured by accidentally putting his arm through a window, that First Sergeant took the CO's vehicle to evacuate the wounded Marine.

Everyone said Burns seemed to be in a daze—the only thing that seemed to explain this was that he was greatly affected by the artillery that had almost killed him and the other company leadership. If the berm hadn't been there, we all would have had a very different first day.

Eventually our platoon received a call to consolidate, to head back to our company. We made the two-mile movement back to the port, then I reported to Burns. He gave me two positions to occupy in order to defend the port.

I was given both the northern entrance and the railroad bridge that led into the port. Lerma immediately set about getting the Marines resupplied with ammo and water. Once we were set, I split our platoon up. I kept two rifle squads and a Javelin team with me at the main entrance, and sent a machine gun and rifle squad with Lerma.

Around midnight we finalized plans, including a security patrol in the immediate area. We got up at 0430 for stand-to, a term used for the time at which the enemy was most likely to attack. We were ready for battle: our gear was secured in our packs, we were loaded up and ready to go.

The sun rose, but brought with it no enemy attack. As a result, we settled into what would become our daily routine: spending our time clearing little outbuildings on the perimeter of the port.

We came upon a small store of weapons. One of the buildings had served as a living space, and it looked like whoever had been living there dropped everything moments before we'd entered the port the previous day. It looked like we even interrupted their meal—there were plates of food and cups of tea. One of the electric hot plates they used to heat their water was still on. Their uniforms were piled up in the corner as though they'd been hastily shed in the instantaneous decision to abandon the position.

Lerma spotted movement above the railroad tunnel, saying that it might be as many as ten Iraqis. He pointed out what he thought might be a spotter on the roof. The Iraqi was observing us through binoculars, calling down to his guys one floor beneath him. A burst of medium machine gun fire erupted from their position. The spotter watched the impacts and yelled down corrections. The method was very similar to the way we employ our machine guns.

We maintained our position at the north entrance to the port. If a large attack was imminent, I felt sure it would come from here. I sent Lerma with a reinforced squad: machine guns, mortars, a Javelin missile team, and eight hundred meters of open ground between them and the Iraqis. Perfect. They began to positively ID targets and engage the enemy.

A reporter moved in to capture the firefight for television. Later, I discovered this was the same coverage Kristine had seen on the news. Meanwhile, our machine gun squad focused on the spotter. He popped up one too many times from the same place, and took a 7.62mm in the chest for his efforts. I saw him go down as I scanned with my binoculars from my position.

The two squad leaders who remained with me wanted to move to the other squad; the one that was "having all the fun." We stayed put. Lerma had everything under control. I called Burns and recommended—as I had done the first time we made contact with the enemy—that I take my other two squads and attempt to flank them. I planned on using Lerma's position as the support-by-fire position to keep the enemy suppressed while we swung around from the north.

Burns denied the request, saying that he was bringing up tanks. I didn't agree, but all I could say was, "Roger, Terrapin Six." I cynically thought to myself that maybe the Marine Corps should change its doctrine, because all it seemed we were doing was blowing the hell out of things instead of ensuring positions were cleared.

Maybe there was indeed pressure from command for zero casualties, but we weren't employing any of the techniques or tactics that we had been trained in. I was all for calling in the tanks, but they should have had infantry support, particularly when entering an urban area.

Lerma brought up the Javelin with two Marines to set up the weapons system. The first missile looked like it was flying true, but it then went errant behind the building.

They loaded a second missile and fired. The missile went right into the window. No enemy machine guns fired after that. We spotted a few men running from the smoking building, heading south towards the trench line from where we had initially taken fire while heading into the old port.

We expected massive surrenders at that point because all of the other Iraqis had given up so easily. We knew that the Iraqi forces consisted of different tiers, and that the majority of them weren't terribly loyal to Saddam. The political officers kept them in check —which was reminiscent of the tyranny the North Vietnamese or Soviet Army would employ—even if that meant telling them their entire family would be killed if they surrendered.

In the end we encountered very few of those loyal Iraqis. Swarms of their forces surrendered almost immediately. When we did engage it was with much smaller elements than I expected we would encounter.

Later that evening I came back to where the first firefight had taken place, the building with the long corridors of glass. One of the Recon teams joined us, and brought their .50 cal Barrett, a large sniper rifle. It was a Special Application Scoped Rifle, SASR. It was massive, weighing near 30 pounds. SASR bullets are eight inches long. It was primarily designed for shooting parked aircraft or vehicles, typically from over a mile away.

Then we began taking more fire from the building. It was one of the few times Burns came to observe one of our engagements. I watched for targets.

The requested tanks rolled up and put a couple of 120mm rounds from their main guns into the building, then peppered it with their coaxially mounted machine guns.

The enemy firing stopped. The tanks turned and headed west to support another company. We began to take fire from another building; they were employing the same tactics, using a spotter and a medium machine gun. The sniper from our Recon team spotted him, applied the data to the scope, and shot at the Iraqi with the .50 cal Barrett from about fourteen hundred meters. He just missed him with his first shot, but the second shot hit. It folded him in half, blowing off his leg.

An hour later we were under fire once again. Burns brought Maidens up this time, and he called for air support to attack the target. Maidens ordered the mortarmen to mark the building with a white phosphorus round known as a WP, or Willy Pete. A Marine Harrier then flew in, firing a Maverick missile right into the building. After that there were no more attacks from that area. The Maverick hit the building full on, but in the end I'm not convinced it did much more than just scare the Iraqis off.

A week later I saw Ross's unit on the news again, this time announcing that the 15th MEU was moving into An Nasiriyah to relieve the Marines of Task Force Tarawa, TFT, so that they could continue further north towards Baghdad.

For me, it was devastating news. While Ross's unit was busy fighting in Umm Qasr, Task Force Tarawa had been in heavy firefights with Saddam's Fedayeen and members of the Iraqi 11th Infantry Division. They had lost several men.

There were also reports of a tragic incident of friendly fire: initial estimates reported 18 Marines were killed. Two A-10 Warthog aircraft flown by Pennsylvania National Guard pilots were ordered on a strafing run, having been told there were "no friendlies north of the bridge" by the Marine forward air controller, or FAC. They fired their cannons on two of our Marine amphibious assault vehicles, AAVs.

All I could do was watch the news and wait for him to come home.

Every name and face I saw on the news was Ross. My heart reached out for him, and I prayed daily for his continued safety. I grieved for every life lost as if it were one of my own friends or family.

Three days later, we left Umm Qasr and traveled 40 miles to another port facility, Azu Bayer. At the same time the rest of the Division—and several other services—were racing towards Baghdad.

Along the way we encountered a huge herd of wild camels traveling in a pack of about one hundred. They didn't have a shepherd, and we smelled them before we saw them—a rank animal stench.

Just shy of our target destination we passed several destroyed enemy tanks. The debris littered a stretch for about one-quarter of a mile. The metal hulls still burned, streaking the sky with towering wisps of black smoke. I'm sure any unit that came upon these vehicles probably shot at them. I imagine that 3/4 came through and added to the destruction, followed by our CAAT Platoon and other elements in 2/1.

Unlike Umm Qasr, the port at Azu Bayer had no surrounding town. We established our post in the northwest corner of the port, where we could observe the entire northern end of it.

The next day, while en route to visit one of my platoons, I met up with Burns. He stood staring at a group of Iraqi women and children through a set of binoculars. They loitered about seven hundred meters out, looking as if they were scrapping for supplies or scavenging near the destroyed tanks. Each one of them carried a white flag tied to the end of a stick.

Concerned that they were engaged in some kind of nefarious act, Burns ordered warning shots to be fired from the company's sniper team. The thing is, at that distance, unless one of them actually saw the impact from the round hitting the ground, it was unlikely they would realize they were being fired upon. The sniper fired half a dozen shots, but the women continued on, completely unaware of the danger. The next order he gave shocked everyone. He wanted to shoot mortars at civilians. Our company XO, Lt Ferreira, called the Battalion Fire Support Coordination Center, CoC, and notified them that women and children were in the middle of the target area. Burns' mission request to fire was denied. When Burns found out what Ferreira had done, he threatened to put him back on ship.

Later that afternoon the company leadership, along with a handful of the platoon sergeants, all huddled behind one of the warehouses, trying our best to figure out how to shield our Marines from Burns. The more we talked about it the more frustrated I felt. We needed a leader to lead us but now we were faced with having to stop and analyze each and every order he gave us. Going forward we were going to have to ask ourselves *is this going to protect our Marines? Is this going to hurt innocent people?*

We all wondered why Burns hadn't been relieved of command by that point. He was trying very hard to sweep things under the rug and make it appear like everything was fine, but it was definitely not.

Burns later pulled Ferreira aside and explained that his intent was a secondary warning to the families. But you don't use mortars to warn innocent civilians.

On our last night in Azu Bayer, I stood on a high perch with one of my team leaders, overlooking the desert. It had just rained, but the dark clouds had moved out quickly, and the air was incredibly clear. We could see all the way to Safwan Hill, one of the only prominent terrain features between Kuwait and Iraq.

There was a sort of peace in that moment, a quiet and stillness I hadn't enjoyed in weeks.

"Sir, I think we should head inside." One of my team leaders pointed off to the north. A 50-foot wall of sand was moving towards us, like something out of *Hidalgo* or *The Mummy*. There was no time to do anything except brace for a massive blast in the face. To our surprise, the sandstorm wasn't the skin-scouring onslaught we expected. Instead, it came in gently and clung to every surface, thanks to the rain.

Surrounded by a cloud of dust, I could barely see more than 30 feet in front of us. I had the platoon gear up for a stand-to, just in case the enemy decided to use the sandstorm to their advantage. No attack came.

We received orders to move to An Nasiriyah. We loaded up on British helicopters to a large logistics area, then transferred onto trucks for a five-hour movement to where the 11th Iraqi Division was headquartered just south of the city. Task Force Tarawa had already made their way through, having suffered significant losses—18 killed in action, and several more wounded.

Two of those killed were later confirmed to have been victims of friendly fire from US Air Force A-10 aircraft.

11

Freedom Isn't Free

April 2003
An Nasiriyah, Iraq
Boise, Idaho

Task Force Tarawa was in the center of the town, and our leadership was there with them working out how the MEU would replace them: TFT was three times our size. We established a defensive position just outside the city utilizing a tower and the Seabees' well-built berms.

That evening, we were tasked to conduct a raid. The MEU informed us that they were going in to recover some of our own from the US Army 507th Maintenance Company who'd been captured after they took a wrong turn in Nasiriyah and were ambushed. Our battalion was tasked with providing a diversionary attack in the operation, while US Special Forces conducted the prisoner recovery.

My platoon hadn't been tasked with anything for this mission, so I stayed back at our defensive position, watching what looked like a fireworks display of tracers flying across the sky accompanied by circling helicopters and explosions. I found out later that this team rescued Army PFC Jessica Lynch and some other prisoners that evening.

Our next mission assigned us to relieving Bravo Company from 1/2 (1st Battalion, 2nd Marines, from Camp Lejeune) at the Saddam Bridge, where the main battle of Nasiriyah took place. Nasiriyah is the closest modern city to ancient Ur, where Abraham lived.

Burns warned us that movement to the bridge was going to be hot, with a lot of potential for enemy contact along the way. RPGs were a real threat. I had 30 minutes to brief my platoon and load up. Once I got to the bridge I was told a tank platoon and CAAT section would attach to us shortly. We would have four to six vehicles and nearly two-dozen Marines to help guard the bridge.

We knew what had happened to the last elements of Task Force Tarawa that had passed through this area. We were preparing ourselves for the worst.

Fortunately, it was an uneventful trip. We linked up with the Lejeune Marines at the bridge a little after dark. Burns met with the outgoing CO while I met with their XO. The squad leaders went with the platoon commanders, and Lerma talked to their company gunny. They asked us to take over in the morning when we had daylight to ensure nothing got left behind, and we agreed that it made sense; there were a lot of friendly units up north. It would be better to wait, since they weren't in a hurry.

We hadn't had a lot of sleep since moving to Nasiriyah and we needed a place to stack our gear and get some rest. The only covered location not already occupied by other Marines was under the bridge itself. Turns out the same location had been designated as the latrine area. It wasn't ideal, but we were desperate for sleep.

Designated latrines are little holes or trenches in the ground for Marines to squat over, so we did our best to avoid stepping into any pits. The stench under the bridge was appalling to say the least, but everyone was willing to ignore the smell for just four hours of uninterrupted sleep. We laid down our iso-mats, and slept five hours straight for the first time since the invasion had begun.

Just before dawn we prepared to stand-to and assume control of the bridge. As the sun crept over the horizon we were better able to survey the surrounding area. Our new sleeping spot was completely littered with human waste.

Designated latrine area, my ass. They might have designated the general area as a latrine, but no one had even made the effort to follow good hygiene practices. The waste was supposed to be collected in one area, where it could be covered up or burned.

We had spent the night with nothing but an iso-mat between us and a field of human waste. Disgusting or unprofessional were words that didn't even begin to cover it. When we found their trash pile, it didn't come as much of a surprise that instead of building actual burn piles, they just threw their garbage and leftover food all over the ground. Flies swarmed everywhere. All I could think about was the potential for the spread of disease amongst our ranks.

I hunted down the outgoing XO. There was nothing he could say that could justify why his unit had failed in its field discipline.

He offered an apology, but that didn't remove the shit from all of our gear.

We took over securing the bridge, and Task Force Tarawa rolled through the city. I was impressed with TFT's size—it took them over two minutes to drive all their vehicles past us. After they went by, it became eerily silent. Now it was just my platoon of fifty guarding an area that was previously occupied by a company of two hundred, plus support from a battalion of one thousand men just around the corner. In the end I was just happy we were able to get away from what drama involved Burns.

Portions of Johnson's CAAT Platoon showed up later that day. We now had three vehicles attached to our platoon to assist us in guarding the bridge. I grabbed a few guys who weren't manning positions, and we went down and cleaned up the shit TFT had left for us. After that I made it a point to sit down with my junior leaders to talk about the importance of keeping things clean.

We hadn't showered in the three weeks since we'd left Bullrush, plus we were still required to wear our chemical suits each day. We found a water pump station and some water tanks, through one of which somebody had shot a hole. This made a spout. Everyone took turns taking a shower under it. Then it was right back into our chemsuits.

While at the bridge we took sporadic, inaccurate fire. We pushed squad-sized patrols out into the immediate vicinity to search the surrounding buildings.

For the most part, our time at the bridge was uneventful, but it wasn't without its challenges. Less than a week after we arrived, our resupply delivery stopped coming. It had been two days since our last drop of clean water and food. In an attempt to stretch our water supply, we reduced our patrols in both distance and duration.

Occasionally, convoys would pass by and we'd trade them our empty jugs for water, asking if they could spare any MREs. We had gone from shit patrollers to bridge trolls. We spent just shy of a week begging supplies from passing units before we received any supplies from our company. We were grateful for all the units passing over the bridge who shared their provisions. We would have been screwed without them.

Once we were fully resupplied, we resumed our regular patrols.

My platoon was focused on keeping the bridge secure and conducting patrols in the area. One night, CAAT team leader Lt Johnson returned from patrol and sought me out. He said an Iraqi civilian had approached him, telling him he'd buried the body of a dead Marine in accordance with Muslim tradition.

It was hard to know what to think of the report. The idea that a dead Marine was buried somewhere in the desert immediately made me consider his family, but it was also entirely plausible that the whole thing had been made up to draw us into an ambush.

"I don't know, man," Johnson said, tucking another dip of tobacco behind his lip, "this guy talked like he had seen the Marine die firsthand." All the details provided by this Iraqi civilian seemed to fit.

As evening approached we noticed a pack of dogs about 50 meters away from where the destroyed hull of the AAV was located. It was morbid to think about what the dogs might be trying to dig up. Johnson suggested using our tanks to surround the area so that we could flood it with white light, and also create cover, in case it really was an ambush. If there was a Marine buried in the ground, we were honor-bound to recover his body and send him home. We are all ingrained with the notion of never leaving someone behind.

In the end, we decided that the risk of using tanks in this situation was too great. It was too close to buildings; an RPG at that range could easily damage them. We scanned both sides of the suspected burial site with our thermals, and called Burns to inform him of our plans.

"I don't want you going out tonight." It was an order.

"Sir, will you authorize us to shoot the dogs, then?" I hoped he would at least say yes to that.

"Negative. Wait until morning."

I fought to maintain my cool as I responded. "Roger that, sir." A few team leaders, all of my squad leaders, and Lerma and Johnson had heard my exchange with Burns on the radio. I turned to them and said, "Alright. I want to discuss our options."

Lerma said without pausing, "What other options are there?" It wasn't a question: he was 100% right, we had to retrieve the fallen Marine. As I digested what Lerma had said, Cpl John Connor spoke up. He had tears in his eyes; he was a little choked up. He said, "If something happens to me, don't leave me in this shithole to be eaten by dogs."

I looked at the faces of the men around me. There was no other option. In my heart I knew it was the right thing to do. My guys were silently telling me, "We're going, sir." So that settled it.

Johnson and I went and briefed the tank platoon commander and told him what we were doing. Johnson pulled his vehicles in a tight square around the search area where the dogs had already begun to dig.

I left Cpl Hollon in charge of the rest of the platoon and took my squad leaders, Makula, Lupton, Breslin, and Warming. Johnson grabbed some of his leadership to assist as well.

We grabbed anything we thought would help with the retrieval of the body. We didn't have disposable latex gloves or anything else to cover our hands, so we donned plastic trash bags and tied them off with boot bands. With e-tools and shovels in hand, we dug as gingerly as possible. Nasiriyah has a very high water table. The ground on top is crisp and hard, but two inches below it's a muddy mess.

It didn't take us long to discover material from a two-man tent. The Iraqi had wrapped up the Marine like he would have done for one of his own, using the only materials he could find. Our fellow Marine had been sitting in the mud and murk decomposing for at least ten days.

His head was missing, except for the lower part of his jaw. His arm and leg were missing on one side, and the other leg was missing its foot. What was left of his flesh was completely burnt and filled with ooze. His body was infested with beetles and worms. The smell was almost as intense as the reverence we felt in that moment.

Even though his flak jacket had helped to keep his cammie blouse intact, there were no nametapes, rank, or dog tags. The rest of his clothing had been burned off, leaving him naked from the waist down.

We placed his remains in a body bag and brought him back inside our lines, standing watch over him the whole night. We said a prayer and tried cleaning up our chemical suits as best we could. One of the guys had slipped and fallen into the decomposing matter as we tried to lift the body out. We burned his suit, and had him break out his spare one so that he could change over into something clean.

I called the company HQ and relayed that we'd recovered the body of a Marine, and that we needed mortuary affairs. I also requested a chaplain in case the Marines wanted someone to talk to.

Burns got on the radio and very plainly reminded me he didn't want me going out until the morning. Before I could give a reply, he said, "I'll be up there to talk to you tomorrow morning. Out."

I thought for sure I was going to be fired.

The following morning we sent a security patrol out at 0200, and they found a human hand. We had no way of knowing to whom it belonged, Iraqi or American, so we bagged it up for mortuary affairs to examine. I imagined that it was from one of the Marines killed in the battle almost two weeks earlier, and that a dog had likely gotten hold of it.

Burns arrived at daybreak. I explained the situation, and how we took action to mitigate the risks associated with recovering the Marine. To my surprise, Burns didn't get too terribly worked up about it, acting as if he would have done the same thing. I later learned that Ferreira, the company XO, had explained the situation to both Burns and battalion. He told them we had to do it to keep faith with the Marines who were still living: they needed to know that every effort would be made to ensure they got back home if they were killed.

No matter how many times we cleaned our chemsuits, the stench and memory of that night would stay with us for the rest of the deployment. We felt like we had made a difference; maybe not in winning the war, but in keeping one of our brothers from being left behind. Later, we learned the name of the Marine we'd recovered: Pfc Nolen R. Hutchings.

12

Down With the Sickness

April 2003
An Nasiriyah, Iraq
Boise, Idaho

A couple days after taking over the position at the bridge, a few guys got really sick with vomiting and diarrhea. Something like dysentery spread across the company. Eighty percent of us were affected.

I suffered from explosive diarrhea; all I could do was lay on my iso-mat and pray for a speedy recovery. From my vantage point I could see our latrine, or rather our eight-foot trench, dug by the backhoe. I watched a Marine as he ran towards it, doing his best to unbuckle and pull his pants down in an effort to make it to the latrine, but he tripped and fell. He managed to crawl a few more feet, but he wasn't fast enough. He ended up puking and shooting diarrhea out at the same time. It ran down his exposed legs and on to his pooled cammies around his ankles.

Any of the Marines who didn't get ill got hosed with standing post for those of us who were, including the staff NCOs and officers. After two or three days, most of us were starting to recover, and the battalion doctor was called in.

"You're not doing a good job of washing your hands. That's why everyone's sick," the doctor said. "Make sure you're being diligent about washing your hands." The thing was, we didn't have a problem with washing our hands. We knew how to live in filthy environs, and the junior leadership was judicious about ensuring the Marines washed their hands.

I walked him around and showed him the cesspool we were living next to, and asked if dumping in some bleach or chlorine would help keep the flies off.

"Lieutenant, we don't need to do that. I don't think that's your problem. The issue is that your men aren't being hygienic. Just make sure everyone washes their hands."

Had I not had firsthand knowledge of the misery of succumbing to a massive illness caused by unsanitary conditions, I might have found a small amount of satisfaction when news arrived a couple of days later that the doctor had gotten sick shortly after his visit. Not surprisingly, shortly thereafter the battalion sent biological/chemical decontamination sprayers.

We were happy to hear a new interim exchange (like a convenience store) was set up back at battalion headquarters, so we rotated squad trips back to buy supplies. Morale computers, plus phones for us to be able to call home, were installed there. But every time I thought I might be able to plan a trip to battalion HQ to call Kristine, something would come up that would require my attention.

All of the Marines huddled around, complaining that Burns never had a problem finding reasons to go back to headquarters. This drove the wedge between him and his Marines deeper. It seemed every time he came back to the company outpost, he had a couple of Marines from headquarters with him. He'd walk them around our camp and point out various things to them. He shared meticulous notes of all the enemy gear and ammunition we discovered along the way, the majority of which was antiquated and inoperable. Never mind the fact that other units had previously cleared some of the buildings, so some of it wasn't technically our company's discovery to begin with anyway.

Burns was rarely around, but when we did see him, it seemed like he was hunting for recognition of some kind. I thought maybe he was thinking that the more stuff he found, it would somehow translate into a higher level of award he would receive. We couldn't prove anything, but something seemed off. The result of it was that Ferreira, our company XO, set up our patrolling efforts and provided a commander's intent with a clear task and purpose, leading the company along with First Sergeant Fantau.

13

Going Back to Cali

June 2003
Somewhere between the Middle East and Hawaii
Boise, Idaho

*I*n the two months since the invasion began, my only contact with Ross had been some very odd-looking postcards. I had to smile at his ingenuity. He'd cut up MRE boxes in order to make his own postcards. His effort made his words all the more sweet, and I will always cherish those first pieces of mail.

When he finally called, it wasn't the conversation I was hoping for. The connection was terrible. There were such long delays and pauses. Anything I said would be echoed back to me, and both of us would talk at the same time—then we'd both stop suddenly, hoping the other person would keep going because we didn't want to talk over each other. I felt a tremendous amount of pressure to try to convey that everything was perfect at home—I didn't want him to lose his focus on his Marines, or to spend one ounce of worry on me.

It was hard not to tell him about what I was seeing on TV, or about how much I missed him and worried about him. When we finally said goodbye I was filled with sorrow, but I tried to remember that for now, he was alive and safe, and that he would be home soon.

Our time in-theater was complete. We flew out of Talil Iraqi Air Base, then on to Bahrain loaded onto C-130's. It was our first stop on our way home after three months in the Middle East.

Just after 0200, we boarded the ship that would take us back to California. The ship's captain, Commander Emmert, woke up his crew to man the kitchen and make food for us. He filled 40-gallon trashcans with beer. He went out of his way to make us feel like we

were part of a team. That's not always the case on amphibious ships: it can sometimes be an adversarial relationship, as if the Marines are a burden to the ship and crew, despite the fact that amphibious ships are made to have embarked troops aboard and can only accomplish their primary mission when they do. Granted, Marines don't always do a good job of endearing themselves to the sailors, and it's not an uncommon occurrence for fights to break out.

We all couldn't have been happier that we were getting a taste of real food again. We had been living on MREs for three months straight.

Battalion had tasked every company with conducting a health and comfort inspection, and we were asked to turn in any unauthorized souvenirs (mostly bayonets, and the pins that adorned Iraqi berets). Everyone I know of complied with this order. The word was convoluted though, on what was authorized as a souvenir; most Marines had a small Iraqi flag or some kind of pin, just small stuff.

But word went back and forth on whether Iraqi bayonets were

authorized. Burns wasn't sure, and he had conveyed that he didn't want the company to suffer a black eye through the possession of contraband; he made it sound as though he was looking out for our Marines.

He stated that he would hold on to the bayonets in a footlocker in his stateroom. If they were authorized, they'd be returned. If not, he'd throw them into the ocean. Later, word came down that bayonets were in fact authorized souvenirs. When Burns was approached and asked if we could give them back to the Marines who had turned them in, he said he had already thrown them overboard.

Later, once we were all home, Maidens said he saw an Iraqi bayonet on the living room wall of someone who was connected to Burns. All Maidens could do was sit there wondering if these were the same bayonets that had supposedly been lost at sea.

Both Thorleifson and Deda got promoted aboard the ship on our way home. They had no love for Burns, so they asked the ship's captain, Commander Emmert, to do the honors. Just before we arrived in Hawaii, Ferreira came in to the platoon commander's quarters and told us the company was going to present a giant Iraqi satin-nylon flag to the ship's captain.

Later that afternoon, Burns saw the company out on the flight deck with the Marines in a loose formation and me standing off to the side. "Why is the company formed?" he asked me.

"I'm not one hundred percent sure sir, but I think it's for some kind of presentation to Commander Emmert."

"The company doesn't have a formation without me knowing about it, Lieutenant."

Ferreira hadn't told us that he'd left Burns out of the loop, but before Burns could do anything, Ferreira was standing in front of the circle of Marines talking with the ship's captain and presenting the flag.

Burns stood by me the whole time with a hurt look on his face, though he tried to disguise it with a half-smile. Once Ferreira was done, Burns went over to Commander Emmert and shook his hand. It appeared to be a veiled attempt at keeping up appearances that he was involved in the event.

He then made a beeline towards Ferreira. I didn't hear what was said, but Burns was livid. Ferreira later told me that he informed

Burns, tactfully, that the Marines didn't want him there, and that they didn't respect him. The truth cut like a knife, but I couldn't help but worry about the repercussions of such brutal honesty.

From: Ross
Date: May 11, 2003 5:05 AM
To: Kristine

We're back on the ship, and I don't think I've ever been so happy to have real food to eat. I've been busy writing up after-action reports and awards. One of the SSgts said it sounds like I'm recommending my Marines for the Bronze Star, but I'm only putting them in for a Navy Achievement Medal. There are some people getting written up for crap that has been totally fabricated.

But there is justice. We've been told Burns won't be around commanding Marines again (not sure what they're going to do with him) and nothing will happen to any of us if he tries to screw with our careers. He'll escape with outward dignity, but the Marines who served with him will know the truth, and I guess we'll have to live with that.

You might not recognize me when you see me. I've lost a lot of weight. Eighty percent of us had a bout with a nasty stomach illness. My stomach is somewhat back to normal, but I had to cinch my belt at least another inch.

Tomorrow we'll get a steel beach picnic. It's where we basically walk around on the flight deck with our shorts and take our shirts off to catch some sun, toss a ball around and relax. We're being allotted two beers apiece! I can't wait to be on a real beach with you. Naked.

In other news, I got selected for Captain, but I won't be promoted until fall 2004. I don't know where I'll be sent next—it's possible that I'll stay with the battalion and deploy again shortly. Otherwise they'll send me on to a B-Billet in the Corps (where you learn to do a different job than your primary MOS, supporting the Marine Corps in making Marines).

Thank you for all the care packages, but unfortunately none of them got to us while we were in Iraq. All those supplies that you sent for the Iraqi kids were sent to our ship instead of coming to theater. It's really out of control.

I guess Mom took it upon herself to have all of the students at her Oregon high school send letters to us. She sent them to me, and now it's quite a burden in a way because we're swimming in them. I would have told her to send them to the Army unit if she would have just asked me about it; those are the guys that are staying in Iraq. At least Dad asked; I gave him the address of an Army unit in-theater that could use the support.

I did read a few of the letters, though. I can't wait for us to have kids so that I can show them how much I love you. I want them to see the affection we have for each other. I want them to know their father is completely infatuated with their mother. That's the way I want them to be raised, knowing that their parents love each other, and that we love them too.

From: Kristine
Date: May 12, 2003 11:08 PM
To: Ross

First off, let me say how much I love you. I'm so glad you're feeling better. I can't wait for you to be home. I'll cook whatever you want for dinner. Start making a list.

Remember how you said you wanted me to keep you up to date with what's going on in my life? I hope you're ready. Your mom is crazy. You have no idea how much I wish you were here!

She has been hounding me, trying to guilt me about letting her be at your homecoming! I told her you wanted it to just be the two of us, but I might as well have been talking to the wall.

I went over last night for another one of my weekly dinners at your mom's house; thank goodness your grandparents were there. We're all sitting around the table and I mentioned that you had been selected for Captain, but you probably wouldn't pick it up until next year. I mostly said it for their benefit because I know they like to hear how you're doing.

Grandma asked where you were going next, and I replied that

you wanted to stay in the infantry, but that if you picked up
Captain before you deployed again, the Marine Corps could
make you move into a B-Billet. Well, Frank was drinking. He
starts arguing with me that he thinks that you can decide where
you want to go, and the Marine Corps doesn't have anything to
do with that.

Ha! I wish that were the case. Anybody who's been around
Marines knows that the needs of the Corps are paramount, and
supersede the desires of the Marine. Even I know that! I just kept
explaining to him that you put in wish lists for your primary and
B-Billet jobs, but then the good 'ol USMC just puts you where
they need you, and it doesn't necessarily have to do with what
you want.

It seems like every time I try to talk about you, about anything
even in general about the service, he argues with me. I am so
tired of it. It makes me not even want to go over there.

Then we got on the subject of you coming back home. I was
talking about how I was flying down to San Diego, how I got
a really good price on tickets and that we'd be coming back to
Boise shortly thereafter.

Then he said, "Well, what about the families?"

I responded, "What do you mean? His dad in San Diego? I'm
going by myself to meet him and pick him up so that we can have
our time together first. We'll meet everyone else later."

Then he started in on an ugly, angry rant. It turned out that Trina
and some other family had planned on going down there to
meet you when you got back. He said, "You can't just tell people
they're not welcome. This is a public event, and we can come if
we want."

All I could think to myself was, *if my husband has been at war
and this is what he wants, you can be damn sure I'm going to
help fulfill his wishes when he comes home. And no, it's not a
public event.*

I tried to explain that you and I are a family now, that our wishes
are that we want to be alone together when you come home,

that we planned meeting up with the families later on that night or the next day for a big reunion.

Then he said, "Well, what if people disagree with that?"

I started to cry a bit. He had been going on for more than five minutes, hollering at me.

Grandma was obviously very uncomfortable. She started telling a story about when Grandpa deployed, and right in the middle of her story, Frank stood up and started yelling at me again, saying, "I just don't agree with that." He slapped the table. "Homecomings are for families!"

The dam burst; I started bawling. I said, "I'm sure I look like the bad guy here, but I'm not the only one making these decisions. It's what *Ross* wants. And it's what I want too."

Then Frank says, "Well, you know, if Ross wants things, I have never been one to go against his wishes . . . "

It was ridiculous. I would have just left if Grandma and Grandpa weren't there. What's even worse though, your mom just stood by the whole time with a smirk on her face, not saying one word during Frank's whole tirade. She didn't try to defend me or stop him from yelling at me.

It's awful. I feel like I can't win. I try to be a really good daughter-in-law. I make more time for them in my schedule than I do for my friends. Nothing I do is ever good enough.

I'm sorry to unload on you, and I wish that we could talk. I'm leaving for Vegas with my mom and dad tomorrow morning, so I won't be able to email until Sunday. I love you more than anything. And just in case you're wondering, YES! You are worth all of her craziness! xoox

From: Ross
Date: May 14, 2003 1:24 AM
To: Kristine

I know you're in Vegas still, but I wanted to let you know that I wrote Mom, and she wrote back. Her version was just like yours, only softened. I know her well enough to know that what happened was plain and simple: she just didn't agree with you.

She didn't mention that Frank was drinking. I think she's starting to stick her head in the sand more and more. I think you were in the right, 100%. Besides, you did the honest thing and that's better. Now I need to hear from Frank.

I mentioned to my mom that no one came to my other two homecomings, so what the hell? Not only that, but Marine homecomings are not as ceremonious as Navy ones. Since my dad was in the Navy, maybe she's a little misinformed about what we do; it's different (and she didn't deal with the Navy lifestyle very long before she and Dad divorced anyhow). I'm sure you don't even know this, but we're slated to offload at Pendleton in LCUs (Landing Craft Utility) and hovercrafts, then load onto buses and drive to Horno, which is where families will be waiting. Our company will probably be the last one off, just like we have been in the past. Mom and Frank are unaware of what goes on during a MEU offload. There's nothing worse than an uninvited guest.

What pisses me off most about this whole thing is that we spent an entire email back and forth talking about this (and rightly so, I'm glad you told me) plus how my mom and Frank's behavior is once again causing strife for us.

I wish it had been possible for you to defer to me, so that I could have protected you from this crap. I know I haven't been accessible to deal with things. Sorry, babe, that it happened that way.

From: Kristine
Date: May 14, 2003 8:39 AM
To: Ross

I've decided to email your mom. I need to stand up for myself and set boundaries. I don't want anyone controlling our lives. I don't want your Mom and Frank (or *my* parents for that matter) telling us how to raise our kids or tell us what to do and how to do it all the time.

I fear this is just the beginning, though, especially if I don't say something. There's going to come a point in time when we have to set schedules for holidays and vacations, there will be conflict down the road. Setting reasonable boundaries doesn't mean I don't care for your folks, but I sure don't have to agree with them.

I'm forwarding the email I sent for the purpose of transparency. One thing I've learned throughout the years of your mom's "misunderstandings" is that I need to use her own words. I want you to read exactly what she wrote so that it's clear as day, so that you get it straight from the source and see how she treats me.

I am looking forward to traveling with you again shortly. I'm excited that we're heading down the home stretch!

From: Ross
Date: May 15, 2003 10:47 PM
To: Kristine

I think your email to Mom was fine. I understand. Frank is argumentative and my mom tries to dictate things. I don't have a problem being confrontational; most of the time it bothers me if I'm not. I don't think my mom understands that I'm almost 30 years old and a husband; we're not little kids.

Just address the things they are saying that you don't agree with. Don't go over there expecting a fight every time, or you're gonna get one. You did the right thing. It was an argument; there will be disagreements in life. Leave it at that.

You rate an apology certainly, but say what you need to say and leave it, don't get wrapped up in the drama for too long. If you go down that path, my mother will just dig her claws in deeper. Trust me. I don't want that for you.

I meant to ask you if you were there when Grandpa emailed me? I haven't received an email since. When you get back, could you check up on them, please?

Thanks for sending those pictures. You look smoking hot in all of them. Something about that picture of you with the hat on . . . you're going to get it, missy.

Can you look into a hotel in San Clemente for when I get back? I don't want to have to drive too far until I can properly ravish you.

From: Kristine
Date: May 17, 2003 10:26 AM
To: Ross

Oh, babe. I just got your mom's email (five pages long!) and there is NO WAY I'm responding to this. I could barely read it all.

I can't deal with this crap anymore—she is clearly blaming me for decisions that you made in the past. You're going to have to respond for both of us because nothing I say will be right for her—or for that matter—be read by her without prejudice.

The fact is that I should be able to say, "This is what we're doing as a family," and that should be it. We are a married couple, and your mom has no right to be asking us to set up an appointment to clear schedules in regard to where we are going and when we will be coming home. This entire argument is ridiculous.

I have way more issues than that with her letter, but let's just deal with one thing at a time.

About your grandpa: yes, I was there when he emailed . . . I typed it for him. For the most part, every email you've received from your grandpa, I typed and sent on his behalf. Of course you know that I will be more than happy to check up on them.

From: Ross
Date: May 21, 2003 4:01 PM
To: Kristine

I'm so sorry that you're dealing with my mom. If I were you, I'd step away from this.

Thank you for sending me her response. My mom's approach to things is very odd. It seems the older I get, the more fixated on getting involved in my life she becomes. She wasn't like this when I was in high school; hell, I was barely around. The same goes for my time when I was enlisted or in college. It's becoming stranger by the moment. It's clear my mom has become overly attached. I wish there was something we could say, but there isn't. She's going to be who she is. I don't want her behavior to affect our relationship.

I'm in port right now. Hopefully we'll be able to get off the ship soon, but the CO is playing some games trying to manipulate us into not getting any free time.

I'll craft something on behalf of you and me and send it on to her. You're right; almost all the things she's been upset about have been my ideas. With any luck this will soon be over.

14

Keep Calm and Aloha On

July 2003
Honolulu, Hawaii

As hard as I tried to hold out for an opportunity for us to spend Ross' first hours alone together when he returned, Trina continued to wear me down. We still wanted to have our own time without interruptions, so Ross and I dipped into our savings, spending money on a plane ticket and hotel room in Hawaii so that I could meet his ship, even though these few short days cost us thousands. We were trying to accommodate her professed need to attend the homecoming.

Ross mentioned that the Chaplain had given all the returning personnel a return and reunion brief. He mentioned to me what he learned, worried there might be some kind of weird awkward pressure when reconnecting physically and emotionally with each other. I hadn't thought about that, but since he mentioned it, I couldn't help but wonder *what if it's different? Or he doesn't want me?* Hopefully, it wouldn't be an issue, but it was just one more thing in the back of my mind.

In the weeks leading up to his return, Ross and I started reading *His Needs, Her Needs* together and answering the questions in the book. It was a great resource to better understand how to strengthen our marriage.

I couldn't believe it, but all of the guys he was rooming with were reading it too. I could imagine a room full of Marines, all of them absorbed in this book. I got a kick out of how they joked with each other that they were "taking away from" or "filling each other's love tank."

Before I knew it, I was packed and buckled into my seat on an airplane, nothing but half an ocean and a landing between Ross and me. The next morning it was the Fourth of July. I couldn't think of a better day to welcome my hero home. I got dressed and walked the few blocks from the hotel to the rental car place. I just hoped I could find Pearl Harbor—and his ship—easily. I was excited and scared. I knew Ross would be Ross, but I also knew he could be different in many ways.

I saw the big, beautiful gray beast of a ship from a distance floating in the harbor. I found a parking spot not far from the gate. I kept popping Altoids and trying to calm my nerves. I climbed out of the car and waited at the gates. Several other family members were already waiting, and by the time the gates were opened, our group had swelled to more than 20. I felt better knowing I wasn't alone. Even though I didn't know any of these family members, there was an instant sense of connection. Every one of us knew what it was like to lay awake wondering if a loved one was okay.

I checked in with the security staff and went aboard.

My heart skipped a beat when I saw him.

They were all standing in formation. Captain Burns was giving them a quick brief; complete with any last minute information they needed before they were released on libbo. Finally, Ross glanced over in my direction, and his eyes locked with mine. *Ah.* I couldn't stop smiling. It was everything I could do to stand still and just wait for him.

Finally, the command was given, and they were dismissed.

We ran to each other, and he grabbed me tightly. It was just like it had always been.

I said the mandatory hellos and goodbyes to all of his friends on ship, then we headed for the car. Once we were there, we could finally say hello to each other a little less formally. We embraced freely without worry or fear of watchful eyes. We both stopped and looked at each other and smiled. He laughed. We were together again.

We went back to the hotel, and we made up for all the lonely nights without each other. Satiated and rested, we went out to discover Honolulu together. The water was beautiful and warm. The sand of the beaches was so soft, it begged you to wiggle your toes deep down and feel the aloha.

Ross looked at me and smiled. "God. You are beautiful."

I blushed. It felt like a first date all over again. Or the honeymoon we'd never had. I was so glad to have him home safe and sound. Until this moment, I hadn't really grasped the depth of what a burden it had been for me to send him off to war, how much faith it required just to keep going every day. And now my reward: *him.*

I snuggled into him as we soaked up the afternoon Hawaiian sun. "It's so good to have you back," was all I could say.

Dinner was our first luau together. We walked around and played the island games that are the staple at luaus. "This is the kind of place where you need to bring kids with you," I said.

"Kids? I kind of like the sound of that. Maybe we should go back to the hotel and put that plan into action." He grabbed me and nuzzled my neck.

I laughed. "No chance, buddy. We paid a lot of money for these tickets. And besides, I still need to be able to walk properly." I laughed.

After the luau we headed downtown. Honolulu was packed with people for the holiday; the city was positively bursting. We went to the top of the bar above Wolfgang Puck's near Diamondhead, had drinks, and listened to their acoustic guitar player. We ate dinner, then, after sunset, watched the fireworks over the ocean in Waikiki.

It was beautiful, and it was enough. We spent two days just soaking each other up.

For the first time since he'd left, I had everything I needed to be happy.

Celebrating our reunion at the Paradise Cove Luau

'd had two whole days with Kristine. Saying goodbye was almost as hard as the first time I'd left her. I threw myself back into the job, knowing I'd be home soon enough. I just needed to keep myself occupied until then.

The rumor mill was in full swing about the kinds of awards being handed out, especially for the officers. The buzz was that the company commanders (Captains) and above were getting the Bronze Star with Combat "V" (for valor): complete bullshit for this deployment. Hardly anyone from any of our units were in the shit. In my mind, none of us rated an award like this.

We were busy tying up loose ends, including combat loss paperwork. This was how we accounted for items that were destroyed during our deployment and how we reported any missing gear. Burns reported that he had lost his NVGs, night vision goggles. But then Lt Maidens did the serialized account, and suddenly they appeared. Some speculated Burns wanted to claim them as combat loss so he could keep them and take them home. It was just another little thing on the long list of reasons why I thought so lowly of the man.

This was the last straw for our company XO, Ferreira. He couldn't deal with such fraudulence and dishonesty from a Marine Corps officer. He went immediately to the battalion XO, a Major, who then assured him that Burns would be dealt with appropriately.

When our NCO Marines discovered that Burns was looking to be awarded a Bronze Star with Combat "V," they lost it. They started circulating a Letter of No Confidence, taking a scene from the movie miniseries *Band of Brothers*. They had the idea that it would eventually make its own way to the battalion commander's desk.

One of my squad leaders brought it to me, and asked for guidance—there were already 20 signatures from our staff NCOs. The letter chronicled a laundry list of infractions, from significant events like the mortar incident, leaving his rifle unattended, to little things like not wearing his Kevlar when required.

I talked to Ferreira about it. He told me the Marines had pulled him aside back in Iraq and had showed the letter to him. He told them not to turn it in, that Burns would punish them for it, that it wouldn't make a difference in the end.

I understood their need to do something, but I knew this wasn't the right way to go about it. The battalion XO had assured us that the matter would be taken care of.

We really thought it would be a dead issue.

15

Together Is a Wonderful Place to Be

July 2003
Camp Pendleton, California

My jaw hit the floor after listening to Trina's voicemail. She wasn't coming. After we'd spent thousands to have our reunion in Hawaii so that she could come to San Diego when his unit returned. She said again and again that it mattered to her "more than anything." After the guilt trip she'd put us through, after everything, she didn't even have the courage to tell me personally. She left the news in a voicemail.

In the end it didn't matter, though. Her selfishness had given us a gift: Ross and I would always have the memory of our two amazing days spent reuniting in Hawaii. Besides, Ross's dad Rick, and his wife Charlotte, were still planning on being there to welcome him home, along with his grandparents who lived in San Diego.

The homecoming itself was a process; Ross and his unit couldn't simply get off the ships and make their way to us. This was the Marine Corps, after all. Though it was my first time experiencing it, at least Ross had told me to be prepared. He was right.

We were asked to show up early: at 8 a.m.

Just before that I met up with his dad, stepmom, and grandparents at the parade deck—the cement pad with the official battalion logo on it where ceremonies and other events took place. There was a large US flag flying, almost as wide as the parade deck, draped from the building. The surrounding area was covered with homemade WELCOME HOME signs. Marine Corps Community Services, MCCS, was there too, manning tables so that loved ones could grab a complementary beverage and small packaged snack.

Marines were offloaded from the ship to the Del Mar Boat Basin at Camp Pendleton. From there they loaded onto buses bound for Camp Horno. Once the buses arrived at Horno, the Marines went to the armory first, to turn in and account for all the serialized gear— things like weapons and radios and NVGs. It was always a tedious and very OCD process. Nobody was going anywhere until *all* the gear was accounted for and locked up.

Five hours after we'd arrived at the parade deck, I finally caught sight of him.

It had only been a week since I'd last seen him, but the minute I spotted him the feeling was exactly the same as it had been in Hawaii. But that elation was immediately followed by sadness: As happy as I was to have him home, I knew there were others who wouldn't be welcoming their loved ones home.

It was a short hello and welcome home from his parents, then Ross whisked me away so that we could reconnect with each other once again.

We didn't have a home in California, and we didn't have much money for a great hotel. Before I'd left that morning I had done my best to make the room a little more romantic. It had been a bit of a challenge, but with a few carefully placed candles and a cooler full of his favorite things, I'd staged the room. I hoped Ross would appreciate my efforts.

Welcoming back the Marines from 2/1 with Mia

Truth be told, what he probably wanted most was me, naked, in bed—or maybe not even in the bed! Most men are pretty simple: they want good sex, good beer, and good food.

The look on his face when we walked into the room said it all.

It didn't matter where we were. As long as we had each other, we could be happy anywhere.

Standing beneath Old Glory with Ross' parents, Rick and Charlotte, and grandparents Pat and Jim.

Our end of deployment leave block was over before I knew it. I didn't think it was possible to miss things like mowing the lawn and taking out the garbage. I had almost forgotten what it was like to sleep in a real bed again, to sleep next to my wife every night. But we still had a lot of work to do, even though we were stateside, including the announcement of unit replacements. Much to my relief, we were told that Captain Banner would be replacing our shitbag CO.

We had a lot of turnover in the company, which was pretty typical for post-deployment. Lt Maidens, Lt Deda, and I were all shuffled around to other companies inside the battalion, as company XO's. Captain Marcus Ferreira went to Norfolk and attached to Fleet Anti-Terrorism Security Team, known as FAST company.

My new boss, Captain Banner and I spent most of our initial meetings discussing the direction he wanted to take both the company and the Marines. It was always helpful and refreshing to have these conversations, but I told him that the bar was very low. I told him as long as he wasn't a liar or weak, he'd do well.

One day during the turnover process, a slew of awards came down from battalion. We sent a clerk to pick them up. Included in the awards was a Navy Commendation with Combat "V" for Burns.

The same Letter of No Confidence I'd found out about on ship then somehow magically appeared under the Regimental Sergeant Major's door. The Regiment started asking questions and delving into things. It was out of our hands as officers, but finally, it seemed like someone was listening. That was good.

While we were in Iraq, most of the lieutenants received great fitness reports (evaluation reports, known as fitreps). We were given copies of them in April, while we were in Nasiriyah. Unfortunately, Ferreira's was not good—it appeared that he was being punished for defying Burns; that Burns was trying to ruin his career.

When the time came, Burns called a meeting, NCOs and above, and we presented the awards. The enlisted Marines who were involved with recovering the body of PFC Hutchings were given Navy Achievement medals—none of the officers involved received one. In fact, none of the officers in our company were awarded a medal of any kind from the deployment. However, each and every one of the officers from all the other companies in the battalion did receive medals.

It was a small matter; all the lieutenants were concerned about was that Burns didn't take out his resentment for us on our Marines. None of the officers were too worried about not getting an award. We were just glad that our time under Burns was coming to an end.

Two days later found us preparing for the battalion change of command: LtCol Olson was replacing LtCol Ingersoll.

Burns walked up to our formation just prior to the ceremony, calling the officers up to the front of the line. He said, "There will be no change of command ceremony for me and Captain Banner. Literally right after this, I'm walking away."

That was some of the best news he had delivered since he'd taken command.

Months later we received our new fitreps. When I initially looked at mine, it seemed low to me. I was happy for one thing, though: I didn't have a gap in the dates of my reports. That can prevent promotions.

I went ahead and showed my new CO my fitrep so that I could glean some of his thoughts about it. Banner said, "What bothers me about this, Ross, is that it's adversely worded, even though it wasn't officially marked as adverse." He pointed to the signature at the bottom. "Let's go talk to LtCol Olson. I'm curious what he'll think of this."

We walked to Olson's office and reported in, waiting while the LtCol read the report. He looked up at the end, completely shocked and angered. "I never would have signed off on this report—whether the low marks are deserved or not—because it's administratively incorrect. I would have never sent this forward because it's not marked as adverse. I hate to say this, but . . . somebody must have forged my signature."

Olson promised he'd immediately investigate why all the Lts in our company had administratively incorrect reports. LtCol Olson was a very meticulous and calculating person; he always stressed the importance of being able to communicate properly, and that anything that went outside the battalion had better be vetted and checked.

Later, I asked how he'd discovered those faulty fitness reports. He said, "Ross, I wear size 34 briefs. Now, you could slip a 32 or a 36 in my drawer, and it might go undetected. But if you put a red thong in that drawer, I'm definitely gonna notice. I've been in the Marine Corps for eighteen years. I've never seen an adverse report on an officer. Those comments would have stood out like a proverbial red thong. I don't know how he did it—if he figured out my password, or something else in the Marine Online, MOL—but I never would have signed off on those fitreps."

Burns was charged with something along the lines of tampering and falsifying reports; they brought in handwriting experts to help analyze the situation. It was inconclusive. Our fitreps were pulled and rewritten with LtCol Olson as our reporting senior officer, and with newly promoted Brigadier General Waldhauser as our reviewing officer.

In the end, Burns wasn't found guilty of anything because there was no evidence that he had done anything wrong. Who knows what happened. The whole situation was certainly odd. He left active duty shortly thereafter, joining the Marine Reserves.

16

Creating a New Destiny

July 2003
Camp Pendleton, California

I was so excited to start looking for our new home. We were going to give base housing a try this time. We wanted to live in the Del Mar neighborhood because it was situated next to the Oceanside Harbor. It had a gate with 24/7 easy access; we were looking forward to being able to walk down to the harbor, grab some dinner and drinks, and wander back in the evening.

We had visited Ross's platoon sergeant's on-base home, in the Pacific View neighborhood. It was gorgeous. A two-level with a two-car garage, decent appliances and a nice layout, their home was exactly what I imagined our future home would look like. It seemed like every house we visited was new and updated, from NCOs on up.

I had only seen Del Mar Housing once, and that had been at night. Streetlights and starlight tend to romanticize just about anything, and our intended neighborhood was no exception. I should have known it would never look as good during the day.

A quick trip to the housing office provided the news that we could pretty much have our pick of the homes available. They gave us a map and marked off a few of the available houses. We set out, keys in hand, ready to find the next place we'd call home.

As it turned out, all the homes available to us were quad homes, attached apartments. I later found out this particular section of the housing area had been dubbed the OG, for officer ghetto. None of the quad homes had garages; they were really beat up. Dilapidated dark brown wood fencing plagued the entire neighborhood, and each unit sported a funny little u-shaped cove in the front. I guess the cove was supposed to be used to hide your stuff? I wasn't sure.

Ross leaned over and smiled at me. "Well, babe—is it all you've ever wanted?" He started laughing.

I didn't even want to look at him. *This whole thing was my idea. Crap.* "No," I said, "it's not." I looked at him, my eyes pleading with him to go easy on me. "But maybe it won't be so bad inside?"

He shook his head and smiled as he unlocked the front door to our potential future home. I let him go in first. I stood on the front stoop, eyes closed, praying by some miracle of miracles that the inside belied the exterior.

Ross's first impression diminished any hope. "What a dump," he called over his shoulder.

I opened my eyes and stepped inside. It was nothing but hospital floors as far as the eye could see—hideous green and white checked linoleum. The stairs sported thick industrial rubber nosing on them.

"I feel like I should take a number and grab a seat to wait for the nurse."

Ross laughed. "Yeah, turn your head and cough, babe."

"More like bend over."

From the looks of things they'd used the cheapest government materials the procurement office would authorize, completely forgetting that the place was actually supposed to be someone's home.

We peered carefully into the cramped galley kitchen with its outdated appliances. "The windows are cheap, too." I said. "And look at the backyard." Through the window we could see what would be our tiny backyard. It was half-concrete, half-grass and incredibly small; it couldn't have been more than four hundred square feet. It didn't bode well for our dogs.

Ross gave me his best Groucho Marx impression. "Wanna check out the bedroom, hot stuff?"

I lightly punched his arm, and we went upstairs. There was one full bathroom upstairs; the master had a half-bath. The second floor's only saving grace was a very large closet at the end of the hallway. *Perfect for storing a Marine's gear*, I thought to myself.

"Well, I guess we're kind of stuck with this kind of apartment, babe. Maybe we can find a more desirable end unit or something."

"I guess that's the price we pay so that I can have friends," I said, laughing and trying to keep my disappointment in check.

We drove around looking for empty houses, but we couldn't locate any empty single end units. It wasn't the cozy two-story I'd imagined. We ended up choosing the quad closest to the gate, so that we could walk to the harbor easily. Just like the other units, the walls had this oily-looking paint on them. The gate in our new backyard was barely connected to the fence.

We informed the base housing office which house we'd decided on.

The clerk confirmed the number and began the paperwork process. She dug through a small file drawer of index cards. She pulled one out, and started typing our information on to it . . . with a typewriter.

I couldn't believe it.

When Ross had told me to expect everything in the Marine Corps to be backwards, I have to confess, I didn't take him as seriously as I should have. *It's 2003, and the government is still using index cards and antique typewriters?* Now I had seen everything.

She added his name to the list: 1st Lieutenant Schellhaas. I asked to see the card. I looked it over. Every Marine who had lived in that house since 1966 was listed there. 1966—the year the quads were built.

In over 50 years, they hadn't changed a single aspect of their administration system, or their houses. It was breathtaking and unbelievable.

I asked how to go about getting our broken gate fixed.

The clerk looked up at me. "Neither the fence nor the gate are technically part of the home. The government isn't responsible for fixing it. That's entirely on you."

I raised an eyebrow, but bit my tongue. *Oh, you're going to fix my fence. You just don't know it yet.*

It was to be the first of several battles I would wage over our less-than-stellar housing.

As we settled into our apartment, I did my best to make it a home.

After more than a dozen phone calls to the housing office, they finally sent someone out to fix my gate (ha!) and after that miniscule but moral victory, I decided it was time for me to find a job. The next deployment wasn't far off, and I would need something to keep me busy while Ross was away. I hadn't found anything in my field, so I was determined to find something fun.

With a scan of the Sunday classifieds, I spotted an ad for a retail employee at the La Costa Resort and Spa. It wasn't exactly the kind of job I was used to, but it would be a good way to get my foot in the company door there, maybe work my way up in the hospitality industry. I thought about all the great perks for travel that came with the territory. That would come in handy, especially considering the life we lived.

I was interviewed and hired on the spot. I would work in their new Lilly Pulitzer store, which was called Pinkalicious. It was still under construction, but it was scheduled to open in the next week or two. I went through training and was excited to have a job again, even though I'd never worked retail.

Ever the over-committer, it was about the same time I also agreed to become the key volunteer coordinator, KVC, for the battalion. That made me the one left leading the families at home when the men deployed. I had been asked several times by Theresa, the former KVC, but had heretofore resisted. What did I know about the Marine Corps? How would I handle some of those infamously hard questions that I knew would come up? How would I figure out what all the acronyms meant?

It took a breakfast invitation and an official request from LtCol Olson to convince me to take the position. Ross thought it was a bad idea, but he left it up to me. I knew it was going to be a challenge, but I wanted to do my part, so I agreed to step up. Part of me secretly hoped Ross was proud of me.

The next weekend we were out running errands, and stopped in a store to grab a couple of picture frames. We ended up running into a senior ranking officer in the battalion, and his wife, Shannon. Somehow in the course of our conversation, Ross mentioned that I'd be the key volunteer coordinator for the battalion.

Shannon's face went sour, but she quickly replaced it with a smile and changed the subject.

I wasn't sure what to think. I'd just met the woman, but there was something about her reaction that left me feeling unsettled. I chalked it up to my people skills being a little rusty, after having spent half a year with my parents.

Things were good at home.

Ross was a happy man because he had won an important argument: I had finally agreed to try for kids. We wanted to get the timing right so that I would be able to give birth shortly after he returned from deployment.

I started my new job at Pinkalicious. I was working just under full time there while holding KV meetings and running the program. At the first meeting, I did the only thing I could do—I was completely honest. I told everyone I still had a lot to learn about the Marine Corps. I admitted to my lack of expertise when it came to military acronyms and the many Marine Corps processes, but I was motivated and excited to lead the group.

I wanted to make sure that they understood that I cared about them and their families. I encouraged them to ask me any questions they had. I promised if I didn't know the answer, I would do everything in my power to get whatever they needed as quickly as possible.

Time passed. We were ready for the pre-deployment brief. It was always difficult getting wives to show up, so we employed any bribery we could to get them to come: 72s (72 hours of liberty, a three-day weekend) would be given by the battalion commander to any Marine whose wife simply showed up. There were raffle prizes too, all donated from MCCS and the local community.

At first I was surprised that we had to offer a bribe to get spouses to attend, but it made sense when I learned it could be a hardship, especially for those with young kids at home, those living away from base, or those who had to take time off from work to attend. As it turned out, the three-day weekend made the personal sacrifice of time and effort to show up worthwhile.

In total there were almost four dozen spouses at the meeting; a great turnout for our first event. This deployment was like many others: There was a deluge of brand new Marine wives, fresh from a weekend ceremony in Vegas or the local Justice of the Peace. These were the spouses who we really wanted to get to know. It was our job to help them navigate through the process of getting a military ID card, as well as healthcare and service benefits.

Powers of attorney were also discussed at the meeting; it was suggested that Marines should give their spouses the necessary legal instruments to be able to negotiate life's administrative hurdles while they were gone. They could choose a general power of attorney, which allowed spouses to do just about everything from signing a lease on behalf of their spouse to filing taxes. Marines could also choose to draft a special power of attorney, which was both more specific and limited.

Some of these Marines, who hadn't known their wives very long, hesitated about handing over the keys to their financial castle, so to speak. It was a case of "I love you with all my heart but I don't trust you with my money." It was our job to talk through the options and educate them that paperwork created stateside (rather than in a far off part of the world) would be easier for everyone, no matter their decision.

Wills were written, too. This was something most young adults never thought about. Who gets what, final wishes, burial arrangements, funeral requests, legacy decisions—these were all issues that needed to be discussed. That scared some people, and we helped them through that, too. Yes, it was completely morbid, but it came with the territory.

Ross and I bought a supplemental life insurance policy this go-around, too. He said, "If we can't be together, the least I can do is set you up to move forward." Ross sounded so matter-of-fact about it all that I hated even thinking about it.

In a twisted way I felt like buying the policy was our way of jinxing war. If you plan for the worst, then it won't happen, right?

17

A Beautiful Gift

February 28, 2004
Fallujah, Iraq
Camp Pendleton, California

I drove Ross to 2/1's headquarters at Horno, where I could once again say goodbye and deliver my heart and soul into the hands of the Marine Corps. It was a terrible thing to say goodbye, but the sooner he left, the sooner the countdown bringing him home could begin. We were both a little quieter than usual. The night before, Ross wanted to go out and celebrate his last night in town. I just wasn't up to it. I'd worked all day and I didn't have the energy. He didn't say anything, but I knew he wasn't happy about it.

It's not common knowledge that the workups prior to a deployment are a killer on relationships. Marines are never home during workup. Any kind of similarity to the regular routine is unheard of. Families are left feeling stressed and nauseated from all the confusion and shifting schedules.

I stood with the other families, waiting for Ross to get on the bus. I remember thinking that something seemed off. Instead of a quick and orderly line, there was some kind of delay. MPs stood at the front of the line shining a bright light on each Marine before they loaded their gear onto the bus. Nobody was saying much, so I just chalked it up to some Marine protocol that I wasn't aware of.

I debated on waiting for the buses to leave, but I didn't want to deal with the emotional rollercoaster anymore. I was trying to be brave, trying to convince myself everything would be okay. The reality was that Ross was leaving me to go to war again. I decided to take myself home instead, and throw a pity party for yours truly. After that, I was going to do things differently this deployment. I was going to connect with friends, help the battalion and other wives on the homefront, and plan a vacation. I wasn't going to let my fear dictate how this deployment was going to go.

The next couple of days brought horrific news explaining the lights and secrecy from the night our Marines had loaded onto the bus: A married Marine from the unit who had been having an affair with the spouse of another Marine confessed he'd tried to break it off with her, but she threatened that she would kill his wife and kids while he was deployed. Long story short, he had taken her out to Deer Park on the south side of Horno—where the PFT, Physical Fitness Test course was—and shot her.

The Provost Marshall's Office better known as PMO, or Military Police, was trying to ID him before he deployed. Eventually he was taken into custody in Kuwait.

At least they got their man. But that was crazy.

A few weeks later, Jessica and Laura, two of my fellow key volunteers—both spouses in the company—invited me over for dinner. I wasn't feeling well; I was completely drained. I almost cancelled, but I really wanted to see them.

We'd met because our husbands worked together. We instantly hit it off. They were both new to the base, plus they only lived about 20 minutes from me, in O'Neill housing. They had a bigger home, wall-to-wall carpet, and newer appliances, but their places felt a bit secluded each time I drove out there. I thought it was nice that they had a few extras to make their house more of a home.

"Hey Kristine, so glad you could make it!" Laura said happily as she pulled me inside. "Do you have any news with what's going on over there?"

"Sorry," I said. "Nothing new." I had signed a confidentiality agreement, a requirement for my KV leadership duties. There were times when I was privy to information that hadn't been released, but the truth at that moment was that I didn't know anything more than they did.

"Can I get you a glass of red?" Laura asked as she took my arm and led me into the kitchen.

"Nope. I think I'm good for now. I haven't been feeling all that great."

Laura winked at me. "What's this? Kristine turning down a glass of red wine? You must be sick or something."

"Or pregnant," Jessica joked, pouring herself a glass.

I had to stop and think. "I don't think that's it. I took a pregnancy test before Ross left; it was negative. I don't know what's going on; I've just been feeling so tired."

Laura and Jessica looked at each other, grabbed my arms and led me to the bathroom. Jessica dug around under the counter, then plopped a pregnancy test into my hand.

I just stared at it.

"Alright already, go pee on the stick!" Laura shouted.

What did I have to lose? I think they were more excited than I was. I indulged them.

The timer went off.

I flipped the pregnancy test over. There was a big fat plus sign staring back at me. I couldn't breathe.

The girls screamed with joy.

I just stood there staring at this little piece of plastic that had silently announced a monumental change in the course of my life. *It's not just about me anymore.* What had I agreed to do? Part of me felt like I should be celebrating, but the truth was that, in that moment, I was really scared. *Ross isn't here.* No, he was going to war again. I was left doing this on my own.

I wasn't ready.

I was going to be completely responsible for another human being, and I had no idea what to expect.

I hadn't grown up around a lot of kids. I wasn't one of those girls who did a lot of babysitting. Babies were a foreign concept; an unknown quantity. I'd never thought we would get pregnant so quickly, so easily. And it's not that I wanted to undo anything, but it meant my life—and especially my relationship with Ross—would never be the same.

There's a military version of Murphy's Law: "Anything that can go wrong will go wrong—as soon as your spouse deploys." I'm certainly not saying this baby was a mistake. But it was a huge surprise. Nothing was ever for certain, and big changes usually seemed to come in threes. So who knew what else 'ol Murphy had in store for me?

It was our first KV meeting since saying goodbye to our Marines. All of our ladies seemed to be doing well. I made sure we had hired babysitters so that the moms with kids would have an easy childcare option.

We were just about ready to adjourn the meeting when Shannon asked some backhanded questions, trying to play on my ignorance of the Corps. She had four years on me, and she wore every one of them like a medal of superiority.

I couldn't begin to fathom what her motivation might be. The truth was, we were all in the same boat. We were all married to service members. We were all compulsively checking our email and carrying our cellphones everywhere we went, hoping we would hear something, *anything,* to know our men were okay. We all prayed that no one in dress blues would come knocking on our doors.

We were preparing to stand by and do whatever we could to serve on the homefront while our Marines went back into combat. That meant seven months of paying bills, wrangling children, and household duties. Seven months of cooking meals, taking care of other people and broken vehicles, seven months of questions from in-laws, and the shouldering of every bit of responsibility our Marine possessed relative to the outside world or his family. In my mind that made all of us all equals, regardless of how many years we'd been married or how many deployments we'd been through.

All of us were waiting.

All of us.

Our last stop before leaving the States was Bangor, Maine. From there we'd fly on to Germany, then to the Middle East. The warm welcome and support we received in Maine was tremendous. I'd never seen anything like it, and certainly hadn't expected it.

We landed late in the evening, but it didn't deter the welcome wagon. The VFW was there, along with many other Veteran's organizations and volunteers; many of them remarked on the new digital cammies that had recently been issued. They came to say goodbye, bringing an arsenal of phone cards and cellphones so that we could all make one last call home.

Some handed out homemade cookies and snacks. They were amazing people, and some of the most patriotic Americans I've ever met. I can see their generous faces in my mind, and would recognize them anywhere.

It took us nearly a week to reach the Udairi Training Range in Kuwait. Once we arrived, I took the first opportunity I had to call Kristine.

"Hi babe, I'm so glad you called!" Kristine shouted over the line. Long pauses and muffled words were still the norm.

"Sorry it's taken me so long. I've been really busy getting ready for everything, and we haven't had a lot of phone access. How are you holding up over there?"

"Things are good—been a bit tired lately."

Even with the delayed connection, I could tell there was something more she wanted to say. I was afraid things weren't going well with the KV, or that my mother had in some way said something to hurt Kristine.

"Ross, I need to tell you something . . . you're going to be a daddy."

"Seriously? Are you sure?"

"Yep, I'm sure. My first doctor appointment is next week."

"Oh my God! Babe! I might be the happiest man alive." I couldn't stop smiling. "I guess this explains why you were so exhausted the night before I left. I knew something was off, but I never imagined it was this. What do you think we're going to have? A little boy or girl?"

"I'd say it's a boy, but it really doesn't matter to me."

"Yeah, me either. All I can hope for is a healthy baby. You know, maybe it's not the best idea for you to be on your feet all the time. Maybe you should think about quitting your job, and just staying home and taking care of yourself."

She hesitated. "I'll think about it. For now it's nice to be able to get out of the house, to have something to do besides focusing one hundred percent on everything the Marine Corps is up to right now."

"I get that, babe, but don't take any unnecessary chances, okay?" I wanted her to stay home. I knew deployments were stressful. I wanted her to relax as much as possible.

"I wish you could have been here in person to find out—I hate that you're so far away right now." There was a pause, and for a second I thought the connection had dropped.

I could hear the emotion in her voice as she spoke. "I know you can't promise to come home . . . but the whole idea of you going to war . . . and thinking there's a possibility that you won't be coming home. I'm freaked out. I don't think I can do this without you."

I knew what she wanted to hear: that I would do the minimum and just get through the deployment, get home no matter what. But my job—my focus—was on taking care of my Marines. I would do whatever I could to do it well, to keep my men safe, as much as the insanity of war would allow. You can't think *I'll do anything to keep my Marines safe.* There'd be no point even having the Marine Corps, or even a military force. If your highest value is safety, you have no business going to war. Of course in the real world, in which there are people who want to kill and destroy us, that's not an option. The next best thing we can do is train hard for deployment, where you learn as a unit to do the right thing. Readiness mitigates some risk, but it doesn't take it all away.

I tried to console her. "Try not to think about that part, babe. I can't even tell you how excited I am to be a dad. I love you so much. You are by far the best thing that has ever happened to me."

She sighed. "I love you, too."

The guy in line behind me cleared his throat. I glanced over my shoulder; the line for the phone was already a dozen Marines deep. "Babe, I've got to go. There's a line of guys waiting to call home and I'm not sure when any of us will have the chance to call again. Promise me you're going to take it easy. I'll be home before you know it. I love you."

After we hung up, I couldn't stop smiling. I told my friends the good news.

We moved out the next morning. A day and a half later, our convoy reached Camp Baharia. I'd thought by then we'd have armored vehicles to ride into Iraq, as IEDs had become the biggest threat, but most units didn't get any. All I had protecting me from bullets, shrapnel, and bombs was a large armored panel secured by lashing-straps, similar to an emergency tow strap, to the door of my Humvee. It was better than nothing.

Camp Baharia was massive, about two thousand five hundred acres, with a lake and small bungalows strewn across the property—a twenty-foot high wall ran the length of its perimeter. Baharia would be our home base for the next seven months.

We had an opportunity to send key leaders from both the company and battalion level to meet with Iraqi leadership at a government building in the center of the city. I accompanied the CO, platoon leadership and a few squad leaders. We would meet up with the US Army 1/505th to plan for movement, security, and immediate action taken, should there be contact with the insurgents.

Insurgents attacked one of our first meetings with the Army. A couple of mortar rounds landed on top of the district center. Several men were severely wounded; one of our sergeants received shrapnel wounds.

We had come over from the States thinking that we'd be working to win hearts and minds in Fallujah; thinking that we'd be doing humanitarian things like trying to get essential services (water, sewer, electric) started, building schools, and generally improving the infrastructure of the area. But after having been attacked on our first visit to the government center, our understanding of how this deployment was going to shake out began to change. If this was indicative of what our time here was going to be like, we'd need more ammo.

We took a good look at the way the Army operated. Their unit was much smaller than ours. Therefore, the ability to stay out for longer durations was limited. The base suffered nightly from episodes of indirect fire, typically from rockets and mortars.

There were a lot of challenges to overcome.

While I didn't always agree with the way the Army did things, we knew we could take a few lessons from the 1/505th, and at the same time gain some efficiency in our operations. Our goal was to try to be more present with our larger force, and stay outside the wire for longer stints. It became imperative to carefully limit any of our patrol patterns, and to use the night to our advantage.

We had been assigned new call signs in the States for use in Fallujah—the company's old call sign, Terrapin, was retired. We were now Pale Rider. Our battalion embraced the principles and fundamentals of counterinsurgency while trying to endear the population to our efforts.

We knew that in order for us to be successful, we needed to help the local security forces and leadership secure populated areas. Once those were secure, we could better assess any other mission-related needs.

18

Into the Fire

March 2004
Fallujah, Iraq
Camp Pendleton, California

I t was game time. The Marine Corps officially took over operations from the Army. The night before, troops moved towards a US air base further west of Fallujah, and an IED erupted on Route Mobile Highway when the fleet passed. A Marine attached to the air wing unit was killed; others were wounded from a subsequent RPG attack on the eastern side of the city.

The entire battalion then began a clearing operation on the eastern side of the city, alongside one of the Joint Special Operation Task Forces so that the insurgents couldn't use the area to attack convoys on that side of the road again.

Our first obstacle was dealing with the fact that Fallujah had never been properly cleared—the Army just didn't have enough people to do it. Hell, the Marines didn't have enough people to do it. We could certainly make a dent, but the Marine Corps put a plan in place when we rotated out that added a reinforced regiment so that we could clear it properly—a tasking that would start in November. It would be known as the Second Battle of Fallujah, Operation Al Fajr, or Operation Phantom Fury.

The first morning after our official assumption of command, we were tasked with securing a strip of the city to deny the enemy the ability to use this portion of the town to conduct attacks. The area we were to operate in was a prime location for attacking convoys traveling west to places like Ramadi, Al Taqqadum Air Base, and Al Asad Air Base. We began clearing the first building on the eastern side of town. It would develop into a running battle; there would be hasty ambushes all day.

Captain Banner took 2nd Platoon on a mission deeper into the city. He didn't have a lot of time to brief me on his plan, and I was left with the other two platoons to continue to clear and patrol our sector. I divided it in half: 1st Platoon operated in the southern half, and 3rd Platoon in the north.

Banner called via radio for the company to consolidate near the eastern entrance to the city sometime late in the afternoon. He gave me a linkup time of 2100, which I relayed via radio to 1st Platoon.

Well after sundown, it was time. I moved out to the linkup point with Lt Wade Zirkle. A Humvee armed with a mounted machine gun brought up the rear.

When we neared our destination I went to the front of the patrol to conduct the linkup with the Captain. "Pale Rider Six, this is Pale Rider Five. We're one hundred fifty meters from the linkup site, over."

No answer. I tried two more times, and still received no answer.

I saw movement to the south, near the main road. I took out my NVGs to get a visual. I used the standard nighttime visual recognition signal for conducting a linkup when radio communications had failed.

As I gave the last flash to say *we're coming in*, a hail of fire came down on us from behind and to our right. My Marines began returning fire. I dropped my NVGs and hit the deck, grabbing my radio to call for a ceasefire—I thought the unit from across the street was shooting at us. I couldn't see where the fire was coming from and I wanted to be sure it wasn't coming from one of our sister companies, just in case they had entered our area and confused us for the enemy.

Shots were definitely ringing from our friendlies, but when I looked closer I could see that they were firing to the immediate right of us, not at us.

As the fire we were under began to wane, I surveyed our position. Pfc Sandoval, the Marine manning the M240 machine gun mounted to the Humvee, was slumped over the cab of the vehicle, motionless. Smoke rose from his machine gun, the barrel almost white-hot from the high rate he'd been firing.

I ran out to check on him, yelling for Marines to assist me in pulling him from the vehicle into cover for triage. Lt Zirkle received the casualty and situation report from his squad leaders. Another Marine had been shot in the butt.

As soon as we had Sandoval out of the line of fire, I dropped to my knees, holding his head in my lap. As I unbuckled his chinstrap I noticed that his face looked distorted. There was dark discoloration across the top of his forehead; one of his eyes looked out of place.

Not having any clue where he'd been hit, I just tried to reassure him. "Everything is going to be fine bud, First Sergeant is on the way."

As I removed his helmet, blood gushed into my lap. I cupped his head, and it felt like I was holding a plastic bag with a bunch of loose Lego pieces; his skull was completely shattered.

I tried to be as quiet as possible in telling Lt Zirkle that Sandoval was gone; I didn't want to distract the other Marines. We needed them to stay focused on their tasks. But there was a lot of noise— Marines were yelling, redistributing ammo, and repositioning to cover avenues of approach. We needed to be ready—even as we tended to our casualties—should another attack come. Our ears were ringing from all the fire we had just put down on the enemy.

"Sandoval is dead, Wade!" I screamed after the third try to relay the message over the noise. Lt Wade Zirkle reported it up to battalion; we still couldn't reach Captain Banner.

Doc Worley, one of the platoon's corpsmen, moved over to Sandoval; he had missed the exchange between Wade and me. He began to check on him. "I've got a pulse!" the doc cried out, but he didn't realize that it was just the last involuntary action of Sandoval's body. I leaned down as Doc was making ready to perform CPR and told him "Doc, he's gone." My words fell on deaf ears. Worley did what he was trained to do; save lives. He had a pulse, and he was determined to save Sandoval.

I patted him gently and let him do his work while I went to check on the other casualty. Thankfully, it was just a superficial gunshot wound to his butt.

I saw Marines bounding forward tactically, from the flank, towards our position. It was a Golf Company squad leader. "This is secure," I told him. "Go back and tell your company where we're at and not to fire in this direction."

First Sergeant Fantau arrived to conduct a Casualty Evacuation, CASEVAC, for the wounded Marine and for Sandoval, not yet knowing he was dead.

Maybe I should have said something. I wanted to hold onto the hope that I was wrong about Sandoval, but deep down I knew the truth. The reality was that he was gone. As much as it goes against my own morality, I wanted my Marines to believe the lie just long enough for us to get back to the FOB, where they could safely let down their guard and grieve this fallen brother.

I took a moment to assess myself. My helmet cover had been split from what looked like a bullet. I had a gash on my hand. The next day, one of my Marines saw the bandages on my hand and asked me if I might receive the Purple Heart for it. "This isn't worthy of the Purple Heart," I said. "It's just a scratch." I wasn't even sure how I'd got it; rounds were impacting all around me. My guess is that I cut it on something on the ground. It wouldn't feel right to wear the Purple Heart for a scratch, especially when one Marine had been shot in the head, another in the butt, and a corpsman wounded more severely by some kind of shrapnel, probably a ricochet.

Our company was the last element to pull out of the city, the last to finish our consolidation, and the last to achieve full accountability.

I brought up the rear of the company as we passed back through friendly lines, and caught sight of both LtCol Olson and SgtMaj Carter. I appreciated the effort they made to be there to greet their Marines as they returned after a long day of fighting.

"Keep your chins up. Sandoval may make it," Olson said encouragingly.

I really wanted to believe him, but I knew better. I don't think LtCol Olson had actually seen him yet.

We got back to the company area around midnight. I took Sandoval's flak jacket and helmet down to the lake and washed the blood out of it. The platoon sergeants cleaned out the Humvee and Lt Patterson later joined me to help clean Sandoval's gear. I left Thorleifson and Zirkle with some alone time in our hooch to write a condolence letter to Sandoval's family. None of us talked very much.

Movies and books have a way of romanticizing war. Everyone loves to watch brave men fighting with valor for freedom, but rarely do audiences see the bloody, emotional truth of war. They don't understand the steps we have to take in order just to be able to move forward to the next day.

After cleaning Sandoval's helmet, I found the tiny bullet hole, just above the front lip of the helmet. It was hardly noticeable. Sandoval had stood completely exposed, laying down fire to protect us. Everyone except him hit the ground when we took fire. He stood fully exposed and bravely fought.

Pfc Leroy Sandoval received a Bronze Star with a Combat "V" for his actions that night.

From: Ross
Date: March 27, 2004 2:59 PM
To: Kristine

> I can't tell you how hard I've been trying to get into contact with you. It's been crazy here, and we've had very little downtime.

> Can you please go out and buy four pairs of digital cammies from Oceanside, so that we can give them to our interpreters? We're not allowed to give them any of ours. Their gear looks completely different, which makes them a target out there. If you get them in Oceanside, they won't have the EGA [Eagle, Globe, and Anchor, the USMC emblem] printed on them, which will be the only way the interpreters will be allowed to wear them, since it's not the official uniform.

> As you know, we lost one of our Marines.

From: Kristine
Date: March 28, 2004 7:43 PM
To: Ross

> I'm so sorry about your losing a Marine this week. I think about you and your men all the time. I don't know if I realized how hard this would be. As the KV leader I know about every single injury and death. Then there are the questions from the KVs and spouses alike.

> I keep wondering what kind of situation you are in. When I do, I immediately picture something like *Black Hawk Down*. I don't like to think of you like that. Sometimes I just want to bury my head in the sand and forget about what is going on there; avoid reading the newspapers and watching the news.

Pretty much all my free time since you went into Fallujah has been spent on KV activities. I hope after this next meeting it will get a little better. There are so many people calling me and emailing me every day that I end up staying up way past midnight most nights, trying to get back to them.

I'll take care of those cammies. In the meantime, take care of yourself, and know that I love you.

Sandoval's flak jacket went to our interpreter, Sammy, as a hand-me-down. His real name was Abdel Noor Mohammed Sayyed Ali, from Asmara, Eritrea, and he looked a bit like Sammy Davis, Jr. I think he liked being called Sammy. The Army had called him that previously, and he asked that we call him Sammy too. He was a small man, around one hundred pounds, probably 5'4" or so. He was about 40 years old—almost ten years older than me at the time.

The DOD was strict on who could wear the new digital cammies. They were implemented because they wanted to offer us a uniform that didn't require dry cleaning and heavy starching; it would end up saving our service members hundreds of dollars a year by allowing us to simply throw our uniforms in the washing machine at home. It was better designed for weather, and more effective at concealment than the old woodland pattern, except when we covered it with our Kevlar vests—which then made a perfect outline of the shape of our torso, defeating the whole purpose of a camouflage pattern. The uniform separated Marines from the other services as well.

All this had proven to be difficult for the interpreters: it made them an obvious target for insurgents and other enemies. We didn't have enough body armor to give to the interpreters, so we couldn't share that either, but I was thankful Kristine was there for us. It was right to help get Sammy and the other three interpreters some gear, even though it would personally cost us several hundred dollars.

All the other services had money, so they got all the gear they needed. We were required to buy our own cammies, although typically boots and eye gear were issued.

In any case, Kristine sending those uniforms for our interpreters helped our mission readiness and probably even saved lives.

—— ○ ——

I'd never met Sandoval, but I knew from Ross's email and the information passed down to battalion that he had been a stand-up Marine.

Our Marines were in River City. That meant, among other things, that our communications with them were disabled until the next of kin notification had taken place. If a Marine dies, a special team is sent to the family listed on the RED—Record of Emergency Data. At least two Marines are sent to the family member's home address, in dress blues, accompanied by a chaplain. They always come in person, and never do anything over the phone.

We at KV waited for the all-clear notification here in the States. Command reminded us of the specifics of the casualty protocols to ensure families didn't talk about fatalities until that all-clear message was passed.

Before these controls were put in place—on more than one occasion—a Marine or corpsman might let it slip in an email or a call home that their buddy had been killed—probably because they might be having a hard time dealing with the situation. Then that spouse would say something to someone, not realizing the information wasn't official. No family should ever hear about the death of their Marine secondhand.

When the first all-clear messages were released, the phone tree was initiated. If you got the all-clear, it meant your Marine was alive and well. Everyone was desperate for details. Was this a one-time thing? Should we be expecting more fatalities shortly? Some assumed the KV network had insider information that we just weren't willing to share, but we didn't have any more answers than they did.

Most of us scoured the news. We were thankful for the reporters who were embedded with the battalion, as they provided a lot more information than we'd ever get from the Marine Corps. Other reporters would describe our Marines as soldiers, so we learned to scrutinize locations, even uniforms. Each new report prompted thousands of questions in our minds. Was it really a soldier, or was it a Marine, or maybe a corpsman? Worst: was it my Marine?

We tried to keep the ratio of key volunteers to military spouses at 1:20. This meant that there were a lot of phone calls and conversations to have, especially when passing the all-clear messages. Each key volunteer was responsible for calling about 20 families. We did our best to answer questions while trying to let them know that we cared and were there for them. Every all-clear message took at least two hours for a volunteer to complete.

Word was passed that four Americans had been killed in Fallujah. We learned that these Blackwater contractors had been shot, severely beaten, burned, then tied to a car and dragged through the city. Their bodies were found hanging from a bridge.

We were going back into the city, this time for a longer duration. During Operation Vigilant Resolve we were under orders to shut down Fallujah. We were tasked with cordoning off all major access roads, stopping insurgents from getting in and out of the city.

We were given 12 hours to prepare. We moved out in the dark of the early morning. The first firefight started before the sun came up, just as 1st and 2nd Platoons neared their assigned positions. Marines from our battalion recovered the Blackwater contractors' bodies.

A few days later we suffered another loss. Cpl Fey, one of the engineers attached to us, was shot in the head.

The Commandant of the Marine Corps, General Hagee, was coming to tour the battlefield. Our battalion commander, LtCol Olson, personally informed me that the Commandant was expected to arrive within the hour. He ordered me to ensure that all my Marines were awake for his arrival.

Two hours passed without the commandant, so I told the Marines in the immediate area to get some sleep, that we'd wake them just before the general arrived. The company gunny and I leaned on opposite sides of a Humvee discussing what we thought the commandant's entourage would be like. Suddenly, a bullet shattered the headlight of a vehicle directly in front of the gunny. Immediately more impacts came all around our position, and we both got down. What was odd was the sound of the bullets: there wasn't the telltale snap (a bullet's sonic boom) of the round as it passed nearby—it was more of a zing.

We deduced that 1/5, on the southern end of the city, was

engaging the enemy from an elevated position, likely shooting from a rooftop to the ground. They were firing in our general direction but they weren't intentionally aiming for us. Listening to the way the bullets sounded, they had most likely traveled a long distance and lost a lot of velocity by the time they reached us, therefore they had begun to spin and tumble, changing the way they sounded as they traveled through the air.

It was clear that we needed to move. Gunny and I moved our Marines to the far side of the berm so that these stray bullets would travel over the top of us. We needed combat engineers to use their bulldozer to dig us in a little deeper as a permanent fix. Once our position was secured, I collapsed to the ground, leaning up against the Humvee's wheel to rest. I quickly fell asleep.

Two hours later I awoke to LtCol Olson nudging my boots, upset and asking, "Why aren't your Marines awake?"

The commandant didn't seem upset that our Marines were sleeping instead of standing-to waiting to greet him. I roused my men, but I knew that if General Hagee had any idea what we were dealing with just prior to his arrival, he wouldn't have expected us to give up our much-needed rest time to stand around and wait for him, especially since it was four hours later than announced.

The general met with Marine leadership from our battalion, as well as the MEF Commander Lieutenant General Conway, Division Commander Major General Mattis, Regimental Commander Colonel Toolan, and one Secret Service agent. It was an impressive group of leaders gathered in one place.

19

Seeds of Friendship

I was physically drained from my first trimester, which was filled with exhaustion and nausea. It was made worse by the continual fallout from the casualties and fatalities of war.

I got a call from Mia, the first friend I made at Pendleton.

It had been a while since we'd talked because she moved out of the country to take a job on a cruise ship. She figured it would be a fun way to stay busy when her boyfriend deployed to Fallujah as well.

I couldn't wait to hear about all the fun she was having in the Caribbean.

Instead, the call was full of tears and regret. Working for the cruise line turned out to be completely disappointing. She left as soon as her contract was over. Her boyfriend had been cut from the deployment because of an injury, and just before she flew home, she found out he was cheating on her.

Mia was left with crushed dreams, no car and no home to call her own. I invited her to crash with me until Ross returned from Fallujah. I looked forward to having a friend and roommate around for the next several months.

It was a blessing having her; she helped around the house and occasionally cooked dinner. I was still working at the resort part-time, plus I spent full-time hours volunteering for the Marine Corps. I loved having a companion around to share the day with and celebrate life.

I held another meeting for the key volunteers in an effort to keep their spirits up, and let them know how valuable they were to the battalion. We scheduled events and get-togethers to try to build unit cohesiveness for the spouses who remained behind.

Life wasn't always easy, waiting for our warriors to return. Many of us were getting phone calls in the middle of the night from strangers who were preying on military spouses. They'd randomly dial the base area code and prefix, and depending on their intentions, they might tell a spouse their husband had died and that they needed to confirm their social security number and birthday, in the attempt to steal their identity. Others would try to coerce a spouse into having phone sex with them, trying to deceive them into believing it was their own spouse calling from overseas.

Some spouses were simply unreachable. We mailed about one thousand newsletters a month. Inevitably we'd get 20 back—sometimes more. I was surprised to find out some Marines just didn't want their wives contacted. I was told many men had the crazy idea that something bad was going to happen if the unit contacted their spouse. In my mind it was completely irrational, even ridiculous. I knew some of them were pretty old-fashioned; they wanted their wives to be subservient in the home. I can't count the stories I've heard about wives living on base without access to a car, or even a joint bank account. It usually backfired: wives who felt their husband had them under his thumb rebelled once their Marine deployed.

One of the most challenging parts of being a key volunteer was helping the family members of fallen and injured Marines. Some were local to Pendleton, and allowed us to do whatever we could to help; often we'd arrange to have meals delivered to these families. It was the least we could do, and many people pitched in as a gesture of thanks and love. We would do anything we could to try to provide comfort in their time of need. We also understood that everyone grieved in his or her own way. Some wanted help and others didn't. Either way, many of us were praying for them.

I shared a great many tears and emotional moments with strangers, many of whom I would never get a chance to meet in person. It was difficult. And it happened too many times over the course of the deployment.

We'd been given orders to watch the river.

Enemy supplies were still getting in, even with all the monitored checkpoints along major roadways. The river seemed the most likely method the enemy would use to smuggle supplies into the city. I was co-located with 3rd Platoon in a three-story house on a bend of the Euphrates. We could look directly over the river and into the Jolan district of Fallujah. I'm fairly certain the house belonged to a former Iraqi Ba'ath party member because much of it had been gutted; he'd probably left quickly after Saddam Hussein's power collapsed. The floor had been stripped of what was likely beautiful mosaic tile work, leaving only tar. I was thankful to have four solid walls and a roof over my head, but the tar clung to our iso-mats—and pretty much anything else we owned.

Even though the house had recently been abandoned, it still boasted a small population of farm animals, including chickens and goats. We freed the goats because we couldn't feed them, but the chickens seemed happy enough hunting and pecking in the yard. We made use of the eggs they laid as a supplement to our MREs. On occasion, our interpreter Sammy would go into Baghdad on his allotted time off, bringing back rabbits for us to cook up. I remember one night in particular one of our Marines cooked us an amazing meal using rice, eggs and rabbit. It reminded me of gumbo. It was the first real meal we'd had in weeks.

Iraqi civilians regularly showed up at our position trying to get into Fallujah via the farmland that flanked the rear of the house. They'd show up with notes written in English "signed" by a "US soldier," wanting through the line. We would search these men, but to honor local customs we never searched the women. As the days passed, they became bolder. They would drive up in vehicles asking for passage into the city. It wasn't uncommon to find small caches of weapons hidden inside these cars. An embedded reporter snapped a picture of one of these detain-and-search situations. I later learned that I made the front page of the *San Diego Tribune;* they wrote an article and published a photo of me filling out a detainee form on an Iraqi trying to smuggle a sniper rifle into the city.

*O*utside of volunteering full-time, I was growing tired of my retail job. Pinkalicious wasn't exactly a booming place, and the hours did drag on. I loved it when it was busy, but when it was empty there was only so much folding, hanging, and cleaning a girl could do in such a small store.

At least at home, my place was filled with fun and laughter. I had a firepit out back. Many of the ladies in the neighborhood came throughout the week to hang out with Mia and me. We hosted dinners, and usually invited wives whose husbands were deployed like ours. Occasionally, we went out to dinner or went dancing. Of course, being preggers, I was the ideal designated driver.

I was happy in that house. I hated that my husband was gone, but the Marine Corps had given me the best gift in the world—new friends. It was no longer me against the world. My friends and I were in this together; we shared our trials and triumphs.

Of course, there were a few bad seeds but it was easy enough to ignore them for the most part. A handful of spouses wore their husband's rank as if it were their own, only they used it as an instrument to try to instill fear. Thankfully, these were few and far between. I've come to realize—looking back through all the years I've spent in military circles—that those women who had an identity distinct from the Marine Corps, were strong enough and secure enough to be themselves. Those without their own identity or their own life story were usually dependent upon their husband's identity to an unhealthy degree. Subsequently, they wore their husband's rank like an expectation of social subsidy.

The great majority of the ladies I met and knew were tremendous. I didn't see Laura and Jessica as much as I wanted, mostly because it was a good 20-minute drive from my house to where they lived. Most of our little get-togethers were impromptu, usually initiated by conversation; maybe when a friend happened to walk by, or we were chatting with someone by the mailbox. Oftentimes, that small conversation bloomed into a hangout, many times with cocktails and iced tea.

Life while Ross away was tough. But it was never dull.

It was our last day in Fallujah proper. We learned that the Iraqi Army, Fallujah Brigade, was coming to relieve us of our positions.

We were told to leave the place as we'd found it, and we did our best to do precisely that.

Our imminent departure really affected our interpreter, Sammy. I was becoming close to him—he was an altogether kind, hard-working and thoughtful person. He was exceptionally accurate whenever we met with the locals; he could tell when people were lying. Our interpreters were still targeted by insurgents, so I worked hard to secure Sammy's safety.

I wanted to bring him back to the States with me. I asked Kristine if she would be okay with offering him a place to live if we could get him home with us. Sammy was almost in tears when I told him he was welcome in our home. He said, "I don't know how I could repay you."

Later he asked me, "Could I also get a job?"

I told him, "Of course you could." Maybe he was thinking that if we let him stay with us, he'd have to live as some kind of indentured servant. I was happy to let him know that we would let him stay on with us until he was firmly on his feet. He was extremely happy about the possibility coming to the States and living the American dream.

We finished emptying our sandbags and backfilling our fighting positions, bunkers, and anything else we had changed in order to establish a defensive position. I headed out on to a large open air roof to observe enemy movements. A mixed convoy of approximately 50 civilian and military vehicles snaked up the road along the river towards us. I called it in. Turns out it was the Iraqi Brigade coming to relieve us.

When they arrived, a man with a head of thick white hair and a well-trimmed white mustache, wearing a three-piece suit, stepped out and handed me his card. He announced he was the general in charge of the relief.

It was an odd position for me to be in—one wouldn't normally salute while in combat gear and in a combat zone, but I felt it would be appropriate at that time, so I gave him a smart salute and said, "The position is yours, General."

We moved out shortly after that, and headed to our next position just west of Saqlawiyah, outside of Fallujah proper. It took us about 45 minutes to get to the enormous 15-acre compound Banner had located. A 12-foot-high wall ran around the entire perimeter.

The compound's main residence boasted a four-story home with about thirteen thousand square feet of living space. That included a small three-bedroom guest house. A purebred Doberman patrolled the property, but it never really bothered us. After a while, the dog became used to us, but we also took care of him as best we could. The house was a perfect base of operations for our company, plus it commanded good visibility of the river, which was to our tactical advantage.

We immediately set about fortifying the compound with sandbag upon sandbag. It took days on end, using about four thousand pounds of dirt in the process. The compound was a good insulator from enemy fire. We took a few potshots from the side of the house facing the river, along with indirect fire from mortars and rockets, but it was minimal considering what we'd seen elsewhere.

The home's electric service was sporadic, and that made the experience almost luxurious. Few Iraqi nationals enjoyed electricity, but we were lucky—we sometimes got as much as eight hours of service. It came on around dusk, but it was not on a reliable schedule. There were no lights, but the ceiling fans would begin spinning when the power came on. It wasn't home. It was, however, better than that which was to be expected.

Patterson, Schellhaas, Thorleifson

20

Weeds in the Garden

★ ★ ★

April 2004
Fallujah, Iraq
Camp Pendleton, California

A week had passed since we'd pulled out of Fallujah. Lt Patterson's platoon was assigned to pick up and escort LtCol Olson to a meeting with the Police Chief. On the way there, Patterson's convoy hit a huge IED. We saw the explosion from where we were standing. It was a lethal combination of three 155mm artillery shells: two were high explosive, and one was white phosphorous. I jumped into a vehicle with Captain Banner and hauled ass over there as quickly as possible.

By the time we arrived on scene, Marines were already being treated and quickly loaded up for evacuation. Everyone in the Humvee suffered white phosphorous burns, including First Sergeant Fantau. Pfc Brandon Sturdy, a machine gunner, was killed.

At first, I didn't recognize Fantau—by the time we got there he'd already been triaged and his face was entirely covered in bandages.

We loaded my vehicle, and one other, to provide security for the CASEVAC that would take our wounded Marines to Camp Fallujah. First Sergeant Fantau flatlined while we were there. I remember thinking *he's the glue holding the company together.* Our Marines trusted him; it was a devastating psychological blow to all of us that the most senior enlisted man in the company was in such bad shape. Fantau lost most of his nose, suffered a broken jaw, and one of his eyes was badly damaged. Thankfully, he would survive and make a substantial recovery.

It was already month two of the deployment. The casualty and fatality list was already too long.

IEDs were everywhere along the roads, usually detonated with a cell phone or a garage door opener. Insurgents would lie in wait for troops or convoys to drive by. Then, with the cowardly push of a button, they would destroy lives and equipment. We had to be on guard against this threat constantly.

In Iraq, it was not uncommon for people to set up vending shops or carts pretty much anywhere. Since we'd arrived though, there were certain areas that the local populace avoided. Admittedly, many Iraqis were nervous around us. We were Marines, we carried big guns, and there was always fear of retribution by insurgents if the locals were spotted talking to us. Therefore, when a soft drink vendor wandered up the side of the highway and stopped under the overpass leading to Saqlawiyah, I was a little more than suspicious.

I took Sammy and a fireteam with me and went to question the man. We made a little small talk. With Sammy's help, we convinced him that it would be safer and more profitable if he moved across the freeway where more people could see him.

I gave Sammy some money to buy a drink from him, and pointed out a better spot where he could go, next to where we had seen others sell drinks. I remember thinking that a return of vendors to the area meant things were getting better, getting back to normal.

The vendor asked if he could wait for his brother to come back with his truck to help move his heavy cart. I told him he could, but that it would have to be quick. I didn't know his true intentions but I suspected he'd decided on that exact position to stop so he could get a better look at our position, or maybe he was simply trying to get out of the sun by being under the overpass.

I left him where he was, talking to the squad leader in charge, giving him the order to ensure that the vendor moved himself in the next 15-20 minutes. I mounted up and rode out to another squad position.

As soon as we got back to battalion, word came down about an explosion. One of the CAAT Platoons had driven up to check on an abandoned cart. It was detonated as they approached. No one was hurt, but it rang a few bells.

Thank God the vendor hadn't been a suicide bomber. I was upset that I hadn't been adamant that he move immediately, or even checked the cart myself. If I had, though, maybe I wouldn't be here.

From: Ross
Date: June 01, 2004 1:06 PM
To: Kristine

Col tasked me with making sure that Toby Keith and Ted Nugent get 2/1 sew-on patches. I made it over there and picked them up, but I never did get to see them. I was busy with an investigation in regard to some of our KIAs. Only a handful of us forward deployed guys got to go. It's fine though; it's the thought that counts, right? Besides, if I went to see any of them in concert, I'd rather have you on my arm than some Marine. So, no cool pictures to show the kids when I get older.

I'm sad to see Col Toolan move on. He's been one of the bright spots in our chain of command. I hope he goes far. He's the kind of man you want to see as a general.

21

Calling In Reinforcements

March 2004
Fallujah, Iraq
Camp Pendleton, California

Most people don't think about what happens when a military spouse gets hurt while her husband is deployed. We learned that a Marine wife stationed at Twentynine Palms suffered a medical emergency and had been admitted to the hospital for several days. Her husband was deployed in Iraq, so the military police called Children's Protective Services to take their children into foster care because they didn't have family in the area.

The leadership from the Remain Behind Element, RBE, immediately asked why PMO didn't call base emergency childcare, the spouse's unit, or key volunteer network. Their response was that they had asked if a neighbor could help out but she couldn't assume responsibility for the kids for days on end.

In the end, the husband was sent home from Iraq to get his kids back. He had to fight to regain custody from CPS, which was unexpected, to say the least. In the next newsletter, we sent an announcement to all of our family members to consider enacting a special power of attorney to designate a caregiver, just in case something like this happened again. I couldn't imagine how it would feel to have someone other than my friends or family taking care of my child in the event of an emergency. I was barely out of my first trimester, and already my motherly instincts were beginning to kick in.

We were surrounded by kids everywhere we went in Iraq, and I often thought about what being a dad was going to be like. You'd often see young preteen girls carrying babies and toddlers around on their hips; it was the norm in their culture that young girls took care of their younger siblings, from about age nine on up. Very few Iraqis trusted us—most were suspicious of our intentions—but I enjoyed being able to interact with the kids. It was one of the positives of being there.

We were out on regular patrol, doing our usual checks. We stopped to talk to a couple of locals, and a group of kids came out to greet us. Our company gunny had them line up single file, and we handed out candy. Out of nowhere, a man on a moped rode up behind the line and kicked one of the kids as hard as he could. He jumped from the bike and started beating him. One of the corporals jumped on him and began hitting the attacker until we could pull him off the child.

The interpreter with us asked the man why he had attacked the child. The Iraqi said he didn't want anyone taking anything from the Americans. It was strange to be so disliked, and yet at the same time, be used as a resource for assistance. Sometimes people would walk up to our positions asking for help. There seemed to be an inordinate amount of genetic-related medical issues in the area, most likely stemming from marriages between cousins, a cultural thing there. We saw kids born with six fingers on a hand, disfigured bodies, and a whole slew of other medical conditions.

A large percentage of the population suffered from diabetes in Iraq. They were upset with the United States because they thought

the cause of their diabetes could be directly linked to the bomb-ings from Desert Storm in 1991. The clinics were always running low on insulin; they couldn't keep it stocked because of the lack of refrigeration.

It wasn't uncommon to see children with substantial injuries. We came across a one-year-old whose eye had been stabbed out by another child. We cleaned the wound and wrapped it with fresh bandages. We did what we could to give instructions for care, and provided some basic supplies to his mother.

Sadly, that wasn't the worst of what we saw. I'll never forget the day we discovered a special needs child chained to a wall. We questioned some locals as to why they had him chained there. They shrugged their shoulders, saying that the boy would run away if they did not. The child was completely isolated, left to sit in his own piss and shit. We didn't have the authority to do anything about it, so we had no choice but to leave.

*F*our months had passed. Families were already war-weary. Most of the wives charged forward, keeping the home fires burning with what grace they could muster.

There were a few who fell apart when their men left. Part of me really felt terrible for these girls. They weren't ready to be left on their own. Maybe they had married their Marines to escape a life that hadn't been so great. Maybe they were just too young and too far from home to find a way to cope. They suffered from the kind of codependent tendencies that made the limbo of deployment like a spark, and bad behavior like a pool of gasoline. The ones that refused to lean in and get involved with their community usually suffered the worst. Without a doubt, isolation bound these women for failure. People need to be connected in a community.

Shannon's behavior started to affect the whole KV network. I couldn't help but begin to think she'd been gunning for me all along. Maybe her plan was to be as disruptive as possible until I finally gave up, gave in, or quit. She started doing whatever she wanted—whenever she wanted—ignoring the rules laid down by the Marine Corps. People would call me, expressing concerns with her divisive behavior.

I often met with my key volunteer leadership to discuss how to best deal with Shannon. I was told to try to shake it off—that she was just being irrational and was probably affected by the stress of war—but even considering that, it just didn't add up.

I couldn't understand where this exceptionally personal hostility was coming from; it seemed like she reckoned me as the enemy. Did she want to take my place? I was doing my part in the overall mission to support our Marine families in the best way I could, running LtCol Olson's program. I was honor-bound to ensure Marine Corps rules were being followed. I was happy I could lean on LtCol Olson's wife, Dawn, for direction and camaraderie.

I began to question my role. I even went as far as considering tendering my resignation. To my surprise though, I received word that Helen and Col Toolan had nominated me as the regiment's Outstanding Ombudsman and Key Volunteer of the Year, sponsored by Governor Schwarzenegger, the USO, and several nonprofits. I was both shocked and honored to receive their nomination.

That nomination was the boost I needed to reshape my perspective. It's difficult to believe in yourself when your opposition is so constant. I often considered firing Shannon; she was creating animosity in the battalion, and that was the last thing any of our families needed. I worried, though, what the aftermath of such a step might be. After all, she wasn't my actual employee. Plus, this duty wouldn't last forever. In the end, I made the decision to just suck it up and keep moving forward, taking her personal attacks without complaint, knowing that the maintenance of a unified front for our battalion family members was most important.

In truth, my troubles were minimal in comparison to the heartache that too many of our families were going through. We were dealing with deaths and casualties on a regular basis. We were thankful for the embedded reporters, who had enabled us to see the war through their lenses and reports. We happily gleaned what we could from their experiences and perspectives, but that was bittersweet too. There was nothing worse for us than seeing on television the hardships our husbands were dealing with, knowing we couldn't do a single thing about any of it.

22

Monster-In-Law

August 2004
Fallujah, Iraq
Camp Pendleton, California

My best friend Christie threw a baby shower for me in Boise. Of course, my mom was invited and so was Trina. I hoped she would be on her best behavior at this party but to be honest, I never knew what I was going to get.

It didn't take long for her to do her usual thing, which left others feeling uncomfortable. We played a simple game of "collect the pink clothespins." Any time someone got caught with their arms or legs crossed, the person who noticed collected their pin. The person with the most pins at the end of the party would win a prize. Most of us forgot about the game in the dazzling array of conversations and cute baby things, but Trina just *had* to win. She'd just walk up to somebody, like a teacher would do to a young student, and hold her hand up in that person's face until she got her pin. Oh, my. The *looks* I got from my friends as she went to walk back to her seat.

I knew that Ross had called and talked to her the previous night, so I wasn't expecting the customary inquisition from her. Ross and I had always known that we only wanted the two of us at the baby's delivery. We couldn't know if there were going to be complications, if Ross was going to have transitioning issues, or if I would be medically ready for company. There were just too many variables.

We wanted time to bond together as a family before inviting all the love and chaos of our family members into our home. I knew it was one of those decisions likely to cause some pushback, but I had a very simple philosophy: If I did something for my parents, I would do for the same for Trina. If I didn't do something for my parents, I wouldn't do it for her. It made the decision-making infinitely easier, and considering my history with Trina, I thought it more than fair.

Trina, however, didn't like this instrument. She wanted to be special.

She had asked on several prior occasions if she could be in the room during delivery. I told her no every time. Then she asked to be outside the room. Again, I said no. Like that would make me feel any better, knowing she was just a few feet away. It would do nothing but stress me out. I thought the issue had been settled, but she cornered me when she found an opportunity, asking again to be present at the birth.

Thankfully, my mom was sitting next to me and quickly came to my rescue. "Trina, no; it's always been like that. You know the kids need their time to be their own family. I'm sure you'll be able to see the baby before you know it."

Trina gave us her usual look—head tilted slightly to the right, plastic smile pasted on. It was the same expression we saw every time we told her something she didn't want to hear. I knew she was fuming underneath.

But my mom didn't let that stop her. She was really just trying to be encouraging, so she went on. "When my first grandchild was born, we waited for them to call. We saw him for the first time after he was a couple of weeks old. It was so great; he was still teeny tiny, they'd had some time to bond, to show him off to her family before we got there. It was still wonderful."

My mom had made a valiant effort to put the issue to rest, but she didn't know Trina like I did. She didn't understand that Trina saw my yet-unborn son not as my child, but as an extension of herself. And that's why she felt she had a right to him. I was merely the vessel that would produce her grandchild.

Celebrating baby at the halfway dinner with Jessica Patterson

She started to probe again, her bloodhound persistence searching for cracks in my resolve.

"Why didn't you bring this up with Ross when you talked to him last night?" I asked Trina, trying to stay as calm and collected as I could.

She stuttered around for a bit, and finally said, "Well . . . I just didn't think about it."

In the nicest way possible, I said, "Ross would be happy to discuss any concerns you have with him." I got up and went into the adjacent room, hoping she would grab a clue.

From: Kristine
Date: August 13, 2004 6:23 PM
To: Ross

> Just came back from the baby shower. It was an amazing time, and the girls really went all out; except things went awry with your mom, as to be expected.
>
> I know this is the last thing you want to read about, but I don't want to see her or talk to her anymore until you get back. She just frustrates me to no end; I need a break from her. I'm sorry to unload this on you.
>
> I can't wait to have you in my arms again. If I can still fit my arms around you with my big 'ol tummy! :) I hope you know that you mean everything in this world to me.

From: Ross
Date: August 14, 2002 1:24 AM
To: Kristine

> I understand your frustration with my mom, and I wish she'd be a little more understanding about our wishes. Is her attachment to me a little odd? Sure. I truly believe she is struggling with something; I don't know what it is, but her behavior certainly points in that direction. I need just a little patience from you; or rather I should say a little more patience. I know you often hold your tongue with her, and I really appreciate it.

As time goes on, I think things will get worse. I need to sit down and talk to her about it. I know that. I'm dreading that conversation. She is going to be hurt, but I know in the end I have to address it. She is one of the few points of friction (albeit minor) in our marriage (that and how loud you are when you gulp water, heh). She needs to know that she's causing problems. I'm going to have to tell her flat out, but I don't know how it's going to affect her or how she'll respond.

You have every right to be mad at her and not want to see her, but please just try to be cordial for a little while longer. She and Frank have had, at times, a very rough marriage (although it seems to have gotten better since I've left). My grandparents' health is deteriorating and they need care, she doesn't have many close friends she can confide in, and after talking to her the other night, she sounded as though she feels she bears the weight of the world on her shoulders.

All that being said, I want you to understand that our marriage and our child come first with me. I'll seek out some professional counseling on how to broach the subject of these issues with her. Mom and I can sit in a session together. Thanks for being so patient with me, and with my mom. I'm so glad I married such an amazing woman.

From: Kristine
Date: August 17, 2004 4:30 PM
To: Ross

It was good to get a chance to talk to you but if I'm honest, today has been the shittiest day I've had in a long time. I'm pretty upset that you think I don't compromise enough when it comes to your mom. I feel like I already go above and beyond for her, I honestly do. I compromise every time I visit your mom because I sit there and put a smile on my face and act like nothing's wrong, but it is. I can't even count the number of times I've included her in things, invited her to events, or spent time with her. I do it all for you.

You KNOW that if you came to town, if you didn't see my parents, it wouldn't be a big deal; but if I came to town and didn't visit with your mom, the world would slip into total chaos. I do a lot of things for you out of respect for you. The fact is, I don't think you give me enough credit.

I don't know if you're going to understand this or respect my thoughts in this matter. I honestly think you just want to please everyone.

I know this email is rehashing a lot of what we already talked about, but when the phone cuts out as much as it does, these constant delays make it impossible to carry on a conversation about anything. I love you very much, and I can't wait to see you again.

From: Ross
Date: August 18, 2004 3:19 PM
To: Kristine

Please ignore my last email. I'm not having a good day. You really are my everything; I'm just venting. I'm really sick of this place. I'm sorry and really, don't pay any attention to that email. We'll talk tomorrow. I really miss you, and you mean the world to me. I love you so much.

From: Kristine
Date: August 18, 2004 1:06 PM
To: Ross

I'm not upset by your email at all. I understand where you're coming from, and I promise I'll make an effort to compromise or at least think about your position, then get back to you. Love you.

P.S. Your mom emailed me again asking me if she could come down for ten minutes to see the baby. She never quits.

From: Ross
Date: September 2, 2004 9:22 PM
To: Kristine

Thank you for forwarding my mom's email. I think you need to
tell her how you feel. I get tired of her sending emails like this to
you and completely avoiding the same topics in her emails to me.
Write up something that just lays it all out there. I don't know if
that would make things better or worse, but I think the
relationship would have a chance at healing if the issues are out
in the open. I need to talk to her soon about this. And when I do
that, I'll tell her to address her concerns to me, not you. Don't let
this tussle with her get you down. I love you more than anything.

From: Kristine
Date: September 3, 2004 8:13 PM
To: Ross

Well, I talked to a counselor today . . . she had really great cre-
dentials; I was surprised she was working for the Marine Corps
(ha!). The office actually made an exception for me. Normally
they only help active duty service members. I really lucked out
there. Otherwise I would have had to wait to get an appointment
with a counselor off-base.

Here's what was said:

We need to create very strong boundaries in regard to your
mom, then stick to them consistently without backing down or
allowing her to change our minds. No exceptions.

You need to tell Trina to quit blaming me for decisions she
doesn't like.

As far as having Trina come down to visit before we give the
all-clear to our family, the answer is no. And this is why:

You and I have already agreed on the way we would like our birth and visitation to be, plus we let our wishes be known. Our wishes are that our family members would wait to see both us—and the baby—until we're ready to receive visitors.

Giving in when she constantly pushes our boundaries is teaching her that she can keep demanding what she wants until she gets her way; it's teaching her to disrespect both us and our wishes. Love expressed from her towards you will be genuine only if she's willing to listen to your needs, then follow through in whatever way is best for you/us.

We need to bond with the baby based on our own parameters. When we both feel we're ready, Trina can fly down for the ten minutes or however long she wants (within reason). She can have her time when we are ready to give her time. We do not know the future and cannot know it. Therefore our decision, asking people to wait until we are ready, is a reasonable one. We may decide we're ready while we're still at the hospital, maybe a few days later or maybe a week later. Who knows? Our "no" should be a firm one, until the time is right for our family.

(The following are side-notes)

She also said that ten minutes will never be ten minutes; it will turn into "just five more minutes . . . " or the next time I'm napping, or she'll hang around until she sees another chance to get what she wants.

If she does come to the hospital, it will create stress and upset me, which is the last thing I need to go through (especially having just given birth to our child) and it will negatively affect both the baby and me.

The counselor said I should NOT reply to your mom's email, even though I have every right to be angry with her and feel the way I feel (even though I carefully crafted a draft response, dangit). I need to stop discussing these kinds of things with her entirely. The counselor said you're the one who needs to address these issues with her, and I agree. What happens when your Mom comes after me is creating a lot of stress/anger/re-sentment, which I shouldn't have to shoulder in the first place. You and I should be the only ones in our little family circle.

She suggested that if your Mom would like to see you, she might buy you a plane ticket to Boise instead of trying to come out here. I know you probably won't want to do that because you're only going to be home for a few weeks before the baby comes. In the end I guess that's something you and your mother are going to have to work out.

Love you, sorry this is so long—wish you could have been there today.

From: Ross
Date: September 4, 2004 5:49 AM
To: Kristine

Thanks for going to the counselor. I agree with what she said. Mom needs to respect our wishes. I talked to Erik Thorleifson and he talked about how the pastor that married them said that the inner circle of family is the married couple and their children. It's not the parents. Mom is going to have to realize that. It's going to hurt her, which hurts me, but she needs to know our boundar-ies. I know you've been saying this the whole time, but I really appreciate you taking the time to step back and think about it. In the end you're right. You usually are.

I'd rather not say these kinds of things to her via email, so I'm going to try to call her tonight, then call you afterward. I want to seek counseling not only for her but for me as well, when I get home. Maybe one session for me, then one with the three of us; possibly Frank, too. These things need to be aired and dragged out into the open.

What I need from you is to not give up on her yet. Please try to give her more chances to change. If in the end it doesn't work, fine. But please give her a chance to get close. Maybe not right now, but once I talk to her or once she/we get counseling. I cannot give up on her. And I don't feel good about telling her she can't come to see us. It might be the right thing to do, but it doesn't feel right.

23

Darkest Before the Dawn

$$\bigstar\ \bigstar\ \bigstar$$

September 2004
Fallujah, Iraq
Camp Pendleton, California

 suicide bomber drove his truck, armed with a five-hundred-pound bomb, straight into one of our company's seven-ton trucks. The truck was on its way to swap out platoons that were positioned along the highway north of Fallujah. The explosion blew the light armor clear off the vehicle, decapitating everyone on one side. The effect was so clean that it looked like a laser had traversed right through the midst of them.

An investigation was immediately conducted because of the atypical circumstances. Ten of the seventeen men inside the truck were killed: three Iraqis and seven Marines.

One of the survivors, and the only one not to be evacuated out of theater, had bent over to pick up his spit bottle for his chewing tobacco at the precise moment the bomb exploded. It might be the one time I can honestly say chewing tobacco saved a life. The man to his right was killed instantly. The guy to his left was struck in back of the head and suffered a significant brain injury. He was flown back to the States to learn how to talk again.

Lt Wade Zirkle was on the front passenger side of the truck, and suffered horrific burns. One of the seven Marines from our company killed in that blast held the morbid, heart-breaking title of being the one thousandth KIA in Operation Iraqi Freedom.

*T*oo many Marines were dying. The casualty reports created a small mountain of paperwork on my desk. No matter how many I read, I couldn't stop the heart palpitations as my eyes scanned each one. I wouldn't know the first thing to do if paperwork bearing the name "Schellhaas, Ross" were to come across my desk. *I don't even want to think about it. He's almost home. He's almost home,* I kept thinking, willing him to come back to me.

I knew the faces and names of those personally affected by the casualty and KIA next-of-kin lists. I was on the phone daily, talking with wives and other family members, doing my best to help them navigate across the open maw of Hell. I knew the stories, the pain-ridden details of countless Marine families. The last thing any of us wanted to hear was the unexpected doomsday knock at the door. It was the knock that preceded the opening of a door revealing a Marine in dress blues presenting you with a flag: "On behalf of the President of the United States, the United States Marine Corps, and a grateful nation . . . "

It was terrifying.

And it could happen to any of us at any time.

Ross had talked casually, as true warriors do, about what he'd like to happen in the event of his death. He said he wanted a Viking's funeral. He was totally serious. I had no idea how to go about making that happen. I tried not to think about, it but I couldn't help wondering how close to death he stood on any given day.

I couldn't know.

Did I want to know?

Yes. And hell no.

His company had been hit hard. The latest suicide bomber had taken seven Marines with him. Bang, just like that, gone in a moment. I imagined all the beautiful wives I had met who would thereafter walk through life without their husbands at their side. I imagined those parents and siblings who'd lost their loved ones.

I learned in this journey that everyone handles grief differently. No one knows how they're going to handle a situation like that until it happens to them. Planning ahead? That's well and good, but when grief grips your heart and soul, you might as well toss your plans out the window.

We settled into our positions along the Tharthar canal.

One of the Marines was cutting something with his knife and

the blade slipped, leaving him with a wound that was serious enough to require immediate higher-level medical attention. He was put in a small three-vehicle convoy and sent back to battalion. Sammy asked to ride along so that he could pick up some supplies.

While Sammy and the Marines were en route to camp, a 155mm artillery round—mounted on the backside of a guardrail along the road—detonated. Insurgents had waited until the last possible moment, ensuring the most devastating impact. The vehicle in the middle of the convoy took the most damage.

Doc Worley, who had been riding in the last vehicle, had escaped injury in the initial blast and immediately ran to render aid to those affected in the disabled vehicle. Seems the enemy was waiting for that.

They detonated a second IED, tearing off one of Doc Worley's legs. His other leg was badly damaged, but saved in part because the pistol on his thigh took the brunt of the shrapnel. Even as he lay on the ground, he kept his wits about him and administered his own tourniquets.

The remaining Marines scrambled to the stricken vehicle to check for casualties. The driver—Jacobs—was hit along the neck, injured but alive. Sammy had been decapitated. The Marine next to him, Cpl Ebert, took shrapnel to the back of his head. Most likely, the blow severed his spine, killing him instantly.

I was heartbroken when I learned of the blast. I made my way to Camp Fallujah to check on the dead and wounded and to secure any serialized gear or personal items on their person. Mingled with all the gear was Sandoval's old helmet. Sammy had been wearing it when he died. I stood there staring at the helmet, recalling the many conversations I'd had with Sammy, how he'd shared his dreams of coming to the United States, how hard he'd worked to help the American people.

A few months before, Sammy told me his only daughter had died. The gas had been left on in the house. She had asphyxiated in her sleep. It hit Sammy hard. I struggled to find words to console him, but he just said, "It was God's will."

I couldn't get those words out of my head as I thought about his death, along with the other Marine who had been killed in the IED blast. Was it God's will? Maybe it was God's will that Sammy should be with his daughter—if indeed any of this really was God's will.

I took the helmet with me back to camp.

From: Kristine
Date: September 18, 2004 11:19 PM
To: Ross

> I've had a heavy heart all day for the loss you must be feeling. I know you thought highly of Sammy, and he will be missed. I am very sorry that I never had the opportunity to meet such a caring and generous man, but I find solace in knowing that Sammy is with his daughter in heaven. My heart aches for all those Marines lost, as well as for their family members.
>
> I'll be very happy when you're home. I need you to come home, I need to be with you again. It is so dangerous out there; I would hate for you to lose your life, to potentially miss out on your child's life, on growing old together with me. I just don't know where I would be without you . . . I thought about that a lot today. All I could think about is moving home to my parents with our sweet little guy. I don't think I would be able to move on . . .
>
> Time can't go by fast enough. I can't wait to hug you and have you all to myself again . . . without worrying about where you are or what you're doing. Every single time someone gets hurt or killed it's a reality check: I might lose you.

*W*e were nearing the end of the deployment. We all wanted our men home. That meant the pace and number of phone calls began to pick up. When would our Marines be out of Iraq and back in Kuwait? What flight would the men be on? Most of the time all these arrangements were TBD.

Rumors were rampant that the deployment was going to be extended, or that they would be allowed to return home only to be called back into the combat zone within months. Command gave us a 1-800 number to which we could refer spouses for official information from command. We often referred families to that phone line for updates.

With the end of deployment nearing, we put together a return, reunion, and integration brief for our families. The command, KV network and MCCS were all involved. This brief would be one of the last formalities to endure before we got our husbands back.

The Marine's reintegration into the family—and the family getting used to having the Marine back in the household —can be difficult for some. It was easy for Ross and me as I was the one who managed everything at home, so nothing really changed when my husband wasn't around, except for the support he provided when he was here.

Some Marines wanted to pick right up where they'd left off, stepping back into managing the household, the money, the kids, parental discipline and more. Sometimes that was problematic, especially for the kids. Most of them just wanted to love on their daddies and get used to having them around again. The Marine was coming off the stress of the deployment, trying to ease back into family life—the transition wasn't always automatic.

Sex was one of the first topics we discussed at the brief. One of the popular mantras used by military spouses during deployment was "sexually deprived for your freedom." The speaker at the brief reminded us that there would likely be a transitional period for every couple, to be able to adjust. I knew others whose husbands wanted to sleep on the couch for a few days before they slept in their beds again. In the end we were told we shouldn't expect our sex lives to pick right up where we'd left off. We were warned not to expect too much.

I think for most of us the advice went in one ear and out the other. At that point most of us had been planning our reunions for weeks. We were all doing our best to welcome our Marines home.

We wanted our home to be as perfect as possible, which meant cleaning the house top to bottom, restocking the fridge with favorite foods, and making sure we had plenty of our Marine's favorite booze on hand. I knew all the comforts of home that Ross had missed; I wanted him to feel like a king. I wanted it to be so different from everything he had been exposed to in recent months that, if only for a little while, he could leave it all behind. It was the least I could do.

From: Ross
Date: September 25, 2004 8:07 AM
To: Kristine

> We're making a hop across the lines. One less steppingstone before I get back to you. I love you so much, and can't wait to see you.

From: Ross
Date: September 27, 2004 3:44 AM
To: Kristine

> The handover is official. Our company has lost 13 men here. We have a memorial today for Cpl. Ebert and Sammy. I'm glad this will be the last; at least I hope it is.

> I've been thinking about you a lot; every time I close my eyes for a short nap I dream about you.

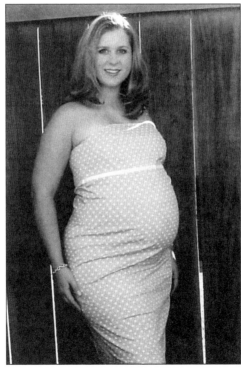

Waiting to welcome my Marine home once again.

24

Happiness Is Homemade

★ ★ ★

September 2004
Camp Pendleton, California

I was a ball of nerves. It wouldn't be long before I could wrap my arms around him. The anticipation of seeing him—of touching him—was almost unbearable.

I huddled with the rest of the families on the parade deck, counting down the remaining minutes that stood between our Marines and us.

Just after 3:00 a.m. our men began marching out onto the parade deck, company by company. After watching what felt like every other unit in the Marine Corps march out and get dismissed, it was time for Ross's company. I spotted him instantly. He didn't see me, but I could make a beeline straight to him from where I was.

Welcoming our boys home: Laura Thorleifson, Jessica Patterson, and me

They were released. I ran up and grabbed him. The first thing he said to me was, "Whoa, slow down! I don't want to hurt the baby."

I laughed. "Babe, we've been doing just fine while you're gone. A tight hug isn't going to hurt anyone."

"Oh, Kristine, look at you. Just look at you! You look so beautiful. Even more than I could ever dream or think while I was gone."

He held me at arm's length and looked at me, then pulled me in close.

"I've missed you so much," I said, resting my head on his chest. "I'm so glad you're back home." I looked up into his eyes. "Are you ready to go home?"

"Hell yes," he said. "I can't wait to get you all to myself so that I can see you naked. And then some."

"You got it," I said. "Follow me."

Finally, my Marine was home.

Upon the entire unit's arrival back home, I sent an email message out to the families letting them know that the key volunteer network was taking a break from taking calls in order to spend time with their families. If they had any questions in the meantime, they should contact the command directly. I also broke the news that I was officially stepping down from my position in order to set up our family for success. I was only three weeks out from my due date, and I knew I would need that time to rest and take care of any final preparations.

Never in a million years would I have imagined Shannon would launch one more arrow my way with this completely procedural email. She asked the family readiness organization to contact me to let me know that the key volunteer network "never goes away."

Well, by God. I'd never said we *did*. I was stepping down, as were a number of ladies, and I didn't want any of them to get calls while trying to come back together with their husbands, especially if they were having a hard time readjusting after this especially harsh deployment. My email was simply to say that if anybody had a need they were to call the command.

I was glad to put some distance between Shannon and me. I wished her all the happiness in the world, and hoped she could get over whatever hang-ups she had. It was going to drag her down in the long run if she didn't. Many may have thought it all boiled down to a personality conflict between Shannon and I, but I later learned that her new KV leaders actually fired her for the same behavior she indulged during my time as KVC. Onward and upward for me, though; I was so glad to leave that drama behind.

Ross and I signed up for Lamaze classes on base. We were the oldest couple in the room by at least five years. After a short intro-duction, we as a class watched what seemed more like a 1970s porn video than an instructional aid about childbirth.

The woman on the screen had no reservations about a camera being focused on her lady parts. Every time a contraction came, her husband gently sang, "She'll be coming 'round the mountain when she comes . . . " Then they got in the shower together and he started singing to her again.

Ross and I just looked at each other saying, "What the hell *is* this?" then busted out laughing.

Everyone else in the room was completely serious, but here we were cracking up: the oldest, and definitely the least dignified. We did our best to keep quiet and to be respectful after that, but it was a bit of a losing battle. We did manage to contain our laughing to a few incidents of snorts and closed-mouth guffaws.

Then there were the partner exercises. The men were supposed to lie down next to us in a spooning position on the floor with the blanket and pillow we'd brought. This was so that the partner could learn how to find ways to provide comfort for his wife as she endured childbirth. The staff turned off the lights and put some calming music on.

The silence was broken by Ross's loud snores. He had confiscated the pillow for himself, and he was dozing away. His body hadn't yet adjusted from Iraq time.

As far as I was concerned, he could sleep through the entire class; he had earned it. He was here, in the flesh, living, breathing. And home.

25

Pain Is Baby Leaving the Body

November 2004
Camp Pendleton, California

*I*t was go time.

We loaded up the SUV and headed to the Camp Pendleton hospital, situated in the middle of the base. My contractions were still sporadic, coming roughly between every five to nine minutes. I wanted to go in and get checked nevertheless because my mom had a history of quick births.

Thankfully, my OB happened to be the doctor on duty that night, so she looked me over and admitted me around 11:00 p.m. Having a propensity for planning, I had written out a detailed birth plan. All the books said I needed to make one, so I had invested considerable time planning out all of the steps.

When I showed the nurse my plan, she laughed at me and said, "We'll do the best we can." She hooked me up to the monitors so that we could see how our little man was doing. They put me on a Pitocin drip to speed things along because I had low platelet counts. As a result my contractions started getting closer and more powerful.

Because I hadn't received an epidural, I was able to get up and go the bathroom. I discovered at that point that my body's new primary mission was to utterly cleanse my colon of all body waste. Thank goodness. The last thing I wanted was for my husband to see me shit myself while giving birth.

Ross did his best to comfort me by implementing some of the techniques we'd read about or learned in Lamaze class. He came over and placed his hand on my leg. I was then quite surprised to learn that the smallest, gentlest touch was excruciatingly painful. I then asked him to quit touching me.

The pain grew worse, which influenced my decision to ask for pain drugs. By the time the anesthesiologist arrived and put the needle in my back I was in so much pain that I couldn't stop my body from moving. I remember the nurse getting really angry with me; yelling at me to stop moving, but I couldn't help it. She then checked me and told me, "Honey, it's too late for meds. Your baby is coming!"

An entire football team of doctors and nurses dressed in scrubs came shuffling into the room, all with different jobs to do. Four male corpsmen in their early twenties mobbed over to one corner and huddled around a baby warmer. Discussing sports. In the other corner were a couple of nurses, the anesthesiologist, and a few other people muddling about. Our nurse snapped at one of them, telling him to get out. He was a new doctor, still in his residency. He ignored her, walked up to me and asked if I would mind if he stayed, saying he'd never seen a live birth.

I looked around the room, chuckled darkly and replied "Hell, what's one more?" But if he was going to stay, I was going to give him a job. "You're in charge of pictures, okay?"

"Absolutely," he said, grinning. I don't think anyone really enjoyed working with my shouty nurse. But he looked happy to be able to stick around. In the meantime, he snapped away.

My doctor took another assessment. "Okay, Kristine. It's time to start pushing."

Ready? "Oh, my God!" I said. "I feel like I have been stung by a million fire ants in places where there should never ever be fire ants!" This just did not feel right at all. The pressure seemed all wrong. "It feels like he's coming out of the wrong hole!" I screamed, never being one to hide what I'm thinking.

"Hang in there, Kristine, you can do this. It's time to push." The fog of pain descended upon me; I couldn't think straight. Push? How did I do that? I had no idea what she meant, so I started doing the mother of all Kegels to get that baby out.

She laughed. "No, Kristine," she said. "You have to push like you're taking the biggest poop of your life."

Ah. Okay then. Not one of the 20 books I had read said anything about pooping a baby out, but it didn't matter now: all I wanted was to get my kid *out* of me.

After a few pushes the doctor announced, "He's crowning!" I looked over and took in Ross's face. The look of disgust was unlike anything I've ever seen. "I can see his hair," the doctor said. "I wonder if it will be more like Mom's or Dad's hair." She cast a smiling glance at Ross.

I blurted out, "It's not his baby!"

You could have heard a pin drop. Everyone in the room started looking back and forth anxiously at one other. But Ross knew I was kidding and started laughing, together with the doctor. "Ah, babe, I'm so glad you can at least keep your sense of humor through this. That's my girl!"

Six enormous pushes and Ryan was here.

I looked at him and waited for the wave of amazing emotion and love to wash over me. That's what had been preached at me for the last eight years: "Only a mother who has given birth could understand." But the only thing I thought was, *it's a baby, and he's mine.*

I was still freaked out about becoming a mom. They placed a towel on my chest, cleaned him up, and asked me if I wanted to nurse him.

That was awkward. And really weird, at least at first.

I had so much adrenaline running through my body that I felt like I could run a marathon—and now I was lying here with a kid on my chest.

This was not at all how I imagined motherhood was going to feel. I felt empty, like a kid who'd been skipped over in the Christmas present line. And I felt guilty for not instantly loving this child.

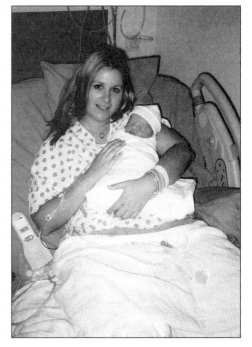

My hospital stay was pleasant; they treated me well, and I had no real issues with it other than a severe lack of sleep: It seemed like every hour they were either checking the baby or me. I felt good, though. Better than I thought I would. We made the call to everyone

informing them that we would be accepting visitors, and for people to start booking flights. Those who were local could come down to the hospital during visiting hours and meet our sweet little boy.

Eventually we made our way home.

My milk came in later that night. I had no breast pump, since the hospital lactation specialists told me that I shouldn't pump for the first 4-6 weeks. My logical side told me to wait until I knew what size my boobs would be before I bought a bra. Big mistake.

My boobs had engorged themselves to what felt like ten times their normal size. They were so hard it felt like my nipples were about to pop off. I was constantly leaking milk; I had wet spots all over my shirt. I was unprepared without a nursing bra and pads to help soak everything up. I was a mess. I didn't realize it would be this bad.

I drove to the only store that was open late, Wal-Mart, to get a nursing bra. I didn't realize that every time I had my shirt off, I would have milk running down my chest. It became a timing game of holding Kleenex over my nipples long enough to make sure I wasn't leaking anything onto the bra I was trying on.

It's one of those things I wish I'd known—anything would have been better than nothing.

After the first few weeks, some of my apprehension began to

abate and I began to bond with Ryan. At first I had trouble getting comfortable holding him, feeding him, and changing him. I was so afraid I was going to do something wrong, or even hurt him. But eventually I got the hang of things, and fell madly in love with my little boy. Like most new moms, I was sleep-deprived. My emotions ran from total euphoria to moments of debilitating self-doubt. It was in those low points that I could hear Trina's voice in my head telling me I wasn't good enough.

My mom came for an extended stay. Her help was such a godsend. I don't think Ross or I had to cook a meal until Ryan was over a month old. Ross was given ten days of paternity leave to be with the baby and me. I was tired and exceptionally happy, but I couldn't shake the feeling that it was going to be over soon. I was terrified that something was going to intervene, that these feelings of happiness and contentment would disappear. Then what?

Frank and Trina flew down to meet Ryan just after Thanksgiving. Their impending arrival felt like a disaster waiting to happen. Cue the dramatic organ music. I knew I'd have to deal with her ear-bleeding advice and unsolicited "know-how." I was glad I had time to get my mommy shit figured out before my personal D-Day.

We decided to take them out to dinner for their first night in town. I put on my best smile and prayed for the best. I don't know how it happened, but somehow we veered into the topic of the family legacy, and wills.

Ross asked, "What's going to happen to the family cabin?" Trina's father had built it years ago.

Trina didn't hesitate. "We'll pass the cabin to Ryan, because if something happens to Ross—meaning if he's killed in the line of duty—then it should go to Ryan."

I asked, "Why wouldn't it go to Ross first?" I was horrified. I couldn't help thinking, *are they banking on something happening to him?*

Ross asked, "Don't you trust Kristine to take care of everything until Ryan is older?"

We were met with blank stares. The answer, unspoken, was deafening.

"Look," I said, "the last thing I want to see happen is for Ryan to be financially hobbled because he has valuable assets in his name that might stop him from receiving scholarships for college. Just as a for-instance." I was met with total awkward silence.

"Or that he might be given a huge responsibility that could wreck him," Ross added, concerned.

Trina and Frank looked at Ross. "Family assets should stay in the family," Frank said.

Trina followed that up by saying, "What would happen if you got a divorce?" Her question was directed only at Ross, but it accused me of one of the worst things possible.

All I could think was *if we were to get divorced, I'm not as petty as she's making me out to be.* I would not try to steal such a meaningful thing from Ross's entire family. The fact that she didn't know—or believe that—about me told me all I needed to know.

After the baby's arrival, we got the green light to move from our dilapidated quad apartment on Nautilus to a duplex on Seahorse.

I was beyond thrilled; even though we still had shared walls, it was a huge upgrade. Now we had a big fenced yard. We even had a one-car garage, plus a large kitchen. I could enjoy cooking more. The best part was the huge park that sat right outside our back door. It was also the first time we could get high-speed internet—which was a total lifesaver.

Moving day came. First problem: we had no idea that the Marine Corps would have paid to move us, if only we had asked through the proper channels from a new policy change.

Not knowing this, we rented a U-Haul and packed up our belongings once again. I asked Ross to grab some muscle-for-hire at the Home Depot, where day workers were consistently available. We were only moving five hundred meters down the street, so it was easy to make a lot of trips without packing everything perfectly.

Two hours later, I was still waiting for Ross to return. Something was surely wrong. I tried his cell, but he didn't answer.

Finally, the phone rang. It was him. "Babe, I've been detained at the gate by the MP's. They think I'm transporting illegal aliens into Camp Pendleton. I've got to sort all this out."

"What? You've got to be kidding me!"

"Seems two of the guys I picked up to help us with the move aren't exactly legal."

"How could this happen? You asked the guys for identification, right?"

"Yeah, and they all *said* they had it. I only checked one guy. I told them we were going onto a military base, and that they needed to be legitimate."

"Tell them to arrest me, Ross; I'll do the time. I'm sure they can't stop me from nursing Ryan in the cell, so just tell them it was my idea."

Ross chuckled, "Yeah, it isn't gonna work like that. I've got to go, I'll call you later. I love you."

"Fight like hell! I love you too."

Thankfully, Ross was able to talk to a senior MP who could clearly see the moving truck from the gate and deduced that Ross had made an innocent mistake. Ross had to call his command and let them know about the situation—pretty embarrassing since he had only been there a week. The MPs called Border Patrol to pick up the illegals.

Eventually, Ross and the one worker the MPs allowed on base were able to move all our heavy stuff to the new house.

Life was always, if nothing else, an adventure.

26

Back to the Grind

January 2005
Camp Pendleton, California

My first assignment as a captain put me in command of Charlie Company at the School of Infantry West. The world was a different place than when I had come through SOI as an enlisted man. We were now responsible for training men who were likely to go to war in the next six to eight months.

My job was to oversee entry-level training for enlisted Marines who had been assigned an infantry MOS. During the first month at school, Marines exercised basic infantry skills: patrolling, zeroing and firing their rifles, fire and movement, and basic land navigation skills. Upon completion of their first six weeks of training, they received their specific MOS selection (0311, Marine Rifleman, for instance). Once they completed all their basic infantry training, they were assigned to a unit in 'the Fleet', also known as the Operating Forces.

My company first sergeant, First Sergeant Coleman, was a good infantryman who hailed from Echo 2/4, quite possibly one of the hardest-hit units in all Iraq (specifically the Ramadi region): 34 dead and more than 255 wounded. They lost 17 in his company alone.

A major part of SOI training focused on the humps because they provided much-needed conditioning, both psychological and physical. We started off with lightweight pack loads, slowly increasing weight and distance. We also carried the crew-served weapons—like the M2 and M240 machine guns, 81mm and 60mm mortars, and TOW and Javelin anti-tank missiles.

Not all SOI units are created equal. Marines graduating boot camp from Parris Island, SC attended SOI East and suffered the scourge of sand fleas and oppressive humidity in the summer, thanks to their close proximity to swamplands, but they humped on flat land. Marines graduating from boot camp in San Diego attended SOI West and dealt with mountains. Honestly, I'd take the steep hills any day over whatever the swamp had to offer. Humps are mostly mental, and for whatever reason, I never really minded the mountains. To me it was one of those things that made you an infantryman.

All Pendleton Marines became familiar with the names of the mountains, like Recon Ridge and Mount Mother Fucker. Most of our humps were on roads—crossing firebreaks cut by bulldozers—and leading the way up the Microwave, aptly named thanks to the small grove of cell towers at the top. It was a tough haul, but the view at the top of the rolling SoCal hills made the Microwave one of my favorites.

In order to graduate, every Marine in the course had to finish the 20k, a 12-mile hump with extremely heavy packs.

The instructors, First Sergeant, and I would carry an 81mm (9 lbs.) mortar fiber (a cardboard container which houses an individual mortar round, similar to a very large Pringles can) filled with dirt to simulate the weight of what a Marine could be expected to carry into combat. The students carried 60mm mortar fibers (4 lbs). We wanted to set the example for the new troops, to demonstrate that it could be done.

Near the end of any big hike, First Sergeant Coleman and I had the same routine. "All right, sir," he'd say. "I'm going shopping. Can I get you anything?"

I'd just smile at him in return. "Surprise me, First Sergeant."

He'd run up and down the long column of Marines, looking for guys who were falling behind. He'd usually grab their .50 cal barrel, maybe an M240 medium machine gun, or something else that was heavy. He would bring it back up to me at the front of the column, then I would end up carrying whatever he brought me for about the last three miles.

The instructors worked their asses off; they were always going twice the distance any of the students completed because they were running up and down the columns keeping our Marines focused and encouraged. They also, however, were ensuring that none of them were in danger of succumbing to physical problems like dehydration or becoming a heat casualty.

Once a hike was complete, we'd have the Marines sit on their packs. The instructors and corpsmen would go down the column inspecting the Marines' feet and looking each one in the eye, making sure they were okay before releasing them to the barracks. The instructors would also ensure the students stretched for 15 minutes, to stave off soreness and cramping. To prevent heat casualties, we'd make sure the Marines were well hydrated the night before humps, ensuring every one of them drank two canteens (half a gallon) of water before bed. The day of, we'd all go to the chow hall prior to step-off, then we'd conduct a dynamic warm-up prior to the hump to get muscles and joints moving in order to prevent injury. We also took plenty of water with us, along with a bit of powdered Gatorade for electrolytes.

The bulk of the training was centered on fire and movement exercises, weapons proficiency, and what it meant to be an individually disciplined Marine. Part of the training was firing live rounds on maneuvering ranges, in order to more realistically prepare Marines for combat situations. We also conducted a lot of non-live-fire exercises in which Marines would use blanks to simulate fighting a thinking, breathing enemy; both in hinterland (rural areas) and urban terrain (cities). They trained in a purpose-built complex of cinderblock buildings or in specially configured arrangements of large shipping containers, simulating the unique challenges of urban combat.

In all, being a company commander at SOI was rewarding and fun. Even though I was home most nights, Kristine was pulling most of the weight with Ryan, and took on the brunt of his parenting. Every night when I got home, I made sure to scoop him up in my arms, trying to make the most of every moment with him, while offering Kristine a break.

*R*oss was one of the only Marines in our group of friends from 2/1 who stuck around for another tour. We talked about it, but I saw how badly the slow economy had affected so many people; he was already almost halfway to retirement, so it didn't make much sense for him to get out. I was ready to support him if he wanted to make it to 20 years. It was who he was, and by that point, I honestly couldn't imagine him doing anything else. He stayed busy with work, and I focused on being a mom.

Ross was a great dad. He would help out with Ryan the moment he got home to give me a bit of a break—although that break usually just meant I had two hands free to cook dinner, put away clothes, or focus on whatever chore I hadn't managed to get done during the day.

He was doing his job as a Marine; I never resented that. I knew every hour he trained Marines he was saving lives. I'm not going to lie and pretend it wasn't difficult having to do so many things by myself. Ross couldn't hear Ryan cry in the middle of the night, since he slept so soundly. I never woke him up. I wanted him to be able to focus on his job. Still, I hadn't intended to raise kids this way. There were days I really wished he had some other profession.

We never thought we would become that couple, the couple that stops going out to dinner together, or going to see movies on dates. We'd always talked about how we'd hire babysitters and still go out on dates several times a month. But we turned into exactly that couple. Sometimes we just didn't want to leave the baby, sometimes we were just exhausted and didn't want to go anywhere, and sometimes we simply didn't want to spend the money.

I did what I thought was best for Ryan, while still keeping an eye on our budget. I made my own baby food, some of which I made fresh throughout the day as needed. I canned most of it. I wasn't trying to be Superwoman; I was just trying to be thrifty. The process was often time-consuming, but it was considerably cheaper than the mainstream alternative.

Ryan was a great kid. He was happy and easy to please. Our dog, Zazu, was incredibly happy in those days. She could always count on Ryan to chuck just about anything onto the floor. If Ryan was running around, she could count on him to have a snack in his hand. She got pretty good about sneaking up behind him and stealthily snatching it away. Ryan absolutely loved her, and she was beyond gentle with him. I loved how the small things in life captured his full attention, how he saw such joy in everything.

When Ryan turned one, we decided we were ready to start trying for a second child. I wanted our kids to be close in age.

Once again we were blessed with a baby as soon as we tried, only on this go-around I was really excited because I knew what to

Just weeks out from my due date.

expect. I knew what I was doing, and this time my husband would be around.

Well . . . sort of.

Time flew. Before we knew it, Ryan was almost two. I was months away from giving birth to our second son when Ross received new orders to a school in Georgia. The report date could not have been more inconvenient for us. He was ordered to report just a couple of months after my delivery date.

After several lengthy conversations about the hassles of moving—and everything it entailed—Ross and I decided to purchase an RV. We figured it would help ease the stress of moving, since we would have a two-year-old as well as a newborn. We also knew Ross would get new orders and we'd be moving again upon his graduation, which would be two moves in one year. Buying an RV felt like the sensible thing to do.

27

Double the Diapers, Double the Fun

September 2006
Camp Pendleton, California

When it came to baby names, we always knew Ryan was going to be Ryan. We weren't sure, however, what our second son's name was going to be. I had it narrowed down either to Warren—just because I liked the name—and George. Ross and I were watching Mixed Martial Arts one night and I saw Georges St-Pierre fighting. I felt like "George" would be perfect, but I decided I'd have to wait to see his face. We could decide when we met him if he was a George or a Warren.

My mom came to stay with us so that we would have childcare for Ryan if and when I needed to make the dash to the hospital for delivery. When the time came, I fully expected a repeat of my last delivery, only with benefits: I knew what to expect.

This time though, the staff that happened to be on duty were a far cry from what I had expected. The doctor on duty informed me that they were going to break my water to get me moving along.

I refused. "My body doesn't need the extra help," I said.

The doctor didn't ask me any questions. Instead, he told me everything he was going to do to me and/or my baby. He was obviously used to telling people what he planned, and he expected them to agree as a matter of course.

This might have been his style, but it certainly wasn't mine. Maybe if this had been my first baby, I would have been more agreeable with him, but by that point I was pretty well informed. I wasn't going to be hauled along by medical technology. I wanted the birthing process to be as natural a progression as possible.

Another doctor came in and introduced herself. She was a young, slim woman who seemed nervous and hesitant. I wasn't sure if it was because of me or because of the pushy doc. She informed me that she would be the primary doctor delivering my baby. I wasn't worried; my delivery the first time was completely absent any complications. I figured the second would be more of the same, maybe even easier.

This time I knew I wanted an epidural. "Yes, *please,*" I said. I asked them to call in the anesthesiologist as I progressed, hoping this delivery would be less painful than the first.

After a while I was moved to birthing room 7, the same room where I had delivered Ryan. I thought that was pretty cool. I was hoping for more similarities—including a healthy baby—only this time of course with drugs.

Lots and lots of drugs.

Ross fell asleep in the corner with his hoodie pulled over his face because just like last time, my body was on fire whenever he touched me. He was better off being in the corner, leaving me alone.

An hour or so later my labor had progressed, so I asked for the epidural. It took several hours for the anesthesiologist to arrive. They got the needle in my back and gave me a test push to check for ringing in my ears.

But then every alarm in the hospital sounded off. The doctors raced away. The woman in the room next to me needed an emergency C-section. I said a prayer for her and her baby, and hoped they would be okay.

Meanwhile, there was still an epidural needle sticking out of my back. I was hoping someone, anyone, would come back and administer the juice.

I knew that the woman who needed the emergency C-section was the priority, and I wouldn't wish the doctor away from her, but a part of me was thinking *if I were in a civilian hospital I probably wouldn't be having this problem right now.* A tear escaped and I sighed, an impotent needle sticking out of my spine. I was going to have another natural childbirth, whether I wanted to or not.

The female doctor came in. She looked extremely nervous. I looked her up and down and asked, "How many babies have you delivered?"

"One or two."

Yeah right, I thought, *if you had delivered any babies at all you'd know the precise number.* I was sure I was going to be her very first delivery. The male doctor stood behind her, watching her carefully. I was conflicted as to whether or not any of these circumstances were in fact good things.

It was finally go time for the delivery of my sweet bundle. I hollered across the room. "Ross! Ross, wake up—it's time!"

Our baby boy was busy making his way through the birth canal, when suddenly his heartbeat sped up. He was under stress.

"Kristine," the doctor said, "the baby's cord is wrapped around his neck. The sooner you can push him out, the better. I want you to wait until your next contraction, then give it all you've got, okay?" That was all I needed to hear. My baby was in danger. It was up to me, and only me, to save him. I pushed with every ounce of my strength, through the contraction and long after.

It was enough—he was out. I beheld his poor little purple face, his wrinkly little body. He looked like he had just gone a few rounds in the octagon.

He was George, for sure.

After I got to meet my tough little boy, they removed the needle and I went to the bathroom. I looked in the mirror. I had broken capillaries in my eyes, face, arms, and chest from pushing so hard. I looked like a horror show freak, but I had my sweet baby and he was alive and well. It was worth all that and so much more.

Mom brought Ryan to the hospital to meet his baby brother not long after he was born.

He was pretty excited about meeting George; he was curious

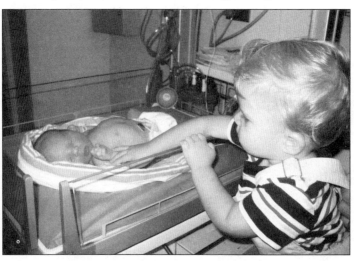

to see what all the fuss was about. Of course, that only lasted a few moments. He was soon much more interested in pushing the buttons that made the bed go up and down.

Once we made it home, Ryan was smitten with the new baby. He wanted to give George kisses and hold his hand all the time. My mom was a great help to have around, as was Ross. And just like before, Mom took care of the cooking and cleaning and Ross helped juggle both kids.

Then Trina came.

The RV, parked out in front of our house, was the perfect place for Trina to stay.

In hindsight, maybe we should have driven the RV several blocks away.

My mom had finally begun to see for herself what Trina was really like. I'd been open and honest with Mom about Trina's unkindness to me, but these recent interactions after George's birth gave her a front row seat to the guilting and manipulation that were part of Trina's arsenal.

It was beyond awkward having the two of them together. I had to admit: it must have been difficult for my mom to witness her own child being treated so poorly and not be able to say or do anything about it.

Mom did her best to engage Trina in small talk and remain polite, but Trina was obsessed with one-upping her any time they discussed kids. Ross was always smarter, faster, more accomplished, or you name it. It didn't take long before Mom stopped trying to engage Trina, and began avoiding her.

Then Trina pulled out what she called *Grandma's Brag Book* to show off her collection of pictures of Ryan.

My mom was really quiet as she looked it over. Then she gave a pallid smile, and gingerly handed it on to me.

As I flipped through the pages, it wasn't long before I realized why my mother hadn't said much about Trina's book. There were no pictures of me.

Not one freaking picture.

It was like I was trapped in a horror movie: I had been utterly cut out.

In Trina's world, Kristine Schellhaas—Ryan's mother—didn't exist. It was as if Ross and I had divorced; every trace of me was gone. Of course there were plenty of pictures of Ryan with Trina's siblings, Trina's parents, and Trina's husband Frank.

It occurred to me then that she had done something similar with our wedding pictures, too. I remember she had an album filled with photos of Ross; she even had a photo of Ross with my bridesmaids! She had cut me, her son's wife, the mother of her grandchild, out of the picture quite literally. It didn't matter that I made Ross happy, or that I had given birth to Ryan. In Trina's fairy tale world, I didn't exist.

I felt sick. I put the book down, excused myself, and went to talk to my husband. "Babe, have you seen your mom's brag book?"

"No, why . . . what's up?"

Where to begin, I thought. "Well . . . anyone looking at it would think . . . I mean, it's fair to say they would think . . . that you and I are divorced. Out of the fifty-plus pictures in there, there's not a single one of me."

Ross said, "Well, you know her. She can be weird like that, Kristine. Maybe it's a subconscious thing."

"Weird doesn't even begin to describe it, Ross. She's awful. And what makes it worse is how she pretends to gush over me when I'm around, but makes up lies and tells terrible stories about me whenever I'm not. Case in point: Remember when all your cousins got together and apologized to me for treating me poorly all those years? They mistakenly believed all the lies Trina had weaved. They didn't see her for how she is until your grandparents got sick and Trina started barking orders and treating her siblings like she treats me."

Ross looked at me but said nothing.

"You know that conversation you said you'd have with her? About her behavior?"

"Yeah, babe."

"Well, guess what. We're doing it," I said. "Before she leaves."

A few days later we sat Trina down, determined to take control of the situation. What I wouldn't have given for a glass of wine to prep myself for the discussion. I had reached my breaking point. She was going to listen, and hear what we had to say.

Trina's behaviors weren't just wrong; they were disturbing. I had no idea if talking to her was going to help or have an effect in the first place, but we had to try. We met her out in the RV, for some measure of privacy.

As she opened the door, there were already tissues in her hand. *I can see where this is going.* She was going to pull the victim card. As we settled around the small table at the front of the RV, Ross began.

"Mom, we wanted to take some time to talk to you about some things that have really been weighing heavily on us."

He reminded her of the emails she'd sent while he was deployed. "I feel like you're placing a lot of blame on Kristine for things that have been my decisions. I was the one who didn't want anyone else at my homecoming. I love you, but you do things . . . and say things . . . that tend to rub people the wrong way. I'm your son, and I want things to be healthy between us . . . but I need you to understand how your actions affect other people around you."

She stared at us, her face blank.

Ross continued. "Do you have anything you want to say . . . about anything?"

"What exactly is it that you think I should say?" She replied. "This is obviously something you and Kristine have been thinking about for some time. You've completely ambushed me. Clearly you think I'm such a terrible person that I will just have to sit here and agree with you."

"That's ridiculous, Mom. We love and care about you. We want to have a relationship with you, but we can't do that unless we can be transparent about how we both feel."

"Then I guess I'll just sit here and listen."

This was her MO when anyone tried to call her out for her behavior. She played the victim so well that we couldn't even have a conversation.

Ross tried to be as gentle as he could; he shared specific examples of situations skewed awry by her behavior. She denied every one of them, insisting she was the one who'd been injured.

We brought up a number of instances in which her actions and words had negatively affected her siblings, her extended family, my family, and more.

"You're mistaken," she said. "All of these people have misinterpreted my true intentions."

Of course! The fault couldn't possibly be hers. She was the victim here.

The discussion, as absurd as it is to attach such a word to such a happening, lasted several hours. In the end I was left emotionally drained, Ross was twice as frustrated as before, and none of it had helped. Not a single ounce.

As we walked back to the house I couldn't help but think I'd wasted three hours of my life. Nothing was going to change.

28

In a Van Down by the River

*T*he coming of the new year meant it was time for us to move. It was our fifth move as a family. Ross's assignment would take less than one year, but living that amount of time in an RV as a family brought a unique set of challenges.

This was the farthest move as a family we'd ever done. It's a huge bummer that the government doesn't pay to ship cars, especially when families move from coast to coast. The small allowance for mileage doesn't begin to balance what it would cost to ship a vehicle. As a result, we had to fork over $1,200 to ship my SUV from California to Georgia.

We were grateful that Ross's dad Rick drove his truck from California to Georgia and met us there. It's really expensive moving all the time; some things the moving company wouldn't pack and move for us. Anything flammable had to be thrown out, which included almost every garage and yard supply item we owned. We had to throw away or give away refrigerator and freezer items. Of course all of it had to be replaced once we got where we were going.

Unpacking boxes the movers had packed was like Christmas: you never knew what you were going to find. But those surprises come at a cost. You hope it's your stuff. You hope it's not broken. And you hope the movers haven't stolen the good stuff. Then of course there are the items rendered unusable by the move. We'd have to replace everything that had been was ruined or broken, and the allowance provided was never enough to break even.

With the RV, at least we'd get to keep some of our condiments.

Packing was difficult; I had to figure out what a year's worth of necessities might be. I brought clothes for George for the next five sizes up, and for Ryan's next two. I prayed it would be enough to get us through.

We packed a few dishes and other essentials. Everything else we owned would be boxed up and kept by the Marine Corps in long-term storage. I was excited about the move this go-around because it was the first pack out for which we had professional movers. It felt liberating, in a way, to know we were going to be living a simpler life (if minimalistic) for the next year. But it was also terrifying to think about living in such a small space with two small kiddos.

Another first: I hired a maid service to clean our house before inspection. It was difficult to part with the money, but the idea of trying to scrub bathrooms and clean the oven while trying to keep an eye on both of the kids sounded like a nightmare.

With the last box loaded onto the truck and a thumbs up on our move out inspection, we said goodbye to our house on Seahorse Lane and drove the RV up to San Onofre Beach, near SOI. We spent the last month of our time in California set up in a little campsite that overlooked the Pacific Ocean. The view was gorgeous. Ross could get to work from there in minutes, and came home a few times at lunch to say hello.

We'd see dolphins swimming regularly, and I enjoyed watching the surfers from the window. I had a million-dollar view, and I could clean my house in 20 minutes or less. I felt like I had won the new mother lottery.

A quick photo op en route from California to Georgia

In my daydreams about moving to Georgia, I envisioned weekends sipping mint juleps, going antiquing, and enjoying a little southern charm. In my mind, Fort Benning looked like a scene from *Gone with the Wind*. I imagined tall trees on both sides of the road, their drooping branches draped with lacey Spanish moss.

Yeah. That didn't happen. Not even a little bit.

Fort Benning was a military base just like all the others we'd seen. We drove through some large historical-looking white homes, but that was pretty much it for eye candy. We wound our way through the base, around a large airfield, then eventually crossed into Alabama. We would live in the RV on the far side of the Chattahoochee River in Alabama, and Ross would work on the Georgia side, about 15 minutes away. Technically his workplace and our house were a time zone away. For the most part, though, everyone within ten miles of the base stayed on Georgia time.

If first impressions meant anything, the RV Park was going to work out great. There were several play parks, a little convenience store, and a pool. We lived within a stone's throw of the Chattahoochee.

Unfortunately, by that point I had already found out that first impressions didn't mean much, especially when it came to moving. The tall chain-link fence that separated the RV park from the riverbank was adorned at regular intervals with small red and white signs that read DON'T FEED THE ALLIGATORS.

Then there were the armadillos. I'd never seen an armadillo before. At first I even thought they were kind of cute. Then Ross's dad told us armadillos are one of the only animals left in the world that carry the leprosy bacteria.

Of course Ross had failed to mention all this to me. In my head I could hear him saying, "What, babe? What's the big deal? Alligators are cool. Armadillos are cool."

This was not working out at all like I thought it would.

At least the RV Park had two great views: the river, and the drop zone for paratrooper training. During our first afternoon on base, we watched the first batch of paratroopers dropping from the plane. It would be the first of many afternoons spent watching the sky bloom with white chutes.

> From: Kristine
> Date: March 11, 2007 11:26 PM
> To: Friends and Family
>
> We're doing great here in Georgia/Alabama (whichever it is). The weather has been crazy. First it was freezing cold, now it's muggy and hot and windy. We had a tornado come through and scare the living daylights out of me (not Ross, so much, because he was in denial).
>
> We kept watching the Weather Channel to see what was going on. There were some tornado warnings and some tornado watches. We weren't sure which one actually meant to seek shelter. They didn't explain that part very well.
>
> So we packed a bag and just waited for the worst to arrive. I started panicking when I heard this crazy whirling noise outside the RV . . . I've experienced very high winds before, but this sounded like a train! We waited it out until about 30 minutes later, when the tornado watch was cancelled.
>
> There was a lot of damage about 12 miles away from us, a part of town where we do our shopping and go out to dinner. It's crazy. I guess that's karma paying me back for making fun of people who live in trailers in the tornado zone. And I just couldn't believe our luck, either. This area hasn't had a tornado strike in about 20 years.
>
> I've enrolled Ryan in gymnastics and Kindermusik on base, which

he absolutely loves. I never knew how broke the Marine Corps actually was until we got here and saw how the US Army lives. You should see the facilities and family care options they have! We're going to live like royals for these next few months.

We came to Fort Benning because I had been selected for a career level school. I requested Fort Benning primarily because it was an infantry-based school centered on ground combat arms MOSs, plus it was three months shorter than its Marine Corps counterpart, Expeditionary Warfare School, EWS.

This meant I could get back to the fleet faster.

I was also interested in gaining new experiences under the Army's educational methodologies. I was one of only four Marines in my class, alongside hundreds of our Army counterparts. There were also quite a few students from foreign militaries as well.

Most of the instructors were soldiers, but they usually had one or two Marine instructors at the school as well, plus a handful of instructors from various US allies.

From: Kristine
Date: April 13, 2007 1:34 PM
To: Friends and Family

It's about time for an update. This place is really starting to wear on me. I thought my biggest challenge would be living in the motorhome, but that's actually wonderful.

We had another big storm come through. Lucky us. We ran into the Laundromat, along with a ton of other people, and there we rode out a really bad hailstorm. The tornado touched down about 30 miles from us.

Everyone else had the right idea: We were busy grabbing documents; they were busy grabbing a few drinks.

After the storm passed, we discovered baseball- and golf-ball-sized hail all over the ground. It had completely beaten the tar out of both of our cars. The hail came down so fast that it broke two of the ceiling vents on the RV. There was hail and water everywhere inside.

Luckily after the tornado warnings had cleared, we had a break in the weather, so we were able to patch the holes and clean the mess up. Now we have a big to-do with our insurance companies' claims department. I never thought I would say this, but I can't wait to get back to California!

The boys are all doing great, for the most part. Ross and Ryan seem to be passing the flu back and forth to each other. It's lasted more than two weeks now! Hopefully this will go away

along with the weather. George has two teeth on the bottom that have popped up. He seems to be handling the discomfort pretty good, all things considered.

Hope all of you are great! Hopefully I'll have a more positive message next month.

*I*t had been five months since our initial arrival at Fort Benning. The kids were getting into everything, and Ross was never around. I loved my children fiercely but to be honest, I wasn't in love with being a stay-at-home mom. I wanted to leave for the day like Ross did, have my own thoughts, then come back to my little guys at the end of the day and get to love on them. Being a mom 24/7 was so much harder than anything I'd ever had to do.

My day literally never ended.

I think the hardest part was that I couldn't count on Ross to get home at a regular time. His schedule was unpredictable, making it impossible for me to manage my day and plan time for doing the chores I couldn't do with the kids in tow. I struggled; I didn't want to feel sorry for myself. I had no career, no life of my own. My life revolved around PBS cartoons, diapers, teething rings, naptimes, and cleaning.

As much as I tried to keep a good attitude and keep a smile on my face, I knew I needed to talk to Ross about how I was feeling. I wasn't happy.

From: Kristine
Date: June 7, 2007 11:43 PM
To: Friends and Family

This month has been filled with all kinds of fun! It's mostly because we haven't spent all of our time in Georgia. We took a trip to St. Louis to visit some family and went to a Cardinals game—George's first pro baseball game. We had terrific seats, thanks to my uncle who works for GMAC. We sat next to first base in the VIP area.

Ross and I celebrated five years this month. We took the kids down to Panama City on the Gulf of Mexico. It was probably the most un-romantic anniversary ever. It was really more family vacation than anniversary, but we were fine with that. We kept looking at each other across a sea of chaos and saying, "Happy anniversary!" to each other.

The boys are doing fantastic. George turned eight months today. It is crazy how fast time is going. Ryan is officially two. He definitely likes the word "no," and is getting a bit rougher with George, though most of the time he's pretty sweet. Zazu takes most of the brunt of Ryan's roughness. He loves to crawl on her and play with her.

Part Three

Discovering Rock Bottom

*"When life gets too hard to stand,
kneel."*

—*Gordon B. Hinckley*

29

Stranded in the Desert

August 2007
Twentynine Palms, California

As our time in Georgia came to an end, Ross received orders to join 2/7 (2nd Battalion, 7th Marines) in Twentynine Palms. There's a saying in the Marine Corps: a Marine's first drive into Twentynine Palms should be at night so that his spouse can't see what she's getting into. At night there will be all kinds of twinkly lights, maybe even the remnant of a spectacular sunset to the west.

Well, Ross—always a man of adventure and daring—didn't subscribe to that rule.

As we drove our motorhome through the bends and crests of the desert roads, all the while watching civilization dwindle from visions of emerald golf courses into stark desert surroundings and backwater dwellings that looked more like meth shacks, I wondered what I had gotten myself into.

When we turned down the main drag, I'm pretty sure Ross felt my eyes burning a hole through the side of his face.

He looked at me. "What?"

"You can't be serious," I said.

"What are you talking about? This place is gonna be great."

"No. Here's what will happen, Ross; I can already tell you. You're going to dump me in the middle of the desert with your two young kids while you get to live your dream, ride off in convoy and shoot big guns on the Marine Corps' largest training base. That seems real fair."

"My two kids, huh?" He paused. "I dunno, babe; all I can say is that I've heard everybody cries when they get to Twentynine Palms but that they cry when they leave, too. Maybe you'll learn to love it."

It took all I had not to laugh in his face. "I hope you're right,

Captain Schellhaas. Because right now you're going to be spending a lot of money on wine every month."

I was only half joking.

After a few days of living in sweltering temperatures—117° outside, 90° inside with both A/C units on full blast—we decided it was time to sell the RV and go shopping for a house without wheels. We settled on building a new house in Desert Knoll, the newest—and one of the only—neighborhoods in the small town of Twentynine Palms. We were banking on being there for the next three years (an eternity) and also on the fact that rental properties would always be in need, with the Marine base being so close. In the meantime, we rented an apartment because base housing was not only full, but also because there was a six-month waiting list.

I was hoping I would make more friends here. When we lived in Georgia, I'd met Amy Hall and learned they'd be moving to Two-Nine as well. Her husband would become Ross's new battalion commander. She and I hit it off instantly, and I was glad to know that at least I wouldn't be in it alone whenever Ross deployed again.

———

I was excited for the opportunity to become a company commander in the fleet, especially with 2/7. The battalion had not yet returned from Iraq, so for the time being I couldn't move into any official positions. In the meantime, Van Osborne,

Ross' Change of Command for Fox Company 2/7

my good friend and fellow TBS graduate, had been assigned to the same unit. He was the acting XO, and I was the acting operations officer until the battalion returned.

We were tasked with preparing for a fireteam-level training exercise with LtCol Hall, our new commander. I was happy to see another friend from Infantry Officers Course, Captain Matt O'Donnell—"O'D," as we called him—when he checked into battalion.

Eventually, I would become the commander of Fox Company. I would be responsible for four platoons: 168 Marines.

We settled into our temporary apartment in Twentynine Palms, and as the days went by it started cooling down into the mid-80s at night—tolerable. I began dealing with the usual headache of finding a new version of everything: dentist, doctors, hairdresser, and more. To say that my options were limited in that small desert town would be an understatement.

Ryan began taking on the enforcer role in the family, telling his little brother what he could and could not do. He tried to look out for George though, trying to be sure he didn't hurt himself. George was as sweet as ever, doing his best to walk. It was hard to believe that he was almost one, and Ryan was almost three.

Ross and I talked about where we wanted to celebrate the boys'

birthdays, which were just weeks away. We didn't have many friends in Twentynine Palms yet, so we decided to head down to San Diego instead, where we could at least hang out with family. I proposed that we go to the San Diego Zoo for the birthday party, but Ross didn't want to do that. He suggested we celebrate at his Dad and Charlotte's house, and in the end I went along.

Thankfully, the kids loved road trips. Ryan's seat faced forward and George's was rear-facing, so they talked the whole way face to face. Of course George couldn't really talk yet, but he loved chatting away in gibberish and Ryan would hold his hand and just talk away, pointing to things that interested him outside, or showing him the toys and books we'd brought along.

When we passed the sign announcing the San Diego city limits, I did a little dance in my seat. It felt good to finally be in a city with all the amenities at our fingertips. We planned on staying the weekend. Charlotte was an amazing cook, plus we could count on a bottle of wine to share, and fun conversation whenever we came to visit. I had a long list of things to buy before the party on Sunday, but I knew I had a great evening ahead of me, with family.

After a quick hello, I sat down and made a list of things I would need for the party. As I was getting ready to leave, Ross and Ryan set up a train set that Charlotte kept at the house. George got into the middle of their progress, and kept trying to play with all the pieces. I could tell both Ross and Ryan were getting frustrated.

It was hard for me to not get upset with Ross. Ryan could have set up the train set on his own; it was George who needed some attention from his daddy. Ross would often come home from work late and wake up Ryan so that he could spend some time with him, but he wouldn't wake George. He loved both of his boys very much, but I had to remind myself that it was just easier for Ross to interact with a three-year-old instead of a one-year-old. George was too young to see it or understand it, but it still hurt my heart and made me angry.

I thought about taking George with me, but then all the pent-up frustration of being a full-time mom kicked in. They were Ross' kids too, not just mine. I deserved a few minutes to myself, to be able to focus on the task at hand without having to worry about who was getting into what.

Ross had no idea what kind of stress I had to deal with on my own, raising two young boys who constantly got into everything in the house. Ryan and George would go in completely separate directions into equally dangerous areas; it worked my nerves to the ragged edge. A complete toddler meltdown could happen in an instant, for reasons as simple as one kid's banana being longer than the other's. I needed a break. I needed to breathe and spend a few minutes being Kristine, not Mom.

And Ross needed to know what it was like to have to chase after two busy, demanding kids. No matter how many times he asked me how my day was, I'd never be able to fully describe it to him until he lived it for himself.

As George took apart the track for the umpteenth time, I hesitated. I thought about taking him with me again, but I was in a mood to get something accomplished and figured I could get it all done faster on my own. I kissed all three of them goodbye, and went on my way.

When the wave of air conditioning hit me just inside the entrance at Costco, it felt like the clouds had parted in the heavens above, and God was smiling on me. I could almost hear the symphony of angels serenading me as I walked through the front doors, membership card on display. It was like a pass into a place only special people could go. It was my first time back in a long time, so I took my time buying what we needed.

As I unloaded everything into the back of the SUV, I went over my list. The last thing I needed to get was goodie bags.

I debated if I really needed them.

Of course I needed them. Good moms always had goodie bags—I guilted myself into purchasing them.

I headed next door into the florescent-lit, linoleum-lined aisles of the Wal-Mart next door. I didn't find much worth buying in the party section, so I explored the nooks and crannies of the store to see if I could find something better.

Finally, when I was all done, I began to make my way back to the boys.

On my way home, Ross called. He was panicked.

"George fell in the pool. He isn't breathing."

"Ross?" Nothing.

"Ross!" That was all.

He was gone; the connection had dropped. I was numb. The world around me slowed to a snail's pace. I dialed him back, but there was no answer.

"Dammit, answer your phone!"

I called the house too, but there was no answer there, either.

My mind raced. *How could this happen? Is George okay? Why wasn't anyone watching him? I shouldn't have left him behind.*

I inched along the highway, agonizing that something was wrong with my baby. A concert had just released from one of the local venues, and traffic was backed up for several miles.

My mind raced with the worst thoughts, then fought to hold on to tatters of hope. I didn't know what to believe. Had I dreamed it? Surely George was okay. Surely I misheard Ross on that phone call. *Please, God.*

Thirty minutes later I pulled into a cul-de-sac overflowing with fire trucks, ambulances, and police cars.

"Oh, no." The tears began in earnest. "No, no, no," I said again. I just kept saying it over and over again.

Ross ran to me as I was getting out of the car. I screamed and shoved him as hard as I could. I couldn't stop crying. "Where's George?" I screamed. "How could you let this happen? Why weren't you watching him?"

Ross hugged me close, crying with me. "I left George in the family room with Charlotte so that I could set up the Pack 'n Play for the night. Ryan followed me . . . I thought she was watching him . . . "

"How did he even get outside?"

Ross told me that in those few minutes, George had bear-crawled past Charlotte and our twenty-year-old niece, making his way down the hallway to the master bedroom, where the dogs were.

What we didn't know was that Rick and Charlotte regularly left their screen door open to the backyard so that the dogs could open it any time they wanted to go outside. Ross had previously barricaded the door in the family room leading to the pool, but he didn't know that the door from the master bedroom was kept open like this. They had an in-ground pool in their backyard. There was no safety fence around it. Rick and Charlotte's dogs didn't like kids, so once they saw George heading towards them, they opened the door and escaped in the yard.

George followed, of course. Ryan had always been scared of the water, but George embraced it. He didn't mind getting his face wet; he loved baths. I could almost imagine his glee when he saw the pool.

I needed to see him. I made my way to the ambulance, barely able to see my son through my tears, through the oxygen mask now covering his face. The paramedic was working on him feverishly, trying to bring him back.

And I could do nothing.

All I could do was think about my beautiful little boy, my George. He rarely cried—he was so full of life, so full of smiles. If memories are like making cash deposits in a bank account, ours was both overflowing and now—entirely too empty at the same time.

I stood there at the side of the ambulance waiting for something to change, a sign that something might be positive, that he could be saved.

But I knew it had been too long. It was all wrong. I wondered why Life Flight hadn't been called. *He should be in a helicopter heading to a Children's Hospital for specialized help,* I thought. *If they weren't able to save him before I was able to get here, which felt like it took forever . . .* but I couldn't finish that thought. After what seemed like an hour had passed, finally Life Flight came and transported him to the San Diego Children's Hospital.

Ross and I left Ryan with Rick and Charlotte, driving quickly to the hospital in our car.

We barely spoke to each other for what amounted to the longest drive of my life. All I could think was that George would be a vegetable, with a miserable quality of life. But he was my joy, the child who loved life, who laughed, who always had a smile on his face. I called him my angel baby.

As soon as we walked through the doors of the hospital, they knew who we were. They led us through the double doors into a private room where they broke the terrible news to us: The miracle I had been seeking, that the helicopter or the hospital would be able to save him, disappeared the instant the words "I'm sorry" formed on the doctor's lips.

He was gone.

They walked us back to a private room, where we had to say goodbye to our perfect little boy.

He was so beautiful. He looked like he was in a deep and peaceful sleep. I felt like I could just pick him up and kiss him good morning, kiss him awake. How does a mother just leave her baby behind and get on with her life? It wasn't fair, it wasn't right that we had been dealt this card; especially after everything else we had faced down and fought through in our marriage. How were we supposed to overcome this?

Good people aren't supposed to lose their kids, I thought.

The hospital asked if we wanted to have footprints or handprints cast. They also asked if I wanted a clipping of his hair. I didn't want any of that. I knew all those things would remind me of this day. They would not be made with joy, but instead with grief. I wanted everything about George's memory to be associated with happiness. Only happiness.

As we walked out of the hospital, I was numb. It was hard to look at Kristine. I felt like I'd failed everyone that day, in the most important duty I had: to protect my family. I didn't have words for anything.

I was so angry and so disappointed in myself that I couldn't cry. I called my folks in Idaho; they were in disbelief. They offered to help in any way they could. My mom knew I was in pain, and that hurt her. I didn't want to talk. She was worried about me, as any mom would be in a situation like that. She wanted me to stay on the phone, keep talking to her, but there was nothing left to say. My son was gone. Mom wanted me to tell her I'd be okay. I couldn't do that. I said, "Love you," and hung up.

I called LtCol Hall. It was late, but the first thing he said was, "I'll be right there." I told him we had family, and that we'd be okay. You could hear the concern in his voice, that he felt our agony. He had ten kids of his own. One of them was the same age as George. I asked him if he could please tell everyone what happened for me, and that I didn't want any phone calls. He told me to take all the time I needed.

To be honest, I wondered if he thought I was capable of being in command after that. If I couldn't keep my own child safe, how could I take care of my Marines?

Walking out of that hospital without George was the hardest thing I have ever done in my life. The drive home was excruciating; vivid. I could see every detail of every plant, fence, and building the headlights shone on. As we drove, I thought about how to let people know what had happened. My first call was to my parents; I chose to call my dad because I thought he might not break down as much on the phone as my mom surely would —I couldn't handle to hear her cry and manage to keep myself together, too. I kept it as short as possible, saying what had happened, then I told him I couldn't talk anymore. I asked him to call my brothers and let everyone else in the family know.

The only other call I made was to my best friend, Christie. She was caught off guard; she remained silent. I thought the phone connection was lost, but then the tears came. "I'm coming now. I'm on my way," she said.

But I didn't want her to come. I didn't want anyone to come. I just wanted to crawl away and die.

The rest of the drive back to the house was done in silence.

Once we arrived back at Rick and Charlotte's house, we had to endure questioning from the police. They separated Ross and me, subjecting us both to a series of questions, looking for clues suggesting foul play. I knew they were just doing their job, but it was all I could do not to scream at them to go away.

The officer asked, "Did George have any cuts or bruises on him?"

"Yes," I said, "a scrape on his toes, but nothing more."

"Has your husband ever been violent with you or the kids?"

"No, not at all. Never."

"Were you concerned for your safety with your husband?"

"No, he's my best friend. He's a great father."

It went on like this for a while. Eventually, and thankfully, my interview was over. Ross's took longer than mine, since he'd been there when George drowned. I was informed that there was a grief volunteer who was available to speak with me if I wanted, but I didn't want to talk to anyone. I couldn't stay in that house one minute longer. Everything was too painful.

The next morning we loaded Ryan into the car for the long drive back to Twentynine Palms—without our beloved George.

Ryan didn't understand what had happened. He knew everybody was upset. He was worried about his brother. "Where's George?" he'd ask. "Where is brother? We need to go find him."

We told him that George was in heaven with the angels, but he didn't know what that meant. How could a three-year-old understand that? He kept telling me not to cry, and continually asked if Daddy and I were okay. I didn't know what to tell him.

I was completely consumed by grief. I didn't want to talk. I didn't want to eat.

I just wanted to shut down and disappear.

30

The Cost of Imperfection

October 2007
Twentynine Palms, California

I t was late Sunday afternoon when we got back to Twentynine Palms. The next morning I went back to work. I needed to focus on something other than my grief and failure. I had my Marines to take care of.

I called a company formation and told them personally what had happened. I wanted them to hear it from me. I told them that they were my therapy, and that I was going to be out for a while taking care of funeral arrangements. I asked them to give my XO, Lt Socci and First Sergeant Sweet all the help they could until I got back.

M y mom came down as quickly as she could; she wouldn't take no for an answer. The truth was we needed her, even though I didn't want anyone around. I just wanted to shut down, to distance myself from the world.

Mom helped take care of us in the wake of George's death.

I had become one of the wives who needed help and support from my military spouse sisters. It was humbling. People I'd never met dropped off meals for our family to show us their love. I was grateful for everything. Not only did I mentally have to come to terms with the reality that my son was gone, but I was also going through a physiological change—George had still been nursing.

We had to start planning the funeral. Never in a million years did I think I would ever have to plan a funeral for my child. In the heart of this maelstrom I couldn't stop myself from thinking of all the things I would have to do if Ross paid the ultimate price. What if I lost him, too? It was something that happened altogether too often in military service. I couldn't avoid it, and although it was perhaps the worst possible time to wrangle these demons, ironically there was also no time like the present.

I was fighting through a haze of misery as I considered his final resting place. Would I bury him in Idaho? Or would I cremate him, and spread his ashes somewhere? I couldn't bear the thought of leaving him alone somewhere. It was a vile road to walk even having to think about what I would have to do if I lost him. After agonizing for what felt like too long, I decided I would cremate his remains and keep the ashes with me. It took every ounce of fortitude I possessed to make that decision, but even as I did so I laid it to rest. I knew I could neither escape the real world nor the immediate question that was pressing me relentlessly: What would I do with my son's ashes?

None of the urns I looked at were right. Nothing was right. Every website I visited to look at vessels broke one more piece of my heart. I couldn't bring myself to order anything.

I called my dad. I asked him to build me something, anything. I just couldn't do this.

He said he would take care of it, and not to worry. I knew my dad would come up with something that would honor my son and help mend a mother's heart.

He enlisted the help of his cousin, an artist, my uncle Dean. The two of them laid out plans to design a special box made of Lacewood. Uncle Dean went on to cast a bronze sculpture of an angel sitting protectively over the box. It was beautiful, and it was perfect.

One of the final details for me was what to wear to the funeral. I didn't have an appropriate black dress, and the last thing I wanted to do was go shopping. My dear friend Nancy Osborne came and held my hand through the process. It's an awful feeling, having to look for something to wear for such an occasion. I was in constant tears trying on clothes in the dressing room. Every dress I pulled on, as I looked in the mirror, revealed an image staring back at me that was broken, clothed in something that was not for me, but for others. We do some things because they're expected of us. I found I was absent from myself, just checking off the boxes of the things a grieving mother is supposed to do.

I broached the subject with Ross, asking him what he was going to wear. He looked at me with tears in his eyes. "What does a father wear to his son's funeral?" I didn't have an answer for him.

We chose to honor George on Veterans Day weekend so that people could more easily attend the funeral. That Saturday was November 10th; the Marine Corps' birthday. This already significant day would now take on new meaning for our family. As we made our plans, we decided we wanted the funeral to take place in Boise, Idaho, at the Vineyard church where my cousins were pastors.

I turned over most of the details to my mom and cousins. I had thought of a couple of songs that spoke to me, but for the most part I let them direct the occasion. The only other thing I managed personally was the flowers. Nothing I found was quite right, so I decided to do something myself. I ordered flowers online, and had them shipped to my parents' home. That evening, when everyone had gone to bed, I sat in the quiet and arranged the flowers one at a time, connecting each to a memory of my son.

Those three weeks before the funeral, I spent almost every waking moment looking at the photos I'd taken of him. I created a slideshow of pictures set to music that ripped my heart out each time I saw it. It was my way of showing my love for George at the funeral; I wasn't strong enough to speak.

I wanted to arrange catering, but my mom knew that we should just have a potluck instead. There's a lot to be said for those women who want to do something—anything—to help in situations like these. The way they express themselves through the gift of hospitality is miraculous. I was humbled and surprised in light of the love of those people who came bringing food to share with all of us.

We requested that mourners bring new and unwrapped toys to donate to Toys for Tots in lieu of flowers. There was a Marine from the Reserve station standing by to collect them. We tried to honor George this way, by giving to others.

We watched the video of his life pass before us on the screen. It was all so fresh, like it was yesterday; this should have been the video that played at his high school graduation. When the music stopped, there was a moment of silence. Then all that could be heard was a long cry, a guttural wail—it took me a moment to realize: it was me.

My cousin Chad spoke to those attending, challenging us to

find ways to do all the things George could not do, to find ways to "Live for George."

I tried disappearing as much as I could whenever Ryan wasn't around. I often thought about an episode I had seen on *Oprah* that featured a family that had lost a child. The mother was paralyzed with grief; she refused to move on, festering in agony until she lost the rest of her family in the process. Her other kids had lost a sibling, but because of their mother's inability to move on, they also lost their mother.

I couldn't lose Ryan, too.

I had to find a way to keep moving forward.

Ross and I began therapy. Our sessions were heavily blanketed in discussions dealing with our loss.

During the weeks and months that followed, I played the "What if?" game, which was massively destructive. But I couldn't help myself.

What if we had never received orders to Twentynine Palms?

What if that day we went to the Zoo instead?

What if we had never gone to San Diego?

What if I hadn't left George behind that morning?

What if Ross wasn't a Marine?

What if I had never married Ross?

Oh, my God . . .

I was a wreck.

Friends suggested I find a therapy group so that I could talk with others who had lost their kids, but I couldn't see the purpose in it. It hurt too much; I didn't see the point. What good was mere talk? Would we all sit around and chat about how we felt like shit? I didn't believe it would change anything. The last thing I wanted or needed to do was try to carry someone else's burdens. It was all too raw. I wasn't ready. And I had no idea if I ever would be.

For a while my life was spent crossing days off on the calendar. Everything became black and white to me; it was either right or wrong. I saw very little gray, and had very little room for compassion towards others when they were ugly, mean, or made mistakes.

My life felt worthless. I became functionally depressive. I ate whatever I wanted to. I didn't care if I got fat, or if things weren't healthy for me. I knew better than to go down that road, but I no longer cared.

The trail of what ifs led me into a death spiral of negativity. I felt disoriented and numb, with only one true string connecting me to the world: Ryan. I knew and believed with all I had left that I needed to stay strong for him.

If I didn't, I would end up losing not one but both of my children.

Around that time, strange events began to occur around the house. The TV would spontaneously switch on at the beginning of George's favorite show on PBS; the lights would flicker randomly throughout the day. It was odd, very odd. My heart wanted to believe it was George saying he was okay in heaven, but my brain insisted it was just faulty wiring.

As for Ross and me, our relationship was hanging by a thread.

We both loved each other very much, but the intensity of the pain we felt was eating us alive; there was nowhere to hide from it. My husband's guilt was slowly killing him, and my anger and resentment towards him and his family for allowing it to happen was ripping me in half.

We went through the motions of daily life whenever he was home.

Ross was gearing up for another deployment. He was constantly training; gone most of the time. I was just trying to survive.

I bounced back and forth between hating him and having compassion for him.

Because of his schedule, we had no time to heal together.

I began to doubt if healing was even possible.

Construction hadn't yet started on our home because the banks weren't granting loans for new builds, so we asked for a refund of our earnest money, and moved into base housing.

I needed a new environment—I had to get away from that apartment; there were too many memories. I wanted to at least try to make a new home for our family, even though we had a huge bleeding hole right through our middle.

We decided to sell the RV. Several months passed, with only a handful of phone calls. We looked at the possibility of trading it in, perhaps for a smaller trailer we might be able to use more often, but the trade-in value was less than half of what we had paid for it. Gas had gone from $2.50 a gallon when we bought it to $3.75 a year later. People were trading in their SUVs and anything else that guzzled a lot of gas. The timing for us couldn't have been worse.

I began to think creatively about the challenge, looking for un-conventional ways to unload this thing.

I knew I needed a change in my life. It all began with small victories; things like taking showers regularly, or just getting out of the house.

I found and adopted two dogs that had been abused and were languishing in animal foster care. Their previous owner was elderly and had passed away. The dogs had gone to the daughter's home, but her husband was killed shortly thereafter in a motorcycle accident. When the dogs were turned in, the children told the staff about how their parents would beat the dogs to discipline them from time to time.

Darla, the older dog, a cavalier King Charles spaniel, was a hospice case. She was deaf, blind, and diabetic. She required two insulin shots daily, she suffered from cancer, and she had a heart murmur, which also needed medication. Lincoln Military Housing bent their two-pet rule, graciously allowing me to have three dogs for a short amount of time, considering Darla wasn't going to live much longer.

The younger spaniel was either Darla's pup or grandpup, we weren't quite sure. It seemed to us like it was meant to be: all of us had grief and death in common. It allowed us to believe that some-how we could pull together and love on each other to get through our heartache.

Ryan adjusted pretty quickly. He got on with life as best he could. He still spent time at preschool, but he cried every time I picked him up. He'd always tell me to go away and come back for him later, that he loved his friends at school.

Just like at the apartment, the TV would switch channels seem-ingly on its own, even with a different cable box and service provider. The lights occasionally flickered, too. Maybe it was George. I wasn't sure if I could trust my heart on that, but I wanted to. Sometimes Ryan was in the middle of watching a show, and the channel would change to George's program. He would get angry when that hap-pened, until we made a game out of it. We'd say, "George is just saying hello."

After a couple of months, it all stopped. Once it had, I found myself longing for the TV to change channels or for something unexplained to happen. Those occurrences made me feel like I had a small piece of him with me. But now even they were gone, too.

It seemed grief had not only come to visit, but also had decided to cling to our family. News that Charlotte, Ross' stepmom, had cancer was just another devastating blow. By the time Ross was ready to deploy, Charlotte was in her final stages. There was still a lot of awkwardness between us. Ross carried the brunt of the guilt for George's death, but Rick and Charlotte were burdened with their own feelings of regret, too.

A couple of weeks before Ross was scheduled to ship out, Rick came for a short visit. They stayed up all night talking. Ross finally shared with his dad some of the difficulties he'd experienced in his childhood. Rick was floored. Trina had always painted such a different picture.

It was then that Rick confided in Ross about why his marriage to Trina had failed. Not surprisingly, the real reason Rick had left wasn't anything like what Trina had told everyone.

Ross shared the highlights of their conversation with me the next morning. The news wasn't shocking to me; it was just Trina. She loved to talk about her days being married to her navy officer; she would whip out her military spouse badge with pride any time it was convenient for her. Now that the truth was verified though, everything Trina had preached to me was mere words. I would never be able to see her the same way again.

31

Broken Crayons Still Color

January 2008
Twentynine Palms, California

Without my cousins Trevor and Chad, I'm not sure Ross and I would be married today. Before they agreed to marry us, they set certain conditions we had to agree to—since we didn't live in town—before they agreed to do the usual pre-marriage counseling with us. We agreed we would allow them to support our marriage for the long haul, meaning we promised to get together on a regular basis, and come to them whenever issues arose between us. After George died, and before Ross deployed, we agreed to sit down for a session. It was hard.

We all cried a lot. It was there in that room that I allowed the spinning wheels of my anger and hurt to slow. I listened to an outsider's perspective. I opened myself up to the idea of forgiveness. It was because of Trevor and Chad that I began to believe that I could build a bridge towards healing my relationship with my husband. It would take work, but it was a start. And I understood that there would be days when I just didn't care if we made it or not. But now that I had opened my heart, we could try to move forward.

It would be one day at time, and it would be together.

Everything else remained out of our control; our lives were on autopilot in Twentynine Palms. We survived by engaging the routine and doing what was expected of us, nothing more. We were definitely using the fake it until you make it method. Thankfully, it was beginning to work.

That is, until we received an unexpected gift.

I found out I was pregnant.

It was the first ray of sun our family had experienced in months. We were bringing new life into our family! By no means did I think this would fix everything, but this new baby offered hope and joy, and I seized the opportunity. I hadn't known just how hungry I was for these things.

We did the math. Ross was going to be overseas when our child was born. Our baby would be a few months old by the time he re-turned. Of course, this wasn't at all uncommon in our Corps; it was something many military families faced.

We were training for Iraq.

Twentynine Palms is the training mecca of the Marine Corps. Here, there aren't traditional ranges like there are on other Marine Corps bases, where ranges are built and designed for a specific purpose. Here, the whole base is essentially a live fire range. As long as the effects of munitions are taken into account, a unit can set up a range and fire nearly everything in the Marine Corps weapons arsenal.

There was the added bonus of weather extremes to train in, which effectively prepared our units for the different environments they'd face on deployment. The only thing lacking was decent vegetation for considerations of rehearsing dismounted patrolling (on foot), but other than that it was the best place in the Corps to be an infantryman.

In a heartbeat, things can change in the Marine Corps, and in this case they did. I got a call on the day we went to pick up the dogs for adoption that word had changed about our deployment. LtCol Hall called me directly and said, "We're not going to Iraq. We're going to Afghanistan." The other Marines and I were excited about that. There didn't seem to be as much of an IED threat in Afghanistan—maybe it would be more of a straightforward fight.

Our training plan changed very little; the basic fundamentals of combat would prevail whether we found ourselves in Iraq or in Afghanistan.

I had been so immersed in my work to that point—it seemed the natural progression of things as a Marine. Thinking about the deployment allowed me reprieve from having to deal with George's loss. I was getting ready to leave my pregnant wife with a toddler, and with the weight of grief over losing George still so painfully fresh, I wondered *but what about Kristine?* I was heading back into harm's way. I felt like I was dumping a pile a shit on her and saying, "Good luck; hopefully, I'll see you later this year."

I'm not sure how much adversity you can throw at one person and expect them to bounce back, but no matter what, Kristine always did. She is a survivor in the truest form of the word.

I wasn't crazy about leaving my son. I knew at this age he wouldn't really remember my time away, but he and I were buddies. We did everything together—I figured he was probably going to weather the deployment better than I would.

——— ⌾ ———

*M*y 31st birthday came and went. It seemed like just another day in Twentynine Palms. Ross was away training, as usual, and I didn't feel like celebrating anything other than the life growing inside of me.

There were good days and bad. I became dog-tired, and felt completely useless. Every inch of me was exhausted, and worse, I suffered nausea and dizziness when I sat upright. I really didn't want to go through another pregnancy alone.

But a few weeks later it was time to say goodbye. Again.

George had only been gone five months. Ross was going to Afghanistan. He was going off to war, and I was left knowing I was going to have to give birth to our child without him by my side.

I'd always heard people talk about how they wouldn't be able to handle losing a child. I was still weathering that storm, but there were pockets of sunshine and hope. Now all I could do was pray that I wouldn't have to deal with losing my husband as well. After everything I'd been through, I knew another loss would destroy me.

I began forming friendships with my neighbors. I couldn't have chosen better people with whom to share our paper-thin military walls. I think God knew that I needed this neighborhood in my life.

I also grew close with the other ladies whose husbands served in 2/7. My small group of friends was like a roll call for the world's most amazing women. I swear each of these ladies could have invented Pinterest because they were always cooking, decorating fabulously, or making something extraordinary.

All of them made motherhood look easy, deftly juggling educational activities, crafts and playtime with their kids. I looked to them for support and for inspiration to become the mom I wanted to be.

They would be the strong arms and open hearts that would carry me through the next three years of my life.

32

No Distance Is Too Far

March 2008
Camp Bastion (Barber/Leatherneck), Afghanistan
Twentynine Palms, California

After we said goodbye to our families, we loaded onto buses and drove to March Air Reserve Base. 747s were waiting for us, along with a few attachments (other units) that were flying out with us. Our first stop, once again, was Bangor, Maine.

I recognized some faces—the same people who had supported us when we flew through on our way to Iraq. Once again, they were there handing out phone cards and letting the troops use their cell phones. It was good to see them again.

From Bangor we continued on to Ramstein, Germany, for a layover, then to the Transit Center at Manas, near Bishkek, the Capital of Kyrgyzstan.

Our mission this time was to train the Afghan police. We weren't deploying as a Marine Air Ground Task Force, MAGTF, which meant we didn't have attached aircraft support. We were as a result relegated to mostly our organic logistic elements.

The Marine Corps had designated 2/7 to serve under the Combined Security Transition Command—Afghanistan, CSTC-A, which was responsible for the training of Afghan security forces. There were two parts to the command: one arm that trained the Afghan army, and another that trained the various federal police forces.

The Afghan police were really paramilitary forces. This configuration meant our battalion would be required to break up into companies and platoons to protect and assist police mentoring teams consisting of DynCorps Contractors (former cops), law enforcement professionals (retired cops, attached to our battalion), and National Guardsmen who were also civilian police officers.

Our job was to teach the Afghan police survival skills within the operational combat environment. The Afghan army would conduct traditional operations to clear an area of Taliban, and the police we trained would hold or retain what the army had gained.

These police forces would be further developed to establish the rule of law on the ground, extending the authority of the Islamic Republic of Afghanistan. The plan was that this government would replace the Taliban, becoming the only government the Afghan people knew.

Training would take place in a central location, and our battalion would support the police who were patrolling the various districts of Helmand Province. We would also aid them and partner with them until they became more tactically capable. We were an interim force until the local police were in full operation in the various Afghan districts.

From: Ross
Date: March 29, 2008 4:54 AM
To: Kristine

Hey babe, already missing you terribly. I'm in Germany. Other than that there's not much to report. I'm not sure how much connectivity I'm going to have. Just wanted to say I love you and to please give our little boy a big hug. When he's tested you to your last nerve, give him a little wiggle room since he doesn't have me to run to. I miss you so much.

The Manas transit center, in Bishkek, Kyrgyzstan, was a sprawling complex. We were housed for a couple of days inside enormous tents that slept about six hundred troops. The chow hall served by far the best food we'd ever had on deployment. There were vendors offering cheap (legitimate) massages, and there were shops where we could purchase supplies. It was almost relaxing. It was a good place to pause for a few days before we headed into Afghanistan. Since there were so many troops moving into and out of Afghanistan, our company spread across several C-130 transport planes for the final leg of our trip. Some of our Marines went to Kandahar Air Field, but I went with the vast majority of the company to Bagram Airfield. We stayed at Joint Combined US Armed Forces and Allied Bagram for three days.

It was like its own little city with coffee shops, restaurants, and incredible chow halls; better than anything we had on our Marine Corps bases back home. Eventually, those of us sidelined in Bagram were sent to Kandahar to meet up with the rest of our battalion. We stayed there for most of April, waiting for our equipment to arrive on commercial ships coming in via Karachi, Pakistan. We needed Humvees, heavy equipment, Mine-Resistant Ambush Protected vehicles (MRAPs), and more. While we were waiting, we did some convoy training and test-fired our weapons.

The waiting gave me time to reflect on everything that had happened back home. All I could think about was how I'd left my wife with all that heaviness to deal with. I thought about how Kristine would be affected if I were killed in the line of duty. As cliché as it sounds, I really wasn't afraid of dying, but I was deathly afraid of leaving my wife alone. What would that do to her? What impact would that have on my son and unborn child?

I went to talk to one of the Navy psychologists who was visiting deploying troops, and explained my concerns to her. I had never told anyone else. I gave her the whole backstory about what we'd been through in the last year. I disclosed how much anxiety I suffered about leaving my wife burdened with everything if something were to happen to me.

She said, "Don't worry about it—nothing is going to happen to you."

What? She can't fucking know that.

But that piece of nonsensical bullshit was all I needed to be able to quit dwelling on those thoughts. A doctor of mental health—or whatever you'd call her—had just told me nothing would happen to me, in Afghanistan, in a war. It was the stupidest thing I'd ever heard.

But what it helped me to realize was that there was nothing I could do about any of it. What good would it do me if I were to allow myself to become overwhelmed by fear for Kristine's future if something happened to me? Was I really prepared to abandon my Marines on the eve of our crossing the line of departure? No fucking way. The guilt I would no doubt feel over that would probably lead to me suckstarting a pistol down the road in the near future.

There was nothing else for me to do but focus on the task at hand. I had to quit feeling sorry for myself. All I could do was hope. If something were to happen to me, Kristine's steel will, the love of her remaining children, and the love and support of our extended family would help get her through that tragedy, too.

If that ever happened, I thought, on the bright side at least I'd be with George.

> From: Ross
> Date: April 21, 2008 4:19 PM
> To: Kristine
>
> I'm three haircuts into deployment. Only 27 left (if we get home on time). I think we might be extended a little bit, but I should at least be home for Christmas. Rumors are that a unit has already been identified to replace us.
>
> I saw the MEU psychiatrist last night. I talked about George and how this overwhelming sense of fear comes over me when I think about how I might not return. I'm not trying to be negative, I feel fine. I just really worry about you. I'm not afraid of dying. I worry about how you would cope with losing George and me in the same year. I do know you'd figure out how to be strong for Ryan.
>
> After I talked to the psychiatrist, I threw myself into planning the unit's next course of action. I felt very good about our plan and how we'll avoid putting ourselves at risk in the same ways the MEU did. This may not be what you want to hear, but I don't have anyone else I want to talk to. Van is too busy, plus I don't want to worry anyone in the Bn. I feel fine.
>
> I wonder what's going through Ryan's mind. I know he understands as well as he can right now. I hope he and I will be able to recover what we once had together.
>
> I miss you terribly and love you fiercely. Give Ryan a hug and tell him how much I love him. You're the best thing that ever happened to me. I love you.

P.S. - I heard yesterday that Toby Keith is coming here. He's actually coming over to our side of the base to eat at our chow hall.

We were getting ready to leave on a convoy to Camp Bastion.

Everyone was concerned about the potential IEDs that were lying in wait for us, as the enemy heavily targeted the main route that coalition forces traveled. We learned that the insurgents in Afghanistan had begun following Iraq's lead, though, and that we were going to face IEDs once again. Our intel had given us a window for the safest times to travel with our convoy of 90-plus vehicles. Two Marines had just been killed a few days earlier while taking this route to Bastion.

We left Kandahar Air Field at 0300 hours.

We hadn't even made it out of the city when one of the wheels completely came off one of our trucks. The US soldiers escorting us got really nervous and radioed—with urgency—"We needed to get out of here right now," that we should "Just tell the driver to throw it into four-wheel drive and get on the move."

I don't think they understood that we had completely lost the wheel.

I radioed back that we needed to get a wrecker on it, which meant that we needed to move all the vehicles off to one side of the road to make way for the wrecker so that it could navigate the narrow road to the disabled truck.

It took a good hour-and-a-half to fix it. By then the sun was just breaking over the horizon.

Locals on mopeds began speeding up to us, slamming on their brakes at the last minute. We quickly figured out that they were trying to incite us to fire on them. They zoomed back and forth, skidding right up to us over and over again. Marines were becoming concerned, but they all kept their cool, and no one fired a shot.

Once we left Kandahar, we were escorted by Kiowa Army Scout helicopters, which would fly extremely low and look into the culverts for explosives.

Echo Company had been the first element of the battalion to

move out. They experienced huge problems trying to get their vehicles refueled during their movement. Since we had the benefit of learning from their trials, we identified a small Canadian Forward Operating Base, FOB, where we could fill up. My buddy Captain Mike Vincent, the S-4 logistics officer, encouraged us to refuel there because he didn't want us to experience what Echo had a few days prior. I asked the battalion for permission to fill up at this base with our Canadian partners.

At 2200 we established a harbor site, a defensive position away from the main highway, allowing us to avoid traveling when the enemy was at their most threatening. Essentially, we circled our wagons in the middle of the desert. In each vehicle, two Marines were on watch, while the other two (or more) slept. It was particularly important that the drivers were well rested.

I began making my way around our 94 vehicles to check our defenses. That's what leaders are supposed to do when we establish a defensive position; walk the lines and talk with the men. I had no idea it would take me so long—it was a stupid decision. It took me four hours to get back to my truck. I got about 15 minutes of sleep before we were on the road again.

We had just made it across the Helmand River to Gereshk when the paved roads turned to dirt.

I got on the radio and called up Bastion, letting them know we were about to enter friendly lines. Once we made the turnoff from Highway 1 towards Camp Bastion, I basically passed out, face-first, in the vehicle. I'd been awake for 45 hours, with only a handful of short naps totaling three hours. The next thing I knew, LtCol Hall had opened my door and was giving me a big bear hug. I thought he'd be mad at me because I was sleeping, but no. We had transitioned our guys safe and sound, and with few incidents.

33

War Torn Afghanistan and the Taliban

May 2008
Now Zad, Afghanistan
Twentynine Palms, California

My company was tasked with providing platoons to Musa Qala, Now Zad, and Washir. There was an Estonian mechanized company and about 15 or so Brits already in Now Zad. The Brits provided a liaison team that augmented Estonian operations with an intelligence cell, an engineer squad, communication team, and fire support team. The Estonians were equipped with wheeled, light armored personnel carriers called XA-180s, Finnish-produced vehicles. The XA-180s would make our lives exponentially easier, as our Humvees and MRAPs weren't designed for the terrain there.

No coalition forces were assigned to Washir, although a British Special Forces mentoring team of about 80 Royal Marines had been there multiple times, and were familiar with the area. Our talks with them revealed that the last police chief had been beheaded, and that it was essentially a hornet's nest of Taliban activity. Trips into the area always brought a sizeable firefight. The Brits believed it was a logistics supply point for the Taliban. That would mean that Washir was probably where arms and ammunition were stored, IEDs were built and distributed, poppy paste was refined into heroin, and Taliban wounded received treatment so that they could heal from their injuries.

Musa Qala was a large city in northern Helmand. The 5 SCOTS Battalion Battle Group was headquartered there, and had been conducting counter-insurgency operations for two years. It was a well-established force with a storied history (dating back to 1794) led and manned by competent folks.

I recommended that LtCol Hall set Fox Company HQ in Now Zad, as it would be the geographical center between Washir and Musa Qala. I hopped on a helo that was resupplying Now Zad, using the flight as an opportunity to recon our future area of operations. The coalition position in Now Zad was the district center. It was obvious that a lot of fighting had taken place there; damaged buildings were everywhere.

We accompanied the Estonians on a few foot patrols, taking in the area around the district center. It was once a thriving town of fifteen thousand people, but it had been completely abandoned for the past few years due to intense fighting between the Taliban and the British. This posed an obvious problem with our mission to train police: If there was no one to protect, why should there be a police force, and what good was the training?

As we were moving about the area, I kept thinking about how different Afghanistan was from Iraq. Now Zad sits in a valley, hugging a giant dry riverbed in the foothills of the Hindu Kush. It looked very similar to Twentynine Palms, with small, sharply cut mountains and narrow ridgelines that looked like jagged teeth.

There were about ten smaller villages surrounding the district center, as well as several poppy fields. The Afghans herded goats amidst the thick, lush orchards of various fruits, including pomegranate. Though the villages were comprised of both noncombatants and Taliban members, most of the population was sympathetic to the Taliban. It wasn't that they favored them; it was just the Taliban rule was, for the locals, better than nothing. The Taliban provided some degree of order—they offered security through a policing unit that could arrest citizens and adjudicate issues. Their rule manifested a shadow government, complete with district and provincial governors. Their political and military heads mirrored the positions of the official Afghan government.

From: Kristine
Date: Wednesday, April 30, 2008 9:40 AM
To: Ross

We just got back from the ER. Ryan's temp was 105.5° so I took him in. We were the only ones there, so that was at least good, but the visit still took a while. He has a small ear infection in his right ear, so we have to give him antibiotics for the next ten days, plus a pain reliever.

Have you seen any poppy fields?

From: Ross
Date: April 30, 2008 10:12 AM
To: Kristine

Poor guy, I hope he gets better. It will make him a little sensitive to the sun (according to the doctor sitting next to me). I told First Sergeant about the fever, and that was the first thing he said: "Is it an ear infection?"

Yes, tons of poppies. Things are quiet here now because of the poppy harvest; the Taliban doesn't do anything because they don't want to interrupt it. It's their funding source. We don't want to destroy the poppies because that's the only real signifi-cant income for the local farmers: if they don't get a harvest, then a lot of farmers feel they have to sell their daughters to the money men. It's a fucked up place.

I tried as best as I could to maintain a front that said, "Everything is fine," in order to support Ross. He needed to stay focused on his mission. Failure to do anything else could cost lives, including his, and I didn't want that weighing on me on top of everything else.

Any emails I sent were positive, as far as it concerned our rela-tionship. I told him I loved him and missed him, which was true: I did. But I was still upset, still hurting from everything that had happened.

I felt my job as a military spouse was to keep the home fire burning, supporting my Marine in any way possible. I was back to the fake it until you make it routine.

From: Kristine
Date: May 06, 2008 5:10 AM
To: Ross

Zazu has been throwing up all day. I cut a watermelon, and she snatched two pieces away from Ryan, and she ate the rinds. She can't keep anything down. The vet said that I need to bring her in if she's still throwing up by tomorrow night.

I'm attaching some pictures of our latest outing. I'm sure Ryan would love some pictures of you too, if you can.

From: Ross
Date: May 6, 2008 10:17 AM
To: Kristine

Wow! That picture of Ryan in the tunnel with his mouth open makes him look like my Grandpa. I can't believe how much older he looks, and it's only been a month. It was great to hear the stories about him. I miss you both so much.

I'll do my best to get some pictures of me to you. So far there's only a couple, and I've got all my gear on, so you can barely even tell it's me. I've got one of Van and me on patrol. We were marveling at how eight years ago we were stupid Lts in Quantico, engaged in all kinds of jackassery, and here we are now as worldly Capts . . . engaged in the same jackassery.

Sorry to hear about Zazu, I hope she recovers well. I love you more than anything.

After returning from my recon in Now Zad, I met with LtCol Hall and explained there weren't any people living in the district center—Now Zad proper—there was literally nothing to police. From what we'd been able to gather, at some point the police had been there, but the logistics were too much for the government to handle. There had been no way of getting them paid, fed, or supplied, so the police ended up shaking down the locals. The people eventually responded by running them out of town.

Hall relayed this information to our higher headquarters, asking for more than one platoon in Now Zad than what was originally slated. The new goal then was to set conditions and limits for the police so that people would want to move back there, which I naively thought I could facilitate.

We sat through some painful days of PowerPoint briefings. Our higher headquarters arranged a long series of briefs on the rule of law and fostering transparency in the police force, alongside which we would be operating. The brief rattled on about chains of evidence and ethical policy procedures, but we were years away from worrying about this fine-tuning kind of stuff. We were just in the infancy phase of this whole mission. We were focused on establishing the police and getting them trained.

Eventually the PowerPoint slides moved on to how the police were going to be paid, and how there were ATMs (located hundreds of miles away), and how we needed to fill out weekly progress on reports for police performance. All I kept thinking was *I don't even have people in the town for the police to police!*

Still though, our mission remained the same.

From: Ross
Date: May 10, 2008 10:29 PM
To: Kristine

> Happy Mother's Day. Please say "Hi" to everyone there for me. Things are very busy here; I'll try calling, but I just can't seem to get a minute.

> By the way, I really like those drink mixes that you sent in the care package. Next month your care packages are going to mean everything to me. V-8, fruit cups, tuna, oatmeal, and anything else you can send that's healthy will be appreciated. Right now it's not a big deal, but it will become huge in the very near future.

> Please email me when you find out if we're having a boy or a girl. If I can't get to a phone to tell you, please know that I love you more than anything. I hope you have the best Mother's Day you can have. I think about you all the time. I love and miss you so much. Give our boy a hug for me.

The living conditions in Now Zad were stark, at best. We had no compound for the whole first week. We needed to start building our tents and shelters, as well as our perimeter.

I walked the area with the engineers and Gunny Kindrick to show where I wanted things to be set up. When I was confident that the Marines understood my intent in regard to the defenses, I headed back to Bastion to insert my other Marines into Musa Qala; I wanted to make sure they had everything they needed, too. On the way, we hit an IED. It blew several tires off the trucks and rang some bells, but there were no substantial injuries.

I made it back to Bastion and was busy grabbing more supplies for our Forward Operating Base, FOB, when news arrived that our backhoe tractor in Now Zad had caught fire. It burned up because it had run out of hydraulic fluid.

The tractor hadn't come with any maintenance equipment because it had been pulled from another unit in Iraq. We had requested that the hydraulic fluid be sent out to us ASAP while continuing to use it, though the fluid was critically low. Since our unit had no shelter, the SSgt engineer made the difficult choice to simply use the backhoe until it stopped. The decision was well intentioned, but now that the tractor was down, the process of getting our command post, CP, built was as a result extended indefinitely. We would have to do a lot of heavy work by hand.

By the time I got back to Now Zad, the towers had been built, and the HESCO barriers were up but not filled. HESCOs are great pieces of gear: they're wire mesh outside, with a cloth interior that can be shaped into different-sized walls, even for buildings. Once they were position, we'd fill them with dirt, and the job was finished. The barriers we used for were for walls seven feet high and three feet wide. The tractor managed to fill 3 of 70 before it caught fire.

We tried filling one HESCO by hand, with shovels and buckets, but it took a platoon of Marines an entire day. We asked to use the Brits' backhoe when we could. They lent it to us for an hour or so here and there, but we were a far cry from getting anything built. We ended up parking our vehicles in strategic places around the wall as a barrier, praying the enemy didn't try to test our defenses.

Our work with the international forces was a convoluted relationship. We had to come alongside them, respecting their wishes and closely coordinating operations, but we also worked independently under Combined Security Transition Command-Afghanistan, CSTC-A, and thus were able to operate under different rules of engagement.

I began speaking more with the Estonians, and learned that they were ordered to maintain their positions—nothing more. They couldn't conduct offensive operations, per the Battle Group's orders. However, if we were engaged and requested assistance, they were required to help. This was how we, F Company 2nd Bn 7th Marines USMC, and C Company Scouts Battalion of the Estonian Defense Force, were able to leverage the considerable combat power we both had.

From: Kristine
Date: May 18, 2008 7:57 AM
To: Ross

> On a whim, I put an ad in the Spokane/Coeur D'Alene Craigslist stating that our motorhome is for sale, and that we might consider a trade for some land. Someone contacted me and said he is extremely interested in our RV. He sent me some pics (attached) and he's working on getting us some new ones. The land is about halfway to Schweitzer Ski Resort. I guess we'll see. I don't want anything too remote, but it's been 8 months of trying to sell this thing, so I'm open to options.
>
> I still feel really tired. Being on my feet for a while really sucks the life out of me. I need to keep my feet elevated, or I become a mess.
>
> Have you thought about where you want to be after this? Do you think we'll stick around Twentynine Palms?
>
> How often do you want me to start sending packages? Every other week, like I did before? I can send the bigger V-8s as well . . . just let me know what size you prefer. I'm getting ready to send one on Monday or Tuesday.

From: Ross
Date: May 19, 2008 2:31 AM
To: Kristine

> It was so great to talk to you last night. I'm so excited we're having a little girl! No doubt she'll have me wrapped around her finger.
>
> I think this land trade will work out. I hope it does. I think it's almost too good to be true. I guess you'll get a better feel when you meet the owners.

It would be amazing if you could send a box a week, if you're up for that. The drink powder was gone in a week, and it's good because it keeps me hydrated. I don't really drink anything but water unless I have that. The Zinc stuff is great, and yes, I've used it. I'm being very careful with the sun; I have yet to get sunburned. I'm doing my best to avoid getting skin cancer like Dad did.

Whatever people want to send is good. Obviously guy magazines are preferred, but even if you send a copy of *Cat Fancy*, it will be read. We get bored. There are so many tabloid magazines being read by Marines, it's funny. Cold drink mixes, nuts, no chocolate since it melts; you know what I like.

From: Kristine
Date: May 24, 2008 9:42 PM
To: Ross

I just got our little boy to bed. If I'm doing the math right, it's already our anniversary where you are, so happy anniversary, darling. I can't believe it's been six years already. It seems like just yesterday we were married, and yet at the same time it seems like twice that long because of all the moves and all the changes in our lives.

If you're happy with this land idea, I'd like to take a serious look at trading the RV for it. I think I'll be happy with that. If we don't like it, we can sell down the road. At least if we trade for land, our money would be tied up in something that retains value, or maybe even gains in value.

Our little girl has been moving around all the time. Over halfway there!

I'm hosting game night at our house tomorrow, so I may not get back to you right away. But if there are messages in my inbox before we start, I will definitely reply. Happy anniversary, my love.

From: Ross
Date: June 2, 2008 5:24 PM
To: Kristine

I got your package two days ago; great job. One of the fruit cups spilled and rotted, it stunk pretty badly. Maybe find canned ones. If you can, send the big packs of unsalted almonds, and lightly salted cashews; that would be great. Can you send some of the breakfast bars I used to eat? I can't even think of the name. The packets of raisins would be a big hit. Please send athlete's foot spray and cream, they have none of that here and I'm starting to show symptoms.

I was supposed to be issued another pair of boots coming over here, but Bn. supply was short, so we made sure our junior Marines had them. My pair is getting ready to fall apart. They're okay for now, and I have a second pair, but can you swing into the uniform shop and see if they have any Bellevilles that would fit me? They stock three different kinds of boots, and they all fit differently. No hurry. I might ask you to ship me some other equipment. My watch died this morning.

I miss hearing your voice.

From: Kristine
Date: June 02, 2008 12:23 AM
To: Ross

Sorry the fruit opened—was it still in its Ziploc baggie? Or did it get all over everything? I tried being really careful about putting everything in baggies, just in case.

I'm glad you emailed me about the things you need. I was getting ready to mail you a box tomorrow, but I will go and get what you asked for and put that stuff in this package.

I took Ryan to a PFT that the base staged for kids whose parents were deployed. It was basically just a bunch of Marines in the gym with baseballs (soft ones), footballs, soccer balls, volleyballs, and some other toys, you know, organized chaos. Ryan didn't want anything to do with it at first. It was pretty overwhelming when we walked in. He wanted to sit on my lap, and wouldn't talk to anyone.

A female Marine came over then, and Ryan warmed right up to her. He was chucking the ball in every direction, like you'd throw it for the dog, and this poor girl and one of her friends kept running after it and bringing it back. They were pretty good sports about it.

From: Kristine
Date: June 02, 2008 9:04 PM
To: Ross

I didn't get around to buying you anything today or sending your box off. I had some light bleeding this morning, but I wasn't terribly worried about it. Then before I went to pick up Maura and Ryan, there was a lot more bleeding, so I had to go to the hospital for an emergency consult. The doctor wasn't sure why I was bleeding, but the good news was that it wasn't my cervix or placenta. It's stopped for now, and he said that if it gets worse to come on in. Otherwise he wasn't worried about it.

From: Ross
Date: June 3, 2008 4:38 PM
To: Kristine

I'm glad the bleeding wasn't anything serious. Can you get a second opinion? I just think back to all the doctors' decisions with George's birth. Navy medicine scares me when it comes to my family.

From: Kristine
Date: June 11, 2008 10:02 PM
To: Ross

The bleeding stopped. I've been cleared by the doctor for normal activities, so that's good. Do you have electricity where you sleep? If so, I can mail a big misting fan to help keep all of you guys cool at night. It needs to be plugged in to an outlet. I think it would help, and you haven't even seen the worst of the heat yet.

34

The Best Way Out Is Through

May 2008
Now Zad, Afghanistan
Boise, Idaho

*I*t was time to head back to Idaho for two things: a friend's wedding, and a summer visit. I left Twentynine Palms and stopped in Las Vegas for snacks and fuel. It was 107° when we left Twonine, but it had cooled down to 95° in Vegas.

When I was done refueling, I closed the door so that the dogs wouldn't hop out. I went around to the rear, and opened the hatch to grab a new DVD for Ryan. As I was walking back to the driver's door, I heard a *click*.

Brendy, my newest adopted dog, stood staring at me, tail wagging, from the driver's seat. In her excitement, she had stepped on the lock button on the armrest. All the windows were up, the doors were shut, and Ryan was completely latched into his car seat.

Step one: don't freak out.

I tried talking to Ryan, demonstrating to him how to unbuckle his seatbelt, but it was no use. He tried, but he wasn't succeeding—either that—or he was just copying me, moving his shirt around instead of releasing the buckles.

I ran inside and asked the clerk to call 911. I ran back to my SUV and tried calling Brendy, the prime offender, back to the driver's door; the scene of the crime. She ignored me, of course. It was just one more thing: my husband was at war in Afghanistan, and now my dog had locked my kid inside the car in the middle of the Mojave.

This time I called Zazu, the dog we'd had the longest, over to the door. I tried to get her excited enough to jump on it. She was my favorite dog, but she'd more than tested my nerves in the past few months. I had recently installed child locks on the pantry door to stop her from opening it and devouring everything inside. One time she tore open a care package and ate one box each of breakfast bars and instant oatmeal. We had the most un-dog-like cow patties in the backyard for the next couple of days.

But the instant Zazu's foot stepped on the unlock button, all was forgiven.

She'd done it. In that moment she became my four-legged hero. Zazu the wonder dog was better than frickin' Lassie and I loved her.

All in all, the ordeal had taken about seven or eight minutes. I was surprised the police hadn't shown up yet. I let the gas station attendant know that we were good to go. Hopefully, this would be the last we would see of the infamous Murphy's Military Law, under which anything that could happen would happen—just as soon as your husband deploys.

It was one of our first patrols. Reports that Besendorfer and Flores had been shot came in via radio, and Doc Hancock went to start field triage.

Doc found that both Besendorfer and Flores had taken hits directly on the Small Arms Protective Insert, SAPI, plates covering their chests; they both sustained deep, baseball-sized bruises. SAPI plates are designed to stop a bullet from piercing skin, but they can do little to dissipate the energy of a bullet traveling at 2,500 feet per second. The impact can knock a man over, depending on how he's standing. While Doc was tending to Besendorfer and Flores, Taliban insurgents snuck up on them. Doc engaged the insurgents.

LtCol Hall was not happy to hear that Doc, a Navy Commander and ER doctor, had ended up in a firefight. He was too valuable to the overall mission to be out there exchanging gunfire. I told Doc Hancock that he wasn't allowed to leave an MRAP vehicle ever again (though he outranked me), and he laughed, but he understood. We had a good working relationship; everyone understood his role.

Our first company-sized operation took place near a large irrigation ditch we had dubbed The Trench Line.

The majority of the company was dismounted, set-in along a ditch at the edge of the town, and the fire support team took up position on top of several buildings to prepare for the operation.

We moved out under the cover of darkness.

Enemy RPG and machine gun fire erupted as soon as we even thought about going anywhere near that trench. Not too long after that, the first casualty report came in: a Marine had been shot.

I ran over to do an immediate assessment. It was Dunkelberger. His eyes weren't fixated on anyone or anything. He was just staring at the sky. I thought we'd lost him, but eventually his eyes looked towards me and I realized he was alive. I left him under the care of a corpsman. I went back out to the operation to check on my other Marines.

At the back of the open field, on the other side of the trench, was an eight-foot-high mud wall. The Taliban would peer through mouse holes in the wall, then poke their muzzle through and fire at us. They had no way to aim accurately using this method; all they could do was fire wildly. Most of the rounds went over our heads.

We finally found a place to cross over the ditch. It was an earthen bridge running over a massive culvert, and it was likely riddled with IEDs. We shot an Anti-Personnel Obstacle Breaching System, APOBS, line charge: a rocket that had a large cord behind it filled with bomblets roughly the size of hand grenades. After the detonation we could safely walk across, stepping in the potholes it had blown, because it would usually detonate any IEDS in the blast.

Once across, we slowly made our way forward, taking one enemy firing position after another, following a trail of expended rounds and blood, destroying bunkers as we went.

Behind the wall, it appeared there were several houses that were still partially inhabited. My guess was that the enemy used them to lay low and rest until they were called into action.

We spent the day clearing positions, but we didn't see a single Afghan civilian. Every single home in the green zone had been abandoned. To sum up the trench line attack: minus Dunkelberger getting shot in the ass, it was a pretty successful day.

There weren't a whole lot of casualties on our side. More importantly, we imposed our will on the enemy and got in their backyard.

From: Ross
Date: June 16, 2008 7:00 PM
To: Kristine

> That is very scary about getting locked out of the car! I bet you
> were scared. I know you called the cops, but if they didn't show
> up, I hope you would have resorted to smashing the window. Of
> course that would have scared Ryan. Was he just smiling as he
> was trying to copy you?
>
> I guess we can keep Zazu, seeing as how she finally did some-
> thing extraordinary, besides eating a whole cake in one sitting.
>
> Yesterday was very exciting. We got into a fight, and my Marines
> did awesome. They are so pumped right now. Some of the
> patrols had gotten into fights while they were out, but we were
> on the offensive this time, and things went really well.
>
> We had one Marine shot, and it looks like it was friendly fire,
> too. He's okay; he was shot in the butt, both cheeks. Seems like
> it missed the really important bits. So that was the worst of it.
> Can't say the same for the bad guys.
>
> It was a good Father's Day. I'm super busy and super tired. I have
> a lot of paperwork to do, so I'd better go get back to it. I love you.

At this point I was running seven dismounted patrols daily, most of which got into firefights every day. We received more information on Dunkelberger and discovered that he was indeed a victim of friendly fire—the doctors pulled a green-tipped bullet from his ass. An inexperienced Marine shot him with the squad automatic weapon, SAW.

I actually don't blame the Marine who shot him—I blame the Marines who'd let their brothers down when we had to scramble to find their replacements two nights before we deployed.

On that night, four salty (experienced) Marines decided to get drunk and have the boots (junior Marines) field day, or clean, the barracks, including their rooms and all the common areas. As the night wore on, the senior Marines started smashing beer bottles and making the boots clean it up.

One of the junior Marines who'd been around a bit longer said he wasn't going to participate anymore. He was a bigger kid, and was at Marine Corps Forces Special Operations Command, MARSOC, for a short period of time in a support role. The senior Marine didn't like being told no, and further, he probably didn't like the fact that this junior Marine was bigger than he was.

The senior Marine told the junior Marine that he was going to keep cleaning or a bunch of guys would beat his ass. The MARSOC Marine walked away. Most of the other junior Marines did not.

The senior Marines ended up shoving one of the junior Marines in his back—he was on his hands and knees— right into shattered glass. It cut him really bad. Another junior Marine got kicked in the ribs while he was down. The night had started out as hazing, but clearly at this point it escalated into assault. Neither is acceptable.

We found out about the incident once the Marines were admitted to the hospital. The four senior Marines who had been hazing the others were immediately cut from our deployment. They would be left behind for adjudication, and they would be charged with assault and hazing. Two of them came to me after the fact, begging to take any punishment as long as they still got to go to Afghanistan.

The last thing I wanted to do was to leave four fully-trained Marines behind: a SAW gunner, a grenadier, a fireteam leader, and a designated marksman (he was trained on—and carried—a Mark 12 rifle equipped with silencer and scope). But the decision was out of my hands: even if I wanted to take them, I couldn't—their actions ran them all the way up to regiment. That being said, even if it were up to me, in the end I still wouldn't have taken them on deployment with us.

We didn't have any choice but to hand the SAW to someone who was completely inexperienced. We did whatever we could to familiarize him with the weapon, but it just wasn't the same. We'd spent five months of intense training with the SAW's original owner. These Marines, who stooped to hazing, let down not just Dunkelberger but the rest of their brothers in Fox Company, too.

From: Kristine
Date: June 16, 2008 12:52 PM
To: Ross

> I went over to your parents' house with Ryan. We ended up going to the Nampa Air Show. Ryan loved it. It was great for him and

good for me, since I didn't have to make too much conversation with your mom.

I ended up staying there till around 3:00 p.m. or so, then we headed back to their house and hung out until 4:30 p.m. I wish I'd left as soon as we got back. Your mom made a comment that was beyond anything she's said so far.

I asked what was going on with the family cabin, just as a way to make conversation. She started telling me a story about how she was fighting with the neighbors about the property line. She says, "Of course, this date doesn't mean anything to you, but we got a call on October 21st from the neighbors to tell us to quit chopping down trees and brush on their land. Of all the days to call and bother us about trees (long pause). Oh wait, I guess the date *would* mean something to you . . . "

She wasn't even a little embarrassed.

The fact that—even for one moment—she could pretend the day that my son passed away should mean nothing to me is just horrific beyond belief. She doesn't see me as his mother. Every single time I go over there she does something to hurt me. It's exhausting. I've had it. I'm not going over there without you anymore.

From: Ross
Date: June 17, 2008 9:32 AM
To: Kristine

I am so sorry about what my mom said. If being around Mom is going to upset you, don't go see her. If you feel up to it, tell her how you feel. I don't know why she'd say something so heartless to you.

I've got to deal with some stuff here. I will email later.

From: Kristine
Date: June 17, 2008 11:30 AM
Subject: From Ryan
To: Ross

(I'm typing what he says to you)

I love you

Are you going to Chucky Cheese?
You clicked R!
You pushed the number R!

nmlkloiiooiyyhr6dre566666r6ydsdfryyyulklllllllllllllll,kkkkkk
kkkkkkkkkkkkkkkkkjyyyyyyyyyyyyyyyyhyzhjkxbnhhmyyteryyhkkjj-
jhhhhhhhhhhhhhhhhhhhhghtggggtrydryttgyygbvbnnvnbvbvbn

I got to play games
You going to type

ypesxzzjhjjjjqnvgtrytrvvbbnmhgfdfrr5sddbgdcfcv-
brrrrrrgqqqqqqqqqqqqffffvvbbbbfbnndee433zxxbnnch
xdfzzzvveyeredgbyhjgjkklloooiiuhhrfdsaaa

Let me see my type, please may I type again?
We both type on ours
Chucky Cheese!
I said Chucky Cheeky!
I love you
I want to see you
I went to Afghanistan

eurueueutoytrt6rw8or6web56wrebr5redxdcxcxzvcvcgfgi-
higuturyfyf6t6t6tytyytfyfrtryyfdhdgert

I love you
I go to Chucky Cheese

(I asked him to tell you what he's been doing in Idaho)

Playing
Playing toys
Drawing
Play with the crayons and put them in the crayon box
Playing kitchen toys
I went to Gaingey and PoPos coke

From: Ross
Date: June 18, 2008 4:01 PM
To: Kristine

I love you too, son. I hope you had fun at Chucky Cheese and at
Gaingey's house. I want to see you too, but I'm helping people

here in Afghanistan. There are mean people that hurt nice people, and I'm stopping them. Sometimes I have to fight the mean people to help the nice people.

Are you being good for Mommy?
Are you having fun at Bodgey's house?
Are you being nice to Brendy and Zazu?

I love you, son; give mommy a big hug and kiss for me.

Love, Daddy

35

War Pigs

★ ★ ★

June 2008
Now Zad, Afghanistan
Boise, Idaho

We were continuing our daily patrols, but we always kept one eye on the upcoming company-sized raid. The major objective was going to be to destroy an enemy observation post, OP, that had been placed up in the canopy of a massive tree. The Brits believed insurgents were directing their mortar attacks from a platform built into a set of thick branches halfway up that huge tree. We dubbed the operation the Tree OP, short for Tree Observation Post.

The night before the operation, Lt Karell was tasked with occupying a compound in the vicinity of where our raid would take place the next day. Karell's squad would be positioned to ambush the enemy if they tried to gain a position of advantage on our main body's movement. The primary objective was to clear a portion of the town and attack the OP while ensuring that we didn't leave our flank open so that the enemy could get beside or behind us.

We reached our drop-off point, and began our clearing operations. My vehicle and its crew would become security for the CASEVAC vehicle. We moved in methodically, clearing row after row of buildings as we continued towards Karell's position. Just before we linked up, two nearby explosions halted our progress.

Two of my Marines had simultaneously stepped on IEDs. Lopez lost one of his legs, and Clenard lost both. The CASEVAC team moved forward to assist with the wounded.

Another explosion. The armored vehicle leading the way for the CASEVAC vehicle struck an IED en route to the platoon casualty collection area. The injuries weren't too severe. The driver and vehicle commander were both knocked unconscious. The vehicle commander suffered a fracture to his foot, and the gunner took shrapnel to the face.

The enemy was shrewd about where they'd placed their IEDs, deploying them at canalizing terrain points—meaning they placed them in areas where if one vehicle was hit, it left no room for another vehicle to maneuver around it.

MEDEVAC helicopters were called. I ordered the rest of my Marines into defensive positions.

Once the casualties were safely moved, the attack continued; we resumed clearing buildings. We moved from compound to compound until we came across an open area in the middle of the town.

Four Marines had bumped (bounding across an area while the partner covers him) across the danger area. I moved to the edge of the opening and tapped the Marine in front of me on the helmet; a nonverbal gesture letting him know I was ready to cover his movement. He did a quick shuffle across the open area. Just as he reached the other side, he disappeared in an explosion and a cloud of dust. He would be the third Marine to lose a leg in just over an hour.

Immediately, four of the team leaders sprang towards the injured Marine across the open field, even though he had Marines on the side closest to him. I was able to grab two of them, ordering them to wait for EOD, explosive ordnance disposal, to sweep the area.

The corpsman put a tourniquet on what was left of LCpl Waters' leg, rushing him to the company casualty collection point and Doc Hancock.

I was done dealing with all this IED bullshit. Karell and I linked up. I told him we'd enter from the open farmland rather than continue through the myriad of abandoned buildings. We, therefore, pushed out into the open, immediately receiving machine gun and mortar fire.

We called in several air strikes. The fire support team helped us pinpoint enemy mortar launch locations. We had discovered earlier that the Taliban wouldn't make their movements in the streets and alleys; instead, they used a series of small holes cut into the walls, no more than two feet in diameter, to transit between buildings.

We wouldn't be able to fit through these holes. The Afghans were short, skinny men about the size of a young teenage girl. We began breaching and making our way through the compounds. We avoided setting foot outside the walls in case of IEDs, booby traps, and direct fire; at least until we got closer to our objective—that big tree. The last wall we came to was on the flank of our objective.

Ten hours had passed since our 0400 departure. Temperatures soared to over 100°. My men were in sore need of both sodium and chow. Reports of heat casualties were already coming in.

We could see the enemy darting back and forth between buildings. The tree—our objective—was still another three hundred meters. I knew we couldn't spend another four or five hours fighting the enemy. I had several damaged vehicles, and my Marines' capability was compromised from the heat and lack of electrolytes. I could see the tree. We were so close, but I knew it wasn't the right time.

I called the mission.

We withdrew under mortar suppression so that our movement was covered. During the withdrawal, one of the CASEVAC element vehicles hit another IED about one foot away from where I'd been lying earlier. Gunny Kindrick was knocked unconscious, suffering a nasty concussion.

It had been a rough day.

We'd suffered a few casualties; three of them would go home. I was a Marine company commander who had failed to reach his objective.

> From: Ross
> Date: June 18, 2008 4:18 PM
> To: Kristine
>
> It gets up to 110° during the day and hovers near the low 80s at night. Sleeping sucks, but I'm so tired I don't care. I took a shower today. I was shaving my head when one of the patrols got into enemy contact. I ran into our command center still wet, soap in my ass and my head 7/8 shaved.
>
> I don't know how much you want me to tell you about what I do here. I don't want you to worry. Tell me what you don't want to hear and I'll leave out anything I can't talk about.
>
> We keep getting communications from the army chain of command. In short they had no idea what they were sending us into. They keep asking why we're attacking trench lines instead of

training police. These villages we're stuck in are, no shit, held by the fucking Taliban, with full complements of enemy troops, fortifications, and bunkers. Of course the army picked wherever they wanted to stick the police station, not realizing it was three miles behind enemy lines. The people we work for have no clue; their intel is crap. It's war here. The police we're training have no idea what they're in for.

Poor bastards.

From: Kristine
Date: June 18, 2008 10:44 PM
To: Ross

As far as what you're doing, you can give me generalities . . . like are you always on the defense? Are you planning your own maneuvers? Are you doing any peace work with the locals? Are you helping any kids? Giving any of my markers away? Building anything?

Attached are some questions that some of the Fox wives have. If you have some time, I will share your answers with the Key Volunteer Network. You know the hardest part of deployment for us is all that we don't know.

Here are a couple of new pictures. Not as good or as personal as the ones I mailed you, but nevertheless, new to you.

From: Ross
Date: June 19, 2008 1:26 PM
To: Kristine

We are on the offensive as much as possible; we dictate the pace of operations to the enemy. They only react. My goal was to get the people back into their town. I don't think that's going to happen on this tour. This mission, for this place right now, does not fit. I'm going to try to work in some civil projects, but we really need to get rid of the Taliban first.

You can start sending pens and markers. We should be getting mail in a few days.

I love the pictures; you look great! It kills me to see Ryan change so much. Here are the answers to those questions you asked me for the Fox Company wives. I love you.

Where are you in Afghanistan and how many square miles is Fox Company in charge of?

We are in Now Zad and Musa Qala districts (districts are like our counties) in Helmand Province (like a state). We are in the northern part of the province; what I like to term the foothills of the Hindu Kush Mountains. We are just under 4,000 feet in elevation. It is hot, but not Iraq hot; it hasn't been hotter than 115°. At night it cools into the low 80s or high 70s. We are working with allies from several European countries, and we share living space with them. We have a great working relationship. (I'm not going into how large our ops area is).

What is a typical day like for you guys?

We're setting conditions for the police to be able to ease into their jobs and not have to fight their way to work. Right now that consists of conducting foot and vehicle patrols to keep the Taliban away from our base. There has not been a typical day yet, but Marines are standing sentry duty and going on patrol. In some places we are providing security for police mentors (former policemen hired by DOD, and National Guardsmen that are police in their civilian profession). But we're all engaged in activities that are very much part of being a Marine infantryman.

Have you heard anything as to when you're coming home?

No. Just rumor and speculation, just like what you're hearing at home. That word will be passed on as soon as we're confirmed. We'll let you know as soon as we know.

Do you have access to phones or computers?

We have limited access. We have very few phones and computers; enough that you should hear from your Marine at least once every two weeks.

How often have you been receiving mail?

We are at a remote location, and mail is irregular. We've been getting mail drops every two weeks so far.

From: Kristine
Date: June 19, 2008 11:07 PM
To: Ross

> I'm glad you're able to dictate how things are going. That's better than being on defense. I can't believe how dumb it is of the army to just chuck you outside a major Taliban stronghold. I hope you're getting the support you need.
>
> Ryan talks about you all the time. We read a book about a daddy bear at night and at the end of the story, I always say, "I can't wait for my daddy to come home and play with me," as if it's part of the book. So we say, "The baby bear's daddy is gone, too," and Ryan just sighs and says, "Yeah, my daddy's gone, too." He always wants to read that story before any of the others.
>
> Your Mom watched Ryan today for four-plus hours. She was an hour and a half late to pick him up, but didn't have the courtesy to call me in advance. She's had him four days this week. Being around her is so annoying; she keeps calling him Ross. Over and over again. It drives Ryan crazy, too. He keeps saying, "My name is Ryan!"
>
> Are we halfway there yet?

On a late morning patrol, Knowles, a combat engineer, stepped on an IED. We sent out the Quick Reaction Force, QRF, with EOD, the bomb and blast experts, to conduct a post-blast assessment, and search for and clear any additional IEDs.

Shortly after their arrival, a second IED exploded. It was so loud we heard it all the way over at the command post. A frantic voice came over the radio saying, "We have a mass casualty. Echo-Six Mike is KIA." SSgt Strickland, our most experienced EOD technician, was dead.

When the QRF returned to the command post, a Marine got out of the vehicle carrying the body bag—in one hand. Strickland had been a two hundred twenty-pound man. The only thing left of him was the lower part of one leg and half his rifle.

We were now down an entire EOD team as we waited for the MEDEVAC bird. Doc Hancock tended to the other ten Marines who had been injured in the explosion. The details about what had happened began to filter in.

While hunting for more explosives, SSgt Strickland had found a large rock that looked to him to be out of place. He took his time, studying the scene. He hesitated to pick it up at first, but in the end he made a fatal decision. The rock sat on a 20-pound pressure plate/pressure release with homemade explosives. It was probably made to destroy a vehicle, not a man.

It was a huge loss. SSgt Strickland was well liked; it was psychologically distressing for us. Strickland knew more about IEDs than anyone else did, and now he was gone.

I brought the company in to talk about it, saying a prayer for Strickland. SSgt West, 3rd Platoon's platoon sergeant, asked if he could say a few words.

West wasn't the most eloquent speaker, but he told the company what they needed to hear: "Strickland was a fucking great Marine; he'd want all of us to keep doing our jobs." He paused, looking around at all the Marines, and said; "Now I'm going to go recover my friend and make sure all of him that's left gets back to his family." SSgt West didn't ask what we were going to do; he simply told everyone what needed to be done, just like Lerma's insistence that we do the right thing when we retrieved the body of one of our fallen on the bridge that night almost five years ago.

Our Armored Combat Excavator, ACE, a small armored bulldozer, led the way. Its blade removed the top two inches of dirt. The idea was that it would blow any IEDs in our path. It takes an incredibly long time to travel that way.

SSgt Stan, the only EOD Tech we had left, swept up to the blast site. He discovered another IED and blew it up. It had only been a couple of hours since the initial explosion, and the Taliban had already planted more.

We found small pieces of Strickland fifty meters away from the blast site. His helmet was almost unrecognizable. It was about two feet in diameter, and looked like a huge flower with petals. All of the flesh and tissue we found was blown in one direction, away from the blast, except a piece of tissue about the size of a milk jug that looked as if it had taken an entirely different trajectory.

SSgt Stan swept around it and immediately got a hit from

the metal detector from something right next to it. The Taliban had moved the largest piece of Strickland and planted an IED under it. SSgt Stan bagged up what was left of his friend, and placed explosives to blow the IED in place.

By the time we made it back to the command post, the devastation of what we'd seen was really hitting us. In the first ten days of operations in Now Zad, we'd suffered four amputees, one KIA, and several other injuries.

The next morning we did what we needed to do—we kept patrolling. Two of the Estonians had also been injured after stepping on IEDs. One of my squad leaders approached me, asking if we could stop the patrols and stay in the compound to fortify it more, to ask the Estonians to do more. I felt for him, but I knew it wouldn't help us.

Despite our losses, we had pushed the enemy away from our base. If we cocooned in our command post, the Taliban would just go back to planting IEDs on our doorstep. Our job was to set the conditions, and hand the police a secure area to operate in when they arrived.

I took the time to talk to each squad. We talked about what had happened, and collectively mourned the men we had lost. I reminded them of the importance of maintaining both focus and mission. We had to stay professional, and we needed to keep doing what we'd been sent to do.

From: Kristine
Date: July 3, 2008 11:17 AM
To: Ross

Hi Daddy, it's Ryan. I wanted to type you a letter.

rt5txes et 35re z t54zv 45vx 53s6v3ss22se4bxx6ycbncxvbzvzx tyc7ibkmopi y 76bifvit7c6tsdx esrw4r4aq421 bxcxvctctfgc f

gbvbbbbbbb[,,[[[7vf7dnh7d7dsn c4 reftujccff

Ryan

Here's what he wants to say:

I love you
(silly sounds)

I want to go away to chucky cheese
play with my stickers
play with my toys

I miss daddy - he's fighting the bad guys
I'm hungry at Bodgey's house
I need to grow big and strong

Mommy, please may I play the hunting game with you?

Now from Mommy:

We're going to meet Christie for lunch today. I called and
texted your mom on July 1st (Tuesday) and said she could have
Ryan Wednesday and Thursday. I called her again yesterday
(Wednesday) and left her a voicemail, but she hasn't called back.
She preaches about courtesy, and yet she can't even commit to
seeing her grandchild. Yet she will find a way to complain about
the lack of time she has with him.

We have a signed offer/acceptance on the land/RV trade.
They're flying down to pick it up on July 8th, then it's a done deal
from there. Ten months of work, and finally this creative plan has
yielded the sale of this dang thing.

From: Ross
Date: July 3, 2008 11:06 PM
To: Kristine

What is the hunting game? I miss you, boy.

I'm still a little worried about how this whole RV thing is going to
work out. I'm glad, but skeptical. I sure miss you. I'm super tired.
I'm going to bed. I love you, babe.

From: Kristine
Date: July 3, 2008 4:13 PM
To: Ross

The hunting game is the Cranium Treasure Hunt game; he really
loves to play it.

He's been feeling baby sister kick for the last two days. He's been
talking about George being in my belly or that George is going to

be in someone else's belly, but I keep trying to explain to him that George is an angel now, and he's watching over us.

From: Kristine
Date: July 9, 2008 10:37 PM
To: Ross

Ryan did awesome today in swim class. I told him that he had to earn the fun kiddie pool afterwards by making good choices and listening to his teacher, and that this included sticking his face into the water. He really tried hard dunking his head in. He didn't put his hair down into the water, but he did his lips, cheeks, nose and face! It is leaps and bounds ahead of his last lesson on Monday. It's great seeing his confidence grow.

They had a CPR class going on next to the pool (you could see through the windows) and people were doing CPR moves on baby bodies. It brought me right back to seeing George. Even though they were practice dummies, my heart couldn't tell the difference. I hate that we've lost our son. I can't think of anything worse than losing a child. I hope that we never have to deal with anything like that again. I don't know that I can make it through anything else.

I wish you were here, even for an hour.

From: Ross
Date: July 10, 2008 11:24 PM
To: Kristine

I'm sorry you had to relive that at the pool. I wish I could have those five minutes back. I wish I could have been there for him.

I'm glad Ryan did well in swim class. I think as time goes on it won't be a big deal for him to get his face wet. Once he gets that down, he'll be fine.

36

Let Go or Be Dragged

July 2008
Now Zad, Afghanistan
Twentynine Palms, California

Ross was dealing with constant danger, injuries, and death. I was trying to deal with an overabundance of emotions. It was all I could do to hold back the tears as I re-read Ross's email from before he was inserted into Afghanistan.

Living in Twentynine Palms wasn't easy with young kids. Trying to keep the kids cool in the summer usually involved a pool: the place I was more frightened of than anywhere else. Add to that the stresses of war, and the despair I felt from losing George, and it was a fertile petri dish for the breeding of negative thoughts. Some days were worse than others. I had to fight the darkness, and keep it from staying in my mind. I often thought about my husband, and what had transpired to get us where we were. The misery would sometimes eat me alive when I thought about him:

Sometimes I hate you.

You get to drop everything, and I always have to pick up the pieces. If I don't know how, I have to figure it out. I'm the one who's keeping everything together, and I'm exhausted.

I'm so angry with you.

For everything and nothing.

It's your fault George is gone.

If I had been there, this never would have happened.

But being mad at you won't help anything. It's eating me up inside.

The worst part is that you're not even here for me to be able to talk to you about this.

We can't even carry on a telephone conversation because someone is always listening or interrupting.

So I'm left on my own.

I know everyone there made an awful mistake that day.

But you're his dad, and you should have known better.

You know that you failed him, failed me, failed everyone.

Sometimes I'm selfish, and don't give a shit about your feelings.

Sometimes I just want to disappear. But I can't.

*I have responsibilities with our children, and can't find any time to be
    alone, though I need it desperately.*

I can't even ask my parents for help.

My family is a thousand miles away.

*I have amazing women in my life here, but I still feel like I've been
    abandoned in the desert.*

And there's no one home to hear me cry.

The good days found me in a better place. Eventually I came to realize that I had been selfish for focusing solely on my own grief. I'd read Ross' words from when he told me about the day he spoke with the counselor. I had refused to take them in. He *had* been there at the house that day. He was the one who had to pull George from the pool. There wasn't a thing in the world I could project onto him that was worse than the loop of guilt and disappointment that surely echoed in his heart and mind.

Now he was in Afghanistan; he was losing his Marines to war. Each time he wrote a letter to a fallen Marine's parents, it reopened his wounds. He knew what it was like to lose a son.

I had finally gotten to the crucial point: I realized, and I had to accept that losing George was a terrible, awful accident.

I thought about our marriage, about everything Ross and I had faced together in life. I considered the wedding vows we had exchanged in the presence of our friends and family. The pain and anger over losing George was a huge reason for me to rationalize leaving; but in truth I had a million reasons to stay. We had already lost too much. I was determined to hold on to what we had left.

As I began the search for my own happiness, I knew there had to be changes. Trina's dismissive comment about the date of George's death was the final straw in our relationship. I would no longer communicate with her. The exception would be reaching out to her so that she could meet her granddaughter for the first time.

Trina treated the loss of George as if he was her own son, but she'd met George maybe five times. The things she said to me, the way she described her loss as equal if not greater than mine, drove deeper the wedge between us. My dark days would sometimes be filled with telling her off:

Don't measure your sadness against mine. He was my child.

Yes, I know you loved him and that you lost him as well.

But don't you dare—don't you fucking dare—try to project your scope of grief on me.

You don't know how I feel.

She was the first casualty in my personal campaign to cut all the negative relationships out of my life. I no longer harbored any sympathy or patience for caustic people, for those who complained constantly about nothing at all. I even went as far as to block and unfriend people on social media.

I was a little surprised at how easy it was.

I had to make peace with the imperfections of others and let go of chaos.

The Marine Corps wasn't going to change, so I decided I would see myself like water: I would move with the ebb and flow of our lifestyle. I would choose to surround myself with positive and inspirational people.

I leaned in, I embraced my military community in a way I never had before.

From that point on, I chose to celebrate accomplishments and small moments. I looked for what really mattered in life.

I made a promise to myself: I wouldn't let what Ross and I had been through destroy everything we had together.

I began to choose to be happy.

As I finished the letter to Strickland's family and added it to the small pile of casualty reports, my determination to destroy the small enemy contingent in Now Zad grew.

We were going back to finish our mission: destroy the OP tree. After a quick vehicle movement up a more direct route to the enemy position, RPGs and small arms fire rained down on us. Explosions boomed on all sides; shrapnel from mortar rounds pelted our truck. We called in our own mortars with pre-planned target solutions.

We drove the ACE tractor out in the open, shovel down, breaking through the handful of compounds in the field. We drove straight through. It was like breaking up a hornet's nest: we got into a big firefight.

After that the onslaught of enemy fire waned, and we cleared our way up to the tree. We had finally gained our objective: the enemy OP. They'd built ladders and platforms on the thickest branches, interwoven with reeds to better camouflage everything. We found water bottles littered all around. We reasoned that they kept men in the tree on rotation all the time.

Giving the order for the engineers to plant explosives and blow up that tree offered at least some catharsis. We had imposed our will on the enemy. We'd sent them running for cover.

I put my earlier failure behind me, and started planning the next operation.

There were periods of time we had British artillery support from our FOB, but eventually they were reassigned. We asked for periodic support from the MEU when we conducted large-scale operations, but those requests were either ignored or denied; I'm not sure which. Whatever the case, several of our battalion officers co-located with the MEU noticed that their artillery and light armored vehicles were just sitting there collecting dust. These officers also had incidental conversations with the MEU officers, who stated they were bored; that they weren't actively engaged in anything. We could have used the help; I don't know why we didn't get it.

Routine could be a Marine's best friend. When it came to things like physical training and weapons maintenance it was essential. When it came to food though, routine was one of the things that could make a deployment feel like it was going to last forever. Most of our food came in the form of Unitized Group Rations, UGRs, which the camp cook boils up over huge trays of water. The steam reheats the food until it's ready to eat. We received several boxes of UGRs from Camp Bastion. We had biscuits and gravy for breakfast, and spaghetti and meatballs for dinner pretty much exclusively. We ate these same two meals over and over and over again for months on end. I felt bad for Echo Company. When I checked in with Captain Matt O'Donnell, he told me they had been dealt the Szechuan chicken, which was, in my opinion, one of the worst meals possible. I was thankful for our good meals.

Our lunches were MREs. Any meals that weren't wanted or desired got dumped into the rat-fuck box. I would eat one of those unwanted items most afternoons. I let the guys have the good stuff.

Mail call was the best because we'd get beef jerky and canned fruit. We loved the bagged packages of tuna and chicken; they were lifesavers. Occasionally, we'd even get fresh fruit from Bastion. Usually when Captain Van Obsorne would come, he would bring boxes of fruit for us. It was a nice treat.

When Marines needed to piss, we had installed giant PVC pipes, about six inches in diameter, that were dug into a berm. There were four of those. When Marines needed to take a dump, they'd walk over to the latrine area. Originally, the UN had built some stalls for who-knows-what, having never finished them. We placed our portable toilets in that area. Marines would clamp the open end of their Wag Bags under the toilet lid. Wag Bags were bags filled with powder to absorb moisture. Each person would bring their own bag with them, and when they'd finished, they'd throw it into the burn pile. The pile would be burned at the end of each day.

When we ran out of Wag Bags, there were fifty-five-gallon drums cut in half. Two plywood stalls, similar-looking to an old outhouse, were built, and the half drums were placed beneath, to catch the waste. Marines would take dumps in the same container, one after the other, then when they were full, someone would pour diesel on the contents, stir, and drop in a match.

Our water came from the Brits. They had a chlorine treatment system with which they pumped in—and treated—well water. They filled up a 550-gallon water tank daily, or every other day, for us. Usually on days when we conducted large operations, we'd run out of water because we came back to base filthy. As a result, we showered and shaved every other day, in order to conserve water. We didn't want to unduly burden the Brits with helping to sustain us.

Some of my younger guys got in pretty good with the Brits, and were allowed to use their shower facilities, which were nice. We built our shower areas from HESCO barriers so that Marines could hang their five-gallon solar shower bag up as they washed. The floor was a wood pallet, and there was no real privacy.

I'd grab one of the big plastic laundry bowls and shower with my PT gear in the bottom of the bowl. As the water ran off of me in the shower, it would catch in the bowl, and I would lightly stomp on the clothes. This acted like the agitator in a washing machine. When I was done, I'd hand-rinse my clothes with any water remaining.

We engaged the enemy in firefights almost daily. Lt Karell asked if he could create a mission to get us into one of the outlying compounds. We had previously set up some ambushes there. I gave him the go-ahead to plan it. The night before his operation, I took with me a small element of Marines so that I could observe the op from the top of a large nearby hill. We dubbed it Mount Olympus because it was from there that our fire support team "cast down thunderbolts" onto the Taliban.

It took us an hour and a half to get to the top of the mountain, but once we were there we had a commanding view of the whole valley. The mountain provided the perfect vantage point for us to observe enemy movements, as well as possible IED planting activities.

The next morning, 3rd Platoon moved out. Along the way, one of our seven-tons hit an IED, which blew up the tire and part of the engine. No one was seriously hurt.

When they reached the compound, our Marines dismounted and started clearing buildings. As they moved, mortar rounds began exploding around them. A mortar round landed one hundred fifty meters from LCpl Ivan Wilson, a SAW gunner. He ran to the nearest wall for cover, inadvertently setting off an IED. It blew him nearly in half.

The engineers immediately began sweeping a path towards him because they knew that the enemy never laid just one IED; they almost always deployed them in clusters.

One of our corpsmen, Doc Ameen, grew impatient because

Wilson was so badly wounded. The moment he stepped out from behind the engineer to run to him, he stepped on another IED. One of his legs was blown off, and the other one was severely injured.

The other corpsman, who happened to be directly behind Ameen, was knocked unconscious from the blast. When he came to, he stood up and began to wander around in a daze. Everyone was yelling at him to stop moving. The Estonians raced their vehicle towards the wounded with Doc Hancock inside to help.

I was still on Mount Olympus, listening to the play-by-play over the radio. I felt helpless watching everything from atop the mountain.

The MEDEVAC helicopters took the wounded back to Bastion. We'd trained and prepared with every kind of weapon and planned for every scenario we could imagine, but the daily dose of amputees and IEDs inflicted a festering wound to our morale.

Despite our telling US Army higher headquarters on numerous occasions that Now Zad was a ghost town filled with Taliban insurgents, they continued to push their agenda for us to train Afghan police, and patrol there.

Eventually the Task Force Helmand Brigadier General came to visit. When he arrived and saw it for himself, he understood why we couldn't do what we'd been tasked with. He finally saw that Now Zad needed infantrymen, not policemen.

The general asked me for my thoughts on the enemy. I told him about the enemy's forward line of troops, stretching from the Green Zone (which paralleled the Wadi) all the way to Pakistani Alley—I believed it was a line of communications for weapons and more. Headquarters agreed that it needed to be cleared.

The Taliban was perfectly content keeping the international troops contained in our little area, and would have never attacked us. But we had been pushing them out, testing their lines, and taking terrain from them since our arrival.

Intel reports indicated that the Taliban was shifting more fighters to Now Zad to protect whatever it was they felt needed protection. While we were not directly training police, we took consolation in the fact that we were helping take pressure off places like Musa Qala, Sangin, and Gereshk.

From: Kristine
Date: July 22, 2008 9:38 PM
To: Ross

> I got a 4D ultrasound tonight; they burned a DVD so I can mail it
> to you. I think she looks a lot like George—she has a lot of devel-
> opment yet to do, but she looks like she has a rounder head, like
> George did. We will see. In some of the pictures she looks like an
> alien, depending on the angle. I'll email you the pics when I get a
> chance, and mail you the video with some more packages when I
> get back to California.

From: Ross
Date: July, 23, 2008 3:48 PM
To: Kristine

> I look forward to those ultrasound pictures of Grace. I was really
> impressed with how articulate Ryan is; he's really come a long
> way in a short time. I love you, babe. I really miss you, and can't
> wait to see you again.

> I think when we get back to Bastion the question will come up
> about who's going to do what on the next deployment. I guess
> the CO is out of here in April, which isn't much time for the next
> battalion commander, if we're leaving in September. It sucks that
> I'll miss a whole round of birthdays again.

> I'm going to forward some pictures. They aren't the best, but I
> can't give away intel on our enclosure. I'm going to have to just
> walk around with our camera guy. He's a really good guy; he's on
> every patrol.

From: Kristine
Date: July 27, 2008 8:39 PM
To: Ross

> We're back in Twentynine Palms. Ryan had his first day of Level
> 4 preschool today. They went to the park, pool, and back to the
> school. They're only doing curriculum Wednesday thru Friday,
> but I don't care. At least it gives him a chance to interact socially
> with other kids his own age, and that's really healthy. I think the

regular school session starts August 23rd, or somewhere around there. At least I can start carpooling with Amy Hall again.

It's crazy that I only have eight weeks left! I'm trying to get the house completely organized; it's amazing that it hasn't been taken care of yet and we've been here since January. When I think about it though, I was pregnant when we moved in, so what can I really expect?

From: Ross
Date: July 30, 2008 12:49 AM
To: Kristine

Sounds like I planned this deployment well, with you knocking out all these chores while I'm gone. I guess I'd rather be shot at . . . kidding.

I hit up the CO about the extension. Still no word.

From: Kristine
Date: July 29, 2008 6:19 PM
To: Ross

You always seem to manage to get out of all the work at home. Well, I guess you'll have time to make up for it when you retire from the Corps. I'll expect a lot more out of you then! :) But then of course the kids will be easy, and will be able to follow directions . . .

Showing the distance from our home to where Daddy is in Afghanistan

I'd like to find another place for Ryan to do gymnastics. The current company is no longer an option because of gas prices. The instructors have stopped coming up to Twentynine Palms, which means I'd have to drive him 80 minutes to Palm Springs.

I did sign him up for Start Smart Soccer. I'm going to try to hire Hannah or Jacob to sit in for me. I really don't want to be chasing a ball around two weeks before the baby is due. Maybe when my mom comes, she can step in.

I can't believe they still haven't decided anything on the extension. Seems hard to believe they haven't picked a unit by now.

From: Kristine
Date: July 30, 2008 9:25 PM
To: Ross

I just got unofficial word that a message came down from the Marine Corps saying you're getting extended as of right now. Nothing official on who's replacing you. That sucks, but again, I was expecting it. Hopefully you can transfer out of your AO [Area of Operations] sooner than later. I'd feel better having you on a base somewhere with big ol' walls.

Our next mission was to take a series of compounds that had been identified as Taliban headquarters.

It was a sprawling complex with a thick outer wall. Our engineers placed a charge, and breached an opening. When we arrived at the target buildings, we began a methodical search of the area. There were stockpiles of wires, batteries, plywood pressure plates, and aluminum powder; everything you needed to make an IED. We also found cases of AK-47 ammunition, journals, and other writings that appeared to be rosters.

I moved around, checking on my Marines, including one of the fireteams who'd taken up position on a roof inside the compound. I took a knee next to one of the SAW gunners to ask how he was doing on water and ammo. An insurgent walked out from an open gate right in front of us, with a rifle slung over his shoulder—he couldn't have been more than ten meters away.

I was doing my best to whisper to my guys, and point out the enemy walking around all nonchalant like he didn't have a care in the world. Karell threw a grenade in the direction he was heading, but missed him by a few meters. As we were preparing to climb down and pursue, the same guy went by going the other direction, his rifle still hung over his shoulder like he was just out for a stroll. This time the entire fireteam lit him up.

We descended the roof to the narrow alley. It led from a gate up to another alley. We wanted to check the enemy body for intel, and grab his rifle. To have walked in like nothing was wrong—all I could think of was that he must have been high as a kite. We found syringes lying around throughout the compound. We figured that they were shooting either adrenaline or heroine.

We cleared the compound, and returned back to friendly lines. We confiscated a small cache of IED material, and we took one prisoner. Added to the fact that we'd suffered no casualties or fatalities, I chalked it up as a good day.

From: Kristine
Date: July 31, 2008 10:28 PM
To: Ross

> Ryan and I made several batches of cookies and treats this afternoon for the 11 Marines and corpsman warriors at Balboa from 2/7. Zazu has figured out how to get food off the counter by standing on her hind legs (I'm guessing) and clawing for stuff. She ate one of the caramel corn bags while we were at dinner. I found the remnants of the bag on the floor. That dog!

> Your Dad called today, and gave me an update with Charlotte. The cancer has spread to her bones, but we don't officially know what that means yet. They haven't met with the oncologist. Seems if it's spreading that fast, it can't be good. You might want to send him an email if you get a chance.

From: Ross
Date: August 4, 2008 1:42 PM
To: Kristine

> Thanks for sending that stuff to the Marines, they're real heroes, and they deserve a lot more. I'm really glad you did that.

It doesn't sound very promising for Charlotte. I have a feeling that this is going to be ugly. I wonder what Dad is going to do once she passes? I'll shoot him an email and see what's going on.

Thanks for the picture. Ryan is such a ham. I miss him a lot.

I miss you both so much. Tell Ryan that I love him, and please know that you are the most important—and best—thing that has ever happened to me.

We were out on one of our daily patrols when we got into heavier contact than I considered to be normal. We spotted a couple of locals gathering firewood at one of the orchards near the city. We were fairly close to them when the enemy opened up on us. We shouted to the locals to get into our trucks so that we could protect them; take them to a safe area.

We called in an air strike. A British Harrier came in and dropped a bomb, but there was a problem: it didn't explode. Neither did it bury itself. That meant there was now a 1,000-pound military grade high explosive device sitting on the enemy's front doorstep.

I thought back to Iraq, when a vehicle-borne IED ran into our seven-ton, killing seven of our Marines in the closing days of the Fallujah deployment.

We needed to address this bomb.

We rotated patrols to keep the impact area secure throughout the night. Dropping another bomb might have been possible, but it would make it extremely difficult to ascertain whether or not the original bomb had actually been detonated. In the end, we decided to take care of it ourselves.

The following morning we moved out in force to destroy the unexploded bomb. Third Platoon had the job of isolating the enemy on either side of the explosive so that we could assess what we were going to do to reduce this ordnance.

We began to take a significant amount of fire almost immediately, from what we estimated to be an eight-to-ten-man enemy group with medium machine guns, RPGs, and light mortars. My guess is they had plans for the bomb, and they had their guys watching it as well. Karell came over the radio to report one of his Marines was shot in the throat, adding, "Fox Six, what is the plan from here?"

Fox Six was me, but I didn't respond. I didn't have an answer for him.

The biggest problem was that we still didn't know exactly where the bomb was, though I'd been led to believe that the squad who'd witnessed the bomb bounce knew its location. Had I known we didn't know the bomb's precise location, I would have planned our maneuvers differently.

I didn't have an answer for Karell. We needed to find the bomb before more of my guys got hurt. I did the only thing I could think of—I took off running across the open field towards the area where we thought the bomb was.

SSgt Solum, the platoon sergeant for Sniper Platoon, plus Guthrie and another sniper, followed after me. I'd covered about two hundred meters when I heard SSgt West come on the radio. "Who the fuck is that? Who is the dumbass running through the field?"

SSgt Buegel got on the radio and told him, "It's the CO!"

West's response called for action. "Start shifting vehicles off to the right. Go give the CO some cover."

At the same time, my gunner SSgt Buegel made his way into the open using our vehicle, waving at me from the turret. Just as I spotted the bomb, Buegel announced over the radio that he could see it as well.

The vehicle couldn't make it all the way up there, so Buegel hopped out and joined us on foot. We split up so that two of us were on either side of the bomb. It had come to rest about 15 meters from the wall. We could see the enemy, not more than 30 meters away, firing through their mouse holes at us.

EOD finally caught up with us. SSgt Stan and Sgt Zambon low-crawled up to the ordnance. We laid down suppression fire towards the mouse holes that were directly in front of the bomb. EOD placed explosives on the unexploded bomb, then primed a non-electric fuse. We had 20 minutes until detonation.

Doc Hancock looked after Nickells, the Marine who'd been shot in the neck, while we waited on the MEDEVAC helicopter.

EOD directed us to move farther back because the bomb was so large. Just before we rounded ANP Hill, SSgt Stan got on the radio, and started the countdown. Right on his mark, the bomb detonated.

The explosion was massive. It was our second successful mission with no fatalities. We then set our focus on planning for a platoon ambush farther north.

We stepped off at 0400 to execute Karell's ambush plan. SSgt Buegel and I accompanied the dismounted elements of 3rd Platoon in one of the blocking positions along the route.

West led a mounted squad into a blocking position to the west. Once the dismounted elements were in place, it was time to call in the mounted elements that would draw the enemy out.

As soon as the vehicles rolled up, they began taking fire. One of the MRAPs reached my position, and we saw muzzle flashes from the mouse holes to the east. Karell anticipated the enemy's reactions to a T. His dismounted elements engaged the insurgent reinforcements and moved to occupy their firing positions, pressing the attack forward. Karell called for machine gun support from one of the mounted elements.

The lead MRAP drove up to about ten meters behind me, slightly to the left. Suddenly a barrage of machine gun fire raked the vehicle, and an RPG broke through the turret's Plexiglas, hitting LCpl Longfellow. We all thought he was dead. SSgt Buegel and Cpl Watson ran over to assist the Marines inside the MRAP.

The driver, LCpl Cookson, was unconscious from the blast, as was Sgt Escobar the squad leader. A CASEVAC vehicle was immediately on scene to take Longfellow away. I was in contact with the fire support team, FST, calling for mortars, redirecting them to our flank.

Longfellow's flak jacket and throat protection had saved his life. He was unconscious, bleeding from a lot of shrapnel to his face and arms, but he would live. Cookson and Espinosa eventually regained consciousness inside the vehicle. SSgt Buegel climbed into the damaged turret, manning the .50 cal and firing at the enemy. Cookson got back into the driver's seat, and drove towards the rest of the squad to support the continuing movement north.

The CASEVAC team made their way to the MRAP to recover Longfellow. As they pulled away, they hit an IED. Doc Hancock was tending to Longfellow inside the vehicle when it hit; the blast forced them forward into the wall of the vehicle. Doc smashed his head and went unconscious for a bit; fortunately he had his helmet on. When he woke up, he continued to stabilize Longfellow while they waited for a seven-ton to pull them out.

Stan's fireteam and I stayed, in order to suppress the enemy. West was on the left flank in the middle of the firefight, along with nine other Marines.

LCpl Matibag took a shot in the abdomen. West quickly brought Matibag to the drop-off casualty collection point so that First Sergeant and Doc Hancock could assist with his injuries. West then made his way to my location with a 60mm mortar. He didn't have a mortarman with him, so I loaded rounds in the tube for him, calling into action what mortarman training I had received while I had been an enlisted infantryman.

We eventually ran out of mortar rounds. Earlier, West had encountered problems with his Mk-19 (fully automatic 40mm grenade launcher), so he moved back to retrieve a working weapon.

Karell continued to press the attack, forcing the Taliban to abandon their fighting positions. They fell back to a small building for cover.

Meanwhile, a British AH-64 Apache had escorted the helicopter that came to pick up Matibag and Longfellow. Our forward air controller linked up with the Apache and directed it to where Karell was engaged.

Once the pilot confirmed the locations of friendly units, he opened up his 30mm cannon against the fleeing Taliban, killing a couple of them. Then he launched a Hellfire missile into the small building that was providing them cover. Those who were left alive came running out of the half-destroyed building. The Apache finished them off with another burst from the 30mm cannon.

We began making our way back, when suddenly West's vehicle hit a huge IED. It knocked me to the ground, along with everyone else within 15 yards. West was thrown from the vehicle. On the way out, he hit the door, snapping his femur—his foot was literally next to his ear.

Matibag and Longfellow would recover fairly quickly. SSgt West would need over forty surgeries and seven years to make a full recovery.

37

Every Picture Tells a Story

August 2008
Now Zad, Afghanistan
Twentynine Palms, California

tCol Ollie North, USMC Ret., and his cameraman arrived to report live from Afghanistan and film a portion of *War Stories,* a military history show.

LtCol North and my dad had been classmates at the Naval Academy. When he stepped off the seven-ton and we shook hands, I asked him if he recognized my surname.

"Of course I do," he said, "and how is Rick? What's he been doing since I last saw him?"

North and his crew had been cleared to go on patrols with us, and tour the area. I told him we were conducting IED sweeps, and that their time with us might provide for them some insight into what our troops were facing all over Helmand. On average, one in four of our dismounted patrols found an IED.

North rode with me in my vehicle. His crew was able to get some footage of the EOD team in action. He rode along behind a dismounted patrol through the middle of town where we'd had contact with the enemy as well.

North interviewed several of our Marines for the show; he was extremely approachable, and all the Marines loved him. He engaged with them and took the time to ask each of the Marines where they hailed from; he showed genuine interest in their lives and stories.

He spent a few days with us and ate dinner each night with First Sergeant, Commander Hancock, other company leadership in the FOB, and me. It was nice being able to talk to someone who understood our company's situation; he'd had a similar experience in Vietnam. We got into some deep and lengthy conversations about dealing with casualties, keeping the mission first, and how to keep everything in balance.

Ross talks with LtCol Ollie North, Ret., for the show *War Stories*. Photo by Sgt Freddy Cantu

From: Kristine
Date: August 12, 2008 11:55 PM
To: Ross

Last night I saw Mollie Gross perform a stand-up routine (Jon's wife from 2/1). She was very funny, and extremely relatable. She said something like, "Ladies, quit planning back-from-deployment BBQs and tell your husbands to stop, too. No one wants to go to that shit, they just want to stay home and have sex with their wives," which is so true. How many more days until you're home again?

I wish there were more programs for military spouses, especially with all the deployments going on. I'm sure MCCS spent some money bringing Mollie here, but it was so appreciated.

Grace is moving around like crazy. Just watching my belly pop in and out—so freaky that there's a human inside of me. You'd think I'd get used to it by now.

I love you so much, and I think of you all the time. Mostly, I think about what a huge baby I am. Here I am managing to find suffering in air conditioning, being off my feet a lot of the time, and you're stuck in desert heat and dirty conditions and you're getting shot at. And you're not complaining! I can't see why not. I could never do that. I can barely handle being pregnant! :)

From: Ross
Date: August 14, 2008 4:13 PM
To: Kristine

I think I'd rather be shot at than have a baby. No: I know I would.

Ollie went on a patrol with us yesterday. They shot a lot of footage. He said we may be on *Hannity and Colmes,* but I don't know when any of the interview stuff will air. He's an incredible person. He and I had a really long talk last night. He was talking about his grandkids, and how they have a pool. He made the comment, "I should probably get a fence up around it before one of them drowns." I told him not to wait, that as soon as he gets back, he needs to make sure it happens. I told him what had happened to George.

He really wants to get hold of Dad. I've asked him to call him when we get back to the States. We just started talking after chow last night; next thing I know we've been sitting there for three hours.

I didn't realize it, but I don't have anyone to talk to here. You're the only person I share anything with. As I talked with Ollie, I managed to get out a lot of stuff I had been keeping pent up. I felt really good afterword. I miss talking with you.

He's getting ready to celebrate his 40th wedding anniversary in November. That'll be you and me some day. I love you so much, and I miss you terribly.

From: Kristine
Date: August 14, 2008 9:52 AM
To: Ross

Hopefully Ollie will let you know when the interview airs. I don't watch much TV at all.

You know what they say; it's lonely at the top. And you probably can't be candid with everyone; it's not as if they're your peers. But I'm glad you've been able to talk to someone. I'm sure with as many life experiences as Ollie has had, he can understand where you're coming from.

It probably did you a lot of good to talk with him about George. Make sure you tell him to also get a floating pool alarm. They're only a couple of hundred bucks, and it will go off if something heavier than nine pounds falls into the water. Funny how everyone worries about gun safety. A child is a hundred times more likely to drown than to have an accident with a gun.

From: Ross
Date: August 14, 2008 11:04 PM
To: Kristine

It will be 6:30 p.m. on Fox News, *Hannity and Colmes* live. I'll get to say "Hi" to you and Ryan.

The mail came, and still no boxes from you. Gunny Kindrick is waiting on 26 boxes!

Honestly, I didn't think I had the need to talk to someone. I know I didn't have the time. I talk to First Sergeant about stuff from time to time. I'm tired, and I have to get up to do this thing live on TV. I miss you and love you.

From: Kristine
Date: August 14, 2008 10:54 PM
To: Ross

When I picked Ryan up from school today, I told him that you were going to be on the TV. He started crying and said that he only wants to love on you, not see you on TV. He said he just wants to watch TV with you.

You're missing at least four boxes, maybe six, from me. And I'm sure others have sent things, too. It's too bad that there's such a problem with the mail getting stuff to you guys.

By the way, I found this picture from the Combat Camera . . . and this looks like you, but I want you to let me know if it is you. I think it is. Are you sitting in the far right side of the picture?

What do the Afghans wear? Is it obvious when you see Taliban among the villagers?

There was a free concert tonight at Victory Field. As we drove by, we rolled down the window so we could hear the band, but instead we got a big whiff of the poop lake [what everyone in Twentynine Palms lovingly calls lake Bandini, the sewage treatment area]. It was really bad. And I mean bad. All of those poor people standing outside smelling shit all night.

From: Ross
Date: August 15, 2008 1:51 PM
To: Kristine

Yes, that's my bald head in the right-hand corner of the picture.

I tried calling Dad so that Ollie could talk to him as well. I didn't manage to get hold of him.

Afghans wear a Dish Dash, a full-length nightgown-looking thing. They don't wear pants or underwear underneath it; they're naked. They don't stand up to pee, either, they just squat down. All of the men dress the same way. The Taliban don't have a uniform or a particular piece of clothing they wear. You can't tell anyone apart, aside from the way the locals react to their presence.

From: Ross
Date: August 20, 2008 4:08 PM
To: Kristine

Sorry we didn't get to talk longer on the phone. I know you're scared when you think of having another baby. I'm sorry that we're in this situation, and for all the anxiety you are having. I think it's going to be that way for a long time, for both of us. It's scary what happened to George, and it's scary that we're starting over with another life—another child—who needs us to be there for her, and all the time. Ryan I don't worry about so much, because he has developed to the point where he recognizes danger . . . most of the time. George was not. I should have been watching him. I still dream about him. All I can do from now on is protect Grace the way I failed to with George.

From: Kristine
Date: August 22, 2008 10:59 PM
To: Ross

Ryan has been a pain, big time. Talk about trying to assert his independence. It's almost been overwhelming. We went to the Officers' Club today for lunch. I took him to the bathroom to wash his hands before we ate. He wanted to use the boy's bathroom by himself, and I said no, that he had to come in with me. So there was lots of arguing and tears.

We went to wash our hands. I said he could use his own sink. I turned the water on for him. He yelled at me. He wanted to turn the water on. So I turned it off, then he turned it on. I put some soap on the tops of his hands. That was unacceptable. He flipped out and, instead of rinsing it off and starting over again, he wanted to wipe it off on a towel. When I told him no, he said he was going to wipe it on his pants. So I gave in and got him some towels . . . do you get where this is going? It's been like this all day. Everything is a power struggle. I hope tomorrow is a better day.

From: Ross
Date: August 23, 2008 11:54 PM
To: Kristine

You're doing a great job. I can't wait to get home and help you out with the kids.

We had a miracle happen today. A roof collapsed on one of our rooms. One Marine has five broken vertebrae (his spinal cord is fine) and a broken ankle, and another Marine sustained only a broken ankle. I thought for sure we'd be pulling out dead bodies from the wreckage. I'm still amazed that those two injuries were the worst of it.

Another Marine lost a leg yesterday. Damn IEDs. I'm down my age minus two Marines since we deployed [34]. Ten of those were partial deployers. It's too many.

*I*t was another ordinary day in Twentynine Palms. It was hot, I was very pregnant, and we were looking for something to do.

We hit up the base movie theater, perfect for a cheap date with my kiddo, and we were having a good time until I realized I wasn't able to take a full breath. I tried again, leaning back in my chair, but I still couldn't get a full breath. I sat up, and it was easier, but still something was wrong. I ignored it for about 30 minutes but it continued to get worse.

I dropped Ryan off at my friend Nancy's house and made my way to the ER. I was taken in right away. They couldn't figure out exactly what was wrong. My breathing was only affected when I laid down or leaned back. They took x-rays but still didn't have any answers.

They told me I needed to arrange overnight care for Ryan. They were going to send me via ambulance to Balboa hospital, all the way down in San Diego. Thank God for good friends I could lean on to help me out in this situation, plus, as luck would have it, Nancy and I had gone out to dinner the night before, and I had left Ryan's extra seat installed in her car.

Not knowing what was wrong was an unsettling feeling. They strapped me to the gurney, rolled me into the ambulance, then we began the long drive all the way down to Balboa. Talk about uncomfortable: being strapped to a wood pallet for a little over two hours—pregnant and twisting through the canyons—is not what I'd call a good time.

Balboa took me to x-ray and immediately discovered what was wrong: I had viral pneumonia. It was hard to believe, because there were no other symptoms.

The Balboa doctors said that the doctors in Twentynine Palms should have been able to see what was wrong, only they didn't take the x-ray properly, so they had nothing to go on.

I was admitted overnight, and released late the next evening. Since I had been driven to Balboa in an ambulance, I had to find my own way home.

Thankfully, Ross's dad Rick swooped in and drove me home. Once again, I was rescued by family and by my military community.

38

"They Sicken of the Calm, Who Knew the Storm"
(Dorothy Parker)

September 2008
Now Zad, Afghanistan
Twentynine Palms, California

September brought Ramadan, a month-long Islamic holiday. We were strictly forbidden from conducting any offensive operations for its duration.

We still conducted security patrols—both on foot and mounted—and we also began to conduct a census of the surrounding villages. I tasked the platoon commanders with gathering tribal and village information. We needed to learn about the key leaders and issues facing the villagers.

Each time we approached the Afghans, we'd try to do so in as nonthreatening a manner as was possible. I made a point to remove my sunglasses, helmet, and gloves, shaking hands any time I spoke with one of the locals. We'd engage the villagers using our interpreters. Unlike in Iraq, the Afghan villagers never offered us tea or invited us to partake in anything they did.

Eventually, the kids approached us, seemingly out of curiosity. The interpreter would always ask the kids questions because they didn't lie about things, such as the Taliban presence.

We knew that members of the Taliban were living in the villages, but it wasn't always obvious who they were. We'd watch for strange or unusual behavior, then isolate the suspected insurgents and engage them separately. Not that it did us much good; we couldn't detain them because there was never any proof that they were Taliban.

From: Ross
Date: September 5, 2008 12:39 AM
To: Kristine

Maybe it's because Grace is almost here, but it's been a really hard couple of days—not with the enemy, but inside my own head. I've been having a lot of dreams about George; he occupies my thoughts all the time lately. I have flashbacks to the moment I pulled him out of the pool. I'm not sleeping; I've lost my appetite.

I had a dream that you left me because I was a horrible father to him. I'm really hurting. It feels just like it felt during the weeks immediately after he died. I should have been there for him. I don't feel right. I've been trying to have a dialog with Jesus. All I can think of is how I failed George. I'm alone with this over here.

I worry that there won't be anything for me once I get home. I'm so glad I have you and the kids. I don't think I could go on like this, feeling guilty and alone. I have so much regret that I wasn't more patient, that I didn't spend more time with George. It just kills me.

Don't let this scare you, I just re-read it and it sounds alarming. I'm fine and I'm going to do everything I can to get home to you and take care of Grace the way I should have taken care of George.

From: Kristine
Date: September 5, 2008 1:39 PM
To: Ross

I don't know if you are still awake, but I thought I should respond sooner than later if possible. I wish that I could just hold you in my arms. Is there someone you could talk to? Maybe Van or LtCol Hall? Rick's a man of God, and you may find some wisdom from him. Maybe guilt is hindering you from being able to hear God speak clearly. I think anger blocked me from hearing him for a long time. You may not get the clarity that you need until years from now, but it'll be worth it in the end. Just try to be still.

I know it's more difficult for you—you were the one who found

George that day. I don't have those images burned into my mind.
I want you to know that I don't blame you. Did I wish that you
had taken George with you when you set up the Pack 'n Play?
Of course. I wish you would have made Charlotte more aware
and more accountable before you left the room. But I don't
know—and nobody can know—if it would have made a difference
in the long run.

We've both learned a lot from loving and missing our George. All
we can do is take the bad and somehow try to find the positive in
the end.

I know that with Grace it will be a new experience, and you won't
take the time you have with her for granted. I don't think George
holds anything against you, even as he watches over you right
now. The time you did spend with him is still far better than what
some kids experience in a lifetime. George knew nothing but
love. He was loved and he was happy.

It's going to take both of us a lifetime to heal from the experience
of losing him. I know that we will both grow into better parents
because of what happened, and in the long run Ryan and Grace
will be the ones who benefit.

From: Ross
Date: September 6, 2008 2:28 AM
To: Kristine

I don't know how you can't blame me. But I know you don't want
to dwell on that. It feels as if this wound is never going to heal.
Maybe Grace will help, but I just can't get past my failures. I feel
like this is even going to affect my health; my heart feels heavy, it
races whenever I think about that day. It's 0230 and I don't want
to go to sleep because I'm scared to see George in my dreams.

One of our Marines stepped on an IED tonight. There was a
malfunction, and the blast was relatively tiny (a blasting cap
went off, which is like a really big firecracker, and he only hurt
his foot). At worst he'll have a hairline fracture. Talk about lucky.
This same Marine was shot thru both femoral arteries on his last
deployment. God is looking out for him, that's for certain. I'll do

my best to be open to the Lord, but all I feel is guilt right now. I think it'll be better once I get home.

From: Kristine
Date: September 18, 2008 10:12 PM
To: Ross

I've been having contractions steadily throughout the day. They are building up in intensity somewhat. I am not ready; the contractions aren't anywhere near regular or strong enough for me to go in yet. But I called Amy Hall because if they progress throughout the evening, then I'm going to have to drop off Ryan at her house. She has been such a blessing to me this deployment. I don't know what I would have done without her.

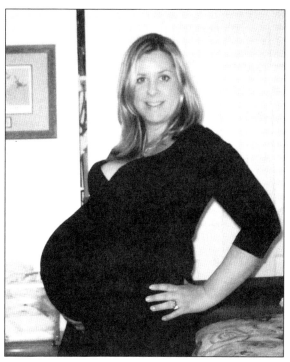

One week away from meeting Grace.

Part Four

Turning the Page

★ ★ ★

"We do not heal the past by dwelling there; We heal the past by living fully in the present"

—*Marianne Williamson*

39

Girl: A Giggle With Glitter on It

★ ★ ★

September 2008
Now Zad, Afghanistan
Twentynine Palms, California

We welcomed our sweet Grace into the world at 8:20 p.m., and my mom cut the umbilical cord in Ross's stead.

I sent out a Red Cross message so that Ross would know we were well, and to call us when he had a moment. He called an hour later, thanks to Amy, who emailed her husband, LtCol Hall, to let Ross know. The minute I heard his voice, the tears started. I held the phone up to Grace's ear so that her daddy could welcome her into the world.

It was in that moment that I realized I needed to stop the what-ifs and start celebrating life again. I wanted to start a new life with our family, live life to the fullest, bring happiness into our lives.

A short 24 hours later I was on my way home, thankful to be away from all the beeping machines and the constant string of interruptions.

From: Kristine
Date: September 28, 2008 11:54 PM
To: Ross

I just wanted to let you know that we're home from the hospital. I've barely had any sleep, so I'm happy to be in my own bed. Just wish you were there to share it with me.

Ryan was happy to meet his new baby sister. He stayed in the room for about three hours. I had Mom bring a DVD that we watched together to help ease any tension he might have had about feeling like he was being replaced, but it didn't seem like he needed it. He instantly loved her.

Here are some new pics. When I was looking at some of these pictures, I couldn't help thinking that she looks exactly like George when he was first born . . . remember his swollen face? Not cute. But she's much better today.

P.S. I sent out a note to both of our families asking people to wait a bit before coming to visit. Hopefully everyone will understand. It's so hard to do all this without you.

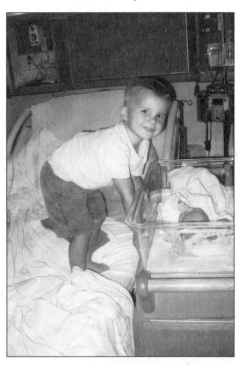

40

Smile Because It Happened

October 2008
Now Zad, Afghanistan
Twentynine Palms, California

*O*n the first day of October, while other moms are starting to think about Halloween costumes, I was thinking about George. It was the first time I would celebrate his birthday without him. And I'd have to do it without Ross at my side.

That day, I had the first of a series of conversations I would have with myself as I tried to figure out how we would continue to celebrate his birthday—his life. I wanted to establish a tradition in which our immediate family could take part, along with us. I didn't want to think about the day he died. I didn't want the memory of it to haunt our family, if that was possible.

Like so many things in life, I knew that the way to get past an obstacle was to battle right through it. So we just lived life and did what we might have done if George had been with us. We made a birthday cake, and I shared stories and memories of George.

I was taken aback by how much Grace looked like him. Maybe God knew that I needed to see a little piece of him in her, even for a fleeting moment. Maybe it was just genetics. But Grace made everything better.

From: Ross
Date: October 1, 2008 11:51 PM
To: Kristine

> It's pretty exciting about the change in schedule. It's never gone this quickly before; I hope it stays this way. I should be out of harm's way on Ryan's B-day. I'll even get to catch three Boise State football games.
>
> Today our little George would have been two. It doesn't seem

that long ago. I miss him so much. I hate that I have what I call
"good dreams" of him, as if he's still alive and we're a normal
family, but then I wake up and he's not.

Sometimes I still can't believe he's gone.

From: Kristine
Date: October 2, 2008 12:21 AM
To: Ross

It is terrible that George is gone. I'd give anything to get him back.
I'm sad that Grace will never know her brother. Ryan won't have
many memories of him, but at least we have a lot of pictures
and videos. I have to believe that he lives on with God—at least
we had him in our lives for a little while, even though now we
can't see him. Hopefully he will live on in part through Ryan and
Grace, throughout their lives and the lives of their children.

I'm not sure when Mom is going to go home. We're just playing
this by ear right now. Grace is lying down on your half of the bed.
Hopefully she'll let me sleep a little tonight.

From: Ross
Date: October 2, 2008 11:07 PM
To: Kristine

What a cute little girl. We do make pretty babies.

I was just thinking about how I'm glad that we don't have
hang-ups about stupid stuff. I think one reason we do so well is
because we have nothing to hide from each other, and one of us
doesn't hesitate to ask the other for whatever we need. I hope
you were able to get some sleep.

From: Ross
Date: October 5, 2008 5:51 PM
To: Kristine

Bad news. The schedule has changed again, this time for the
worse. Looks like we won't be home until after December. I'm
sure it will change again, too; just wait.

One of the companies will be home very early, but it doesn't

look like we'll be home until after Turkey Day. That's just the way
it is, babe. Sorry. I was looking forward to being home for that
weekend.

From: Kristine
Date: October 6, 2008 10:26 PM
To: Ross

Nancy brought us dinner; she's been so amazing. She's bringing
us dinner tomorrow, too because she has to make dinner for
someone else, so she's going to make a big batch of something.

Oh, before I forget to tell you, it seems we've got a bit of a bug
problem in the kitchen. I thought they were beetles at first, but
I found a picture of them online. Turns out they're German
cockroaches. Yuck! I think they're living either in the dishwasher
or behind the stove. They're even in the electrical outlets! I un-
plugged the cell phone charger, and five of them came scurrying
out! I had pest control come and spray before Grace was born,
but now I've got a bunch of bugs on the counters. I need to get
rid of them before they breed and we're infested. I can't believe
it; the house is always clean, especially the kitchen! The sprayer
said he thinks they may have come into the house on cardboard
boxes or paper grocery bags.

It's one more thing on my plate, but I'll get it figured out. I just
wish I wasn't feeling so tired. My energy level is still really low,
but it's much better than when I was pregnant. I played soccer
with Ryan today, so that's a start.

Grace is doing great. She's still feeding every couple of hours
throughout the night, so that breaks into my sleeping pattern.
I'm trying to decide if I want to go to the Christian Women's
Fellowship tomorrow; it's from 9:00 to 11:00 a.m.

You should see our girl; she really is a good mix between George
and Ryan. When I compare photos of the kids, she has more of a
Ryan look to her, only with George's eyes.

She even has your angry scowl. :)

I just went in and checked on Ryan while he was sleeping. I think
this last week, every time I've looked at him, he looks like such a

grown up little boy. He's not the toddler we once knew. You will probably be overwhelmed after having not seen him for so long.

Sucks about the schedule change . . . but hopefully it will change again, only for the better.

Grace is very alert and very happy. It's hard to believe she's almost two weeks old!

From: Ross
Date: October 7, 2008 11:59 AM
To: Kristine

Great, cockroaches. They are so hard to get rid of. And the pesticides they use are really potent. I had them in an apartment in Oceanside, and to get rid of them I had to put the entire kitchen in another room. What a pain. You need to act quickly, before they breed. It doesn't take long.

I think this schedule will be the one we stick with. It keeps us to our targeted boots-on-the-ground date. That's three days after my birthday. By then, 50% of the Task Force plus one Marine need to be back in the States. We would be the 50% plus one. I can't wait to meet our baby girl.

From: Kristine
Date: October 7, 2008 2:20 PM
To: Ross

Your mom wants to visit. I really would have liked it if I could have told her I didn't want her to come, but I'm doing everything in my power to be kind to her. Would I be horrible if I told her not to stay for more than three days?

She sent me an email and said, "I'd fly into Palm Springs and rent a car, if no public transportation is available. But I can't see the value of that expense if I also were required to stay in town. Just let me know your mother's plans, Kristine, and whether you want me visiting at all."

I told her that we would love for her to come and visit, but that we're not making any plans for birthday parties, homecomings, or anything else as a result of your frequent schedule changes.

Plus there's the fact that my mom is staying at the house, so we don't have a guest room for Trina. Funny; she would do *anything* to meet her grandbabies in the past, and would harp on me about it time and time again, but now she can't see the *value* in it if it's not done her way.

From: Ross
Date: October 8, 2008 9:43 PM
To: Kristine

Put Ryan on the floor, and let my mom sleep in his room with him. Do that until your mom leaves; a couple of days won't kill him. I know you're not crazy about it, but if you're a little more liberal now, you won't have to hear about it later. You want help with Ryan; put Trina to work with him. That will keep her busy. All you have to do is ask, "Would you want to take Ryan to the park?" She'll say yes.

My guess is that you'll disagree with everything I just said. And you're not going to like my answers. If that's the case, don't ask me for my input; just do what you want.

I love you.

From: Kristine
Date: October 9, 2008 11:03 AM
To: Ross

If your mom wants to come around Halloween, I'll pay for her hotel room. I'm not inflicting her on anyone else. Love you.

From: Ross
Date: October 9, 2008 2:45 PM
To: Kristine

What about once your mom leaves?

From: Kristine
Date: October 9, 2008 4:56 PM
To: Ross

She can stay at the house once my mom leaves. I just want her to ask for what she wants instead of being passive-aggressive. I already emailed her my response two days ago, saying she was welcome to come. Here's the thing about your mom, too; she could have experienced just about everything with the kids when they were born if she'd only booked a hotel out in town instead of insisting on staying with us. She didn't get her way because she insisted on staying with us right away when I wanted my mom's help. About her staying only three days, I was kidding.

Today I had to run around and get all the paperwork done for Grace. I had to get her enrolled in DEERS [the Defense Enrollment Eligibility Reporting System], then stopped at the law office to get her birth certificate notarized so that I could mail it in. My last stop was IPAC [Installation Personnel Administration Center] to be sure your dependent information got updated. It was 3:40 p.m. by the time I got there (they close at 4:00). I walked up to the Admin Section help desk, and this Marine says to me, "You're wearing flip-flops; you can't be in here, and we can't help you." I was dressed in dark blue jeans and a nice shirt, so overall, I looked fine. Any upscale steakhouse wouldn't have turned me away in those clothes.

I asked them if I would be allowed to step outside, give them the paperwork, then maybe sign the forms outside. Of course that wouldn't work either because "it takes too long to do that." I told them that you were deployed, and that I'd just had a baby, so could they please work with me? The bureaucracy didn't care. The thing is, they probably just wanted to go home at that point, since it was so close to four o'clock and closing time. It seems they didn't want to have to help me.

On a side note, I wasn't wearing flip-flops, either. I was wearing $60 hiking sandals with three straps across their tops, not crappy shower shoes. And not only that, but I just gave birth: My feet are swollen; they don't fit into my regular shoes.

When I came home, I searched online for two hours for the Twentynine Palms civilian dress code. I couldn't find it. I did find Camp Pendleton's code, though, which states that civilians are authorized to wear flip-flops. There were no signs posted anywhere at IPAC stating their anti-flip-flop policy OR anywhere on the Twentynine Palms website. So I'm pissed. The good news for me is that I'm not going to deal with IPAC anymore. The bad news is that you get to go see them when you get home. Be sure to wear your flip-flops.

It will be great to have you home. I hope you get those other boxes soon. And I remembered that I sent you two boxes from the PX online (shipped 9/16 USPS), and two boxes from me here at home (shipped 9/24 . . . and that's all she wrote, as far as boxes go.

From: Kristine
Date: October 10, 2008 5:12 PM
To: Ross

We had our two-week well-baby checkup today. Grace has gained two pounds since she left the hospital.

Ryan has been great this week! But it's been crazy since the fall preschool session started.

It seems like every time I go, there are issues with kids biting, dirty classrooms, and just general overall chaos. I've stopped in a couple of times, and the student to teacher ratio was down-right illegal. There are always supposed to be two teachers in each classroom. I'm sure it's practically impossible for just one teacher to manage 20 kids on her own. I don't want to have to pull Ryan out because of behavior problems, but that means I'll have to take more time at home to work with him and correct his behavior. It might be more effort than it's worth to keep him there. Especially if they don't have the staff to run things the way they're supposed to.

I've got a KV meeting at 6:00 p.m., so I need to get going. I won't email you tomorrow because the power is going to be out—who knows why, but they're leaving notices on a regular basis telling us there's another outage planned.

From: Kristine
Date: October 12, 2008 12:15 AM
To: Ross

Well, your beautiful daughter is lying in bed next to me. She did pretty well last night. It's amazing to me that she wants to stay awake for a whole hour after eating; it's almost like she read the *Baby Wise* book, and knows what she's supposed to do. Thank goodness though, because once my mom leaves she needs to be sleeping through the night so that I can keep up with both Ryan and her.

Charlotte sent an email out about a Christmas get-together. She didn't say it was to discuss her last wishes, but I'm sure that's what they have in mind. When you get back, if Rick and Charlotte don't come up here, we can always go down to San Diego and see them. Rick asked me if I (or you) wanted anything from the house. I told him it wasn't our place to be considered; it should go to Charlotte's kids. He said that she sees us as her kids too, but really, we're short on the list. I'm not worried about anything. I'd just like to see that your Dad is set up so that he's comfortable.

That's the best thing Rick ever gave us—him marrying Charlotte. I love that we gained such an amazing family.

From: Ross
Date: October 12, 2008 4:59 PM
To: Kristine

I want the same as you for Charlotte and Dad; just to make sure Dad is taken care of. I think he probably likes the idea of having the apartment. If he can keep a dog, that's all he'll care about.

I can't believe how lucky I am to have married you, and how lucky we are to have two healthy children. I'm very excited to see Grace.

I sent an email to IPAC to let them know that what they did to you was not appreciated. I'll try to get clarification on their policy.

From: Kristine
Date: October 13, 2008 10:19 AM
To: Ross

We watched the BSU football game here at home. Last night, Ryan and I hung out and ate snacks, cheering on our Boise State Broncos. Too bad you weren't here to hang out with us. There will be a time for us to hang out as a family, and I'm really looking forward to that.

I haven't heard from anyone else as to whether or not they're coming (including your Mom. It's been about a week). Dad said he'd like to come meet Grace and help Mom drive home, so we'll see him shortly. I'll send an email to follow up.

From: Kristine
Date: October 13, 2008   7:43 PM
To: Extended Family

Hi All,

Since I haven't received a confirmation that any of you will be staying at the house in early November, I just wanted to let you know that my mom and dad booked a flight to come and visit, and stay until Wednesday, November 5. If any of you want to come to visit during that time, you are welcome, but you'll need to stay at a hotel in town.

It looks like Ross won't be home until later in November because the schedules have changed once again. As a result, I've had to push the family visitation window to come to the house to November 20.

41

Grab a Straw—Because You Suck

October 2008
Now Zad, Afghanistan
Twentynine Palms, California

*T*he days centering around George's birthday had been an emotional rollercoaster, but it got exponentially worse as the first anniversary of his death approached. I felt raw. I was trying to keep my emails to Ross mostly positive, but there were times that I needed to share what was going on.

I felt entirely alone. I was struggling just to cope with my feelings of loss and grief. I missed Ross. It hurt physically, believe it or not, to be deprived of the ability to hug him, or to feel his arms wrapped around me. I had friends I could talk to, and there was always my mom, but there were no words to explain how I was feeling.

Sometimes I'd just go into the bathroom, shut the door, and cry. Other times grief would sneak up on me while I was out shopping or running errands, triggered by a song or a memory. All I could do was sit in the car or sneak off to a corner to deal with my emotions until the worst of it had passed.

On top of everything else, I was going through the usual post-pregnancy physiological changes, hormones and all. I didn't think it was possible to feel any worse, emotionally or physically.

But I couldn't have been more wrong.

On the eve of George's death, Trina hit a new low, sending me the following email:

> Since you aren't needing any help, you can breathe easy . . . I won't be coming.

I thought *this is going too far.* Her words cut me. I was done. At a time when I most needed to feel secure and supported, she had decided to manipulate my vulnerability, to kick me on the day I was suffering most.

I sat, hands poised over the keyboard, ready to unleash a torrent of emotion. I wanted to throw every manipulative, passive-aggressive, self-centered thing she had ever done or ever said to me right back in her face. I wanted her to feel what it was like to be on the receiving end, wanted her to feel just a single, solitary ounce of the pain she'd caused me to suffer.

But as I calmed myself, I knew no matter what I said it would only be lost in her narrow and skewed world. She would find a way to do what she always did; she would make me out to be the bad guy. In the midst of my grief and anger, my only option became abundantly clear. The lingering threads of connection between us had to be cut. I was done.

I closed my email and sat for a moment, solidifying my resolve. I decided I would no longer communicate with her in any way until Ross came home, until we could get professional counseling. And even then—I promised myself—I would never let my guard down against her particular kind of warfare. She used her words and wickedly timed passive-aggressive interpersonal communication as weapons. Her lack of consideration and her failure to understand how negatively her actions affected others were too destructive.

From: Kristine
Date: October 20, 2008 10:29 PM
To: Trina

> This response is completely unwarranted. I hope you're happy to have caused yet more hurt and emotional pain to an already overburdened person who is grieving the loss of her son, as well as missing her husband terribly. Your timing is perfect, if that was what you were aiming for.

> Spread your misery elsewhere; I'm done. You can correspond with Ross from now on.

From: Kristine
Date: October 20, 2008 10:41 PM
To: Ross

> I emailed your mom last night. I couldn't even sleep, I was fuming

so badly about how she's always saying terrible shit to me while I am the one who sits and suffers. I have endured years and years of her attempts to control, manipulate, and guilt us into doing everything her way.

She could have waited to deliver the email to me, but no. Instead, she didn't care to consider the emotions I'm dealing with in regard to George. Since you're not here to talk to, we can't work through any of this together.

She's incapable of putting herself in anyone else's shoes. She doesn't understand that I don't need her help. And, since the way she does things isn't the way I do things, I prefer to just do them myself (or ask for my mom's help). My mom actually asks and listens to how she can best help me, instead of bulldozing me or arbitrarily rearranging my kitchen.

I know that crossing the Rubicon like this makes things more difficult for everyone, but I refuse to take her abuse anymore. How you want to handle this is up to you. Her comment about George this summer was completely inappropriate. I should have stood up for myself then; I should have grabbed Ryan and walked out the door immediately. I'm angry at myself that I did not. It's healthier to my own sanity if I cut her out of my life.

From: Ross
Date: October 21, 2008 4:09 PM
To: Kristine

I'm at a loss about my mom. I wish I knew what to say. I can tell you now how our conversation is going to go when I mention her email. She'll say that she was innocently responding to the schedule change, that she didn't mean anything by it. I think in some ways, she overthinks so much that it becomes different in her mind. What bugs me is that when I'm visiting, she'll always says, "I wish Kristine were here." Yet she resents you for not bending to her will. Frank and I are the only ones she allows to do that—to get away with refusing to allow her to run the show. Since the guilt trips no longer work on me, she really no longer has any effective manipulation techniques.

I love my mom. She's caring and loving (admittedly this is

conditional for some). But she is affected by something; whether it's innate or environmental, I don't know. She will never be able to see why she can't be allowed to get everything she wants in every situation. She's not rational all the time.

You were right to finally tell her off. Her comments were almost unbelievably ill-timed and inappropriate. I won't ask you to spend any extra time than expected at family functions like holidays, kids' events, and the like. I mean, no dinners or anything else casual. I give up on you two having a cordial or even a functional relationship. She made her bed.

I'm sorry you have to go through all this about my mom. I wish it were different. I wish it weren't exacerbated by George's passing. I miss him so much.

We were preparing for another attack. Both sniper teams were sent out with an engineer armed with a metal detector to sweep in front of them. Our mission was to clear Pakistani Alley. To mitigate risk, we devised some very noisy patrols in the opposite direction to draw the enemy's attention away from our sniper teams' movements towards the real objective. Fortunately, these two teams were competent and very mature; they had my full confidence to accomplish this difficult task.

The snipers set in for the night. Even though they had my full trust, it was still a little unnerving to have them that far away: it would have taken us a while to get them support if they needed it.

The next morning, we headed around to the western side of Now Zad, making it look like we were then going to head north towards another village that was well beyond our targeted objective. Just as we were starting to hear enemy chatter on the radios—them trying to predict where we were going—we made a hard right turn towards Pakistani Alley.

During this time, our snipers observed the enemy from six hundred meters away. The Taliban were talking on radios. One was holding an RPG over his shoulder.

We continued our forward progress. Two more fighters with

rifles joined the insurgent with the RPG on the roof, watching our slow-moving vehicles meander in the open desert to the north of them.

We had aircraft on-station. Our snipers relayed the enemy target to our forward air controller Capt Jordan. In short order, one of the aircraft dropped a bomb on the building and killed them.

We eventually circled around behind the northernmost part of Pakistani Alley. The local Afghans started quickly making their way out of the area; it was as if they sensed what was coming. We drove right past our objective in order to deceive them, while the Estonians set up their mortars and a casualty collection point. We circled back around.

The moment we cleared the first compound, we began taking fire. We made our way to an alley that we had intended on driving through, but it was too narrow for our Humvees. Unfortunately, the intel images caught by our Scan Eagle had shown what we thought was a tractor driving down the alley, but now looking at the space in person, it had been most likely a motorcycle with bushels tied to it.

We amended our plans, sending the Humvees around another way.

We resumed our assault on foot. The enemy began to fall back as we made our way towards them. We were clearing buildings, and bounding. We discovered IED-making material, ammunition, and small bedding areas where insurgents had slept on the floor. There was literally nothing else over here; it was a whole row of housing completely abandoned.

At one point the insurgents were hitting us with 60mm mortars. One landed on the hood of a Humvee, and a combat replacement gunner took shrapnel to the neck, but it wasn't life threatening.

We intercepted some Taliban chatter. One of them said, "If they take 15 more steps, we have a surprise for them." We held our positions to orient where everyone was. We weren't certain who the Taliban were referring to because we were spread across a hundred meters through rows of buildings.

We had a B-1 Bomber on station. The plan was for our guys above to hit the compounds all around us. It took some time to get the GPS coordinates delivered. The B-1 could drop a dozen bombs, nearly simultaneously, on all the correct targets.

Now it was a waiting game. Everyone was quiet, holding in place. Suddenly, two insurgents came running out into the open, firing on us in the alley. A hail of fire rained down on them. One of the Taliban killed was around 5'6" and overweight. We rarely saw fat men in Afghanistan. His condition likely meant that he was a prominent leader. Since he was well fed, he was probably also well paid. I stood over him as a Marine searched him, figuring this dead fat guy was my Taliban counterpart—their commander. We found a regular cell phone, a satellite phone, and an ICOM radio—for local comms.

During our push, we also retrieved a camcorder. We checked the tape: they had captured video of our Cobras flying overhead as we attacked. Our intel guys would get more good information from this device.

Finally the B-1 was ready to deliver the requested ordnance. We conducted a thorough accountability, then moved back to safe areas. This was going to be a massive strike. After they dropped the bombs, we restarted our assault.

We continued clearing buildings. We saw about eight insurgents firing in retreat; one of our squads could see them. Another squad was engaged with insurgents on the other side, but because we were closer, we shot them and watched them drop.

Photo by Sgt. Freddy Cantu

This attack had taken literally all day. While we were still on enemy ground, we took the opportunity to register targets for our mortars so that we could hit them exactly where we wanted, in future attacks. The data would stay on the gun, so it would always be accurate. One squad was still on Mount Olympus, watching for enemy troop movement and calling for fire.

Photo by Sgt. Freddy Cantu

Finally we withdrew, blowing up another dozen hardened positions on our way out. We would have blown up more, but we were running low on demolitions for the destruction of bunkers. As we moved back, we met up with the Estonians at their blocking position. They had gone into the Wadi to look for routes into the mountain range that formed the eastern boundary of the Now Zad valley, checking to see if a more direct route existed to Musa Qala through the ridge. While the Estonians were there, they took 107mm rocket fire, but fortunately they sustained no damage, and zero casualties.

While we were making our way back to the FOB, the mobile trauma bay seven-ton at the rear of our convoy hit an IED, blowing a tire. I took my own vehicle back in order to provide support while everyone else continued on to the FOB. We waited for another seven-ton to come back and tow this damaged one.

During that time, the insurgents came back to reoccupy the positions we had just cleared and registered on our mortars. Marines on Mount Olympus called for fire, resulting in several enemy casualties. In the end, our operation dropped the most bombs in all of Afghanistan that day.

From: Kristine
Date: October 27, 2008 11:37 PM
To: Ross

Ryan mentioned today that his daddy was coming home after his birthday. He said, "My daddy sure is taking a long time to come home." It was cute/sad at the same time. We talked about how you were helping all of the other kids who had to live near the bad guys.

Do you have a date yet when you'll be back in Bastion? Can you tell me in a coded way? I'm just wondering.

Here are some more pictures. Ryan took the one of me and my mom today. He's getting to be quite the photographer! He's really good at using the camera.

In other news, I've become addicted to shopping on Amazon. Driving 30 minutes each way has become a waste of time and fuel just to get supplies. The closest Wal-Mart and the base don't have everything I need, anyway. I order everything I can from Amazon. The result is that we're all getting to know the UPS guy very well around here (here's where you can insert the inappropriate comment about spouses and the UPS driver, heh).

Mom and I ran some errands today, and we came back to a mess. Zazu chewed open a box of protein powder that was sealed inside of another box! In Mom's defense, she didn't think Zazu could get to it, but come on, she still hasn't figured out that she can't leave anything edible in her room unless she's going to close the door. Another huge mess to clean up. I had to steam-clean the carpet in several rooms. For the record, I'm so over this deployment.

From: Kristine
Date: November 5, 2008 10:47 PM
To: Ross

Can you believe our little boy is four years old? Crazy! What's even harder to believe, for me, is that I have been steadily making and nursing babies for the past 5 years! It'll be seven straight years and finally, I'll have my body back to myself.

Your Mom hasn't sent Ryan a birthday card, made a phone call, sent him a package, or anything. Your mom did email me a lengthy response to my talking-to, which was to be expected. I'm not planning on emailing her back because I've asked her to correspond through you for all her needs and questions. I forwarded it to you, and I blocked her email address from my account.

I know it's been rough lately. Know that I love you.

From: Kristine
Date: November 13, 2008 11:08 PM
To: Ross

Amy Hall and I just put in our two weeks' notice at the preschool. Things are out of control there. They just mailed a letter to all the parents saying, "Whoops, we hired a pedophile but no worries because he no longer works here."

Amy and I have been talking with Beth Vincent about starting our own home school co-op, and we're going to ask Erika Cuevas if she wants to get involved too, since we all have four-year-olds; two boys and two girls. Seems like it would work out, if we each take all of the kids one day per week. Plus it would consist entirely of 2/7 Marines' kids, so that is awesome in and of itself.

We'd all get together and work up the weekly lesson plans, and I could teach a bit of French and music here at the house for the kids . . . so they're getting something different than they're getting at the school. Overall, their time spent learning in the home would be about three times more than what they're getting currently, plus it would be free. We're excited about it.

From: Kristine
Date: November 18, 2008 12:04 AM
To: Ross

I'm getting so excited! Probably not as excited as you are to meet your sweet Grace, but still, very excited. It will be great to have you home. I'm missing you something fierce. If you get information on any Fox Company flights, can you please let me know so that I can pass it on, through the KV network?

I went to the reunion brief tonight. It was a comedy of errors. Because I went to the hospital today, I purposely didn't put a onesie on Grace because of all the changing and undressing.

Big mistake. So while I'm hanging out with her at the meeting, she had a ginormous poop. It went out of her diaper and up her back—about the size of a Post-it note. And it stunk really badly. So I took her out and changed her diaper, which was of course the last diaper I had with me. I was hoping she wouldn't need to go again.

She seemed content. I wrapped her in a blanket from the car, and put a hat on her to keep her warm. As the MCCS reps were talking, I was holding her, at which point she began farting really loudly. She was doing it over and over again; it echoed in the church. We were all busting up in our seats: Amy, Laure, Beth, Nancy. After a bit she wanted to eat, so I fed her. Of course, I had no burp cloth with me. So I was using my breastfeeding cover sheet, which isn't really thick. Yeah, she soaked right through that.

Then Sue asked the KVs to stand up to be recognized. I stood, and while I was burping her, she turned her head and puked down the front of my shirt, all over my bra and boobs. I guess she got even with me for taking her to get shots today. Touché little one, touché.

From: Ross
Date: November 18, 2008 7:55 PM
To: Kristine

Our flight number is the same number of kids that your parents had. I will let you know times and dates when I get them; they haven't told us anything yet. I'm not sure of the timeline, but I'm hearing we'll leave theater in the early morning, four days after my birthday.

From: Kristine
Date: November 21, 2008 9:05 AM
To: Ross

So it totally slipped my mind that you're a day ahead of us! Woo-hoo! Let me know when you make it back to Bastion.

Ryan didn't want to go to bed last night. He was up till 10:00 p.m. He finds every excuse to come downstairs. One night he didn't want to eat dinner, and when I put him to bed, he said he was hungry. I decided to let him come downstairs to eat. Now that's his new excuse; he wants a box of raisins, a granola bar . . . I have to keep saying no. But it's nice that he's so persistent.

From: Ross
Date: November 24, 2008 10:55 PM
To: Kristine

Okay, I'm back at Bastion. I got back two days ago. We're just doing the out-processing. We sat through a good class on combat stress. I decided to get all the squads together and have them talk through what they saw out there; it's a start. I am making myself available so that the troops can ask me honest questions in an informal setting. Last night was the first session; it went really well. I was able to explain the big picture to the Marines, and I think they went away feeling like what they do matters. At least I hope so.

It's nice being back in the rear, just relaxing and working out. I'll try to get to a phone, but I can't really get on like I used to because everything has been turned over to 3/8. So we have to wait in line to get on the computers. I'll find a phone and try to call tomorrow or tonight. I love you so much, babe, and I can't wait to see you. Give the kids a hug and a kiss.

42

Hey I Just Met You and This is Crazy
But She's My Momma and I'm Your Baby

★ ★ ★

November 2008
Camp Bastion (Leatherneck) Afghanistan
Twentynine Palms, California

Before we began the journey home, both First Sergeant and I talked through what it was going to be like readjusting to home. We encouraged Marines to tell their stories, to talk about things that were bothering them, or things that they were having difficulty processing. I knew this deployment had left its mark; what was worse for many, its true impact wouldn't fully manifest until we were home. In Now Zad alone, battalion documents showed 181 killed, 87,000 pounds of bombs dropped from aircraft, 2,200 mortar rounds expended, and a great number of missiles, rockets, and guns fired from aircraft.

When we reached Manas, the Marines were given authorization to drink, but they were limited by base regulations to a strict two-beer maximum. It was good to relax, without having to worry about anything. It had been months since we'd had that kind of luxury. Along with great chow and cheap (legitimate) massages, our time in Manas offered space for the continuation of reintegration discussions, and some cooling-off time. We even played some dodge ball at the gym, trying to return to a bit of normalcy.

Out of the 175 Fox Company Marines who had deployed, 54 were awarded Purple Hearts. Two men had made the ultimate sacrifice. Some of Fox Company's wounded warriors were with us wives stateside, waiting to welcome their brothers home. In true Fox

Company style, we were the last group of loved ones left on the field waiting for our men. Eventually, even the band went home.

Finally, just after 4:00 a.m., we saw the men marching towards us. I ran over to the fence to watch them make their way to Victory Field. Ross marched at the front, leading his men in our direction. They rounded the corner to walk on to the field. I took Ryan and Grace and positioned us towards the back; I'd attached a bouquet of pink balloons to the stroller so that Ross could easily find us.

After the company was released, he made his way through the crowd. As I made eye contact with him I couldn't help but smile and tear up.

Ryan, in his pajamas, ran up to greet his dad, immediately breaking down into sobs. "I miss-ted you, daddy."

Ross was crying, too.

Photos were snapped as tears flowed freely. We were just happy to have our own personal hero home again.

I gave him a quick kiss hello. I didn't want him to wait a minute longer to hold his little girl. He held her close and kissed her gently.

We were a family again.

I indulged in a few more moments with Ross, then his Marines who had been injured made their way over to him. He was thrilled to

Waiting to welcome my Marine back with friends Stephanie and Nancy.

see them, and embraced them. His men were so important to him. Watching him interact with them made my heart swell with pride and love. We stayed for almost an hour, but I needed to get the kids home and back to bed. I offered to come back and pick him up, but he was ready to go. He was ready to be home.

43

Be Brave Enough to Start a Conversation that Matters

 ★ ★ ★

November 2008
Twentynine Palms, California

After a couple of weeks spent getting reacquainted with each other again, Ross and I made our first counseling appointment. A lot had transpired between the two of us over the past year, and the deployment had put much of it on hold. Both of us knew how important it was to talk things through, to try to understand each other, to recommit to our relationship. Ross was crazy busy doing write-ups, beginning the prep for the next deployment, but he always made sure I felt like I was a priority.

We bared our hearts and souls in this process, and even after everything that had happened in our marriage, it came as no surprise to me that we still deeply loved and cared for each other.

But that didn't mean the road ahead would be filled with rainbows and unicorns. It was going to require both of us, working every day, to keep our family together. We had to do our best to leave the pain behind, while at the same time, being willing to keep an open dialogue whenever those feelings were dredged up. Nothing we were able to do could ever completely remove the pain we had suffered. What happened had happened. Going forward, I would have to choose either forgiveness or resentment and anger. It would be a decision I'd need to make every single day.

And then there was Ross's mother.

Those who know her have probably never seen her as anything but a perfectly nice—albeit quirky—person. Most had never seen what happened when things didn't go Trina's way, or the problems that arose when she lost control of a situation. They'd never been on the receiving end of her unfulfilled expectations. To her, everyone who had ever disagreed with her either misinterpreted, misconstrued, or misunderstood all her good intentions.

For years I'd been angry about her ill behavior towards me. It's a wonder I didn't have permanent bite marks on my tongue from all the things I'd left unsaid between us.

I could only hope that with professional counseling, we could help her understand how badly her negative behavior was affecting others.

We printed off all the email correspondence between us, giving it to the doctor in the hope that it would help paint an unfiltered picture of our relationship. We wanted to see if the therapist saw what we were seeing.

It took her some time. The counselor led off the first session with the observations she'd made through reading our email correspondence: Trina violated boundaries, felt entitled, made things out to be all about her when they weren't, used manipulation tactics, played the victim, and more. The doctor couldn't diagnose her without meeting her, but from what she'd read, all signs indicated that we were dealing with a narcissist.

Finally. Now, a word for all the turmoil I had been dealing with. I discovered that those suffering from a narcissistic personality live in an artificial, self-invented world, where their fantasies of grandiose talents fuel their need to be admired by others. Narcissists are authoritarians who feel entitled simply because they feel they have the most informed and educated opinion. They lack empathy and understanding, they are envious and contemptuous of others who stand in their way, and they therefore alienate people who regularly interact with them.

I didn't think Trina was a full-blown narcissist, but she certainly had tendencies. She has a kind and giving heart, but it was oftentimes lost with her methods. In the end, I learned that everything came down to conflict, power, and rights—and that I, as a human being, had a basic right to choose not to live in poisonous relationships.

I also learned that setting appropriate boundaries had nothing to do with coercion or pressure. Setting limits in relationships is simply a statement about what kind of behavior I'm willing to accept in my life. For the first time in a very long time, I felt a sense of relief. Counseling had vindicated my feelings, providing us with the tools we needed to be able to move forward.

Ross worked with the therapist to craft a letter to his mother in which he shared our thoughts, and encouraged her to seek help. I know it was hard for him, but it was what we both needed if we wanted to try to salvage some kind of normal relationship with her in the future.

The holidays were upon us. As much as I was looking forward to spending time with family and friends in Boise, I wasn't looking forward to the drama that would no doubt erupt with Trina. It was just a matter of time before she'd throw another dart at her favorite target—me.

The skies opened up, and snow flurried in Twentynine Palms—there is something strangely beautiful about Joshua trees covered in snow. In the desert it was easy to forget that there were any other colors but shades of brown. I looked forward to showing Ryan how to make a snow angel, maybe even a snowman.

It's snowing in 29 Palms, photo taken in front of our home on base.

With as much trepidation as there was excitement, we loaded up the SUV, and headed to Boise. Ross had finished his letter to his mom, but he was conflicted about when he should give it to her. We didn't want any further drama to ruin anyone's holidays, so Ross decided to call his stepdad from the car to prep him for the blowout that was sure to follow the letter. They had an honest conversation; I could tell by the tone of his voice that Ross's heart was heavy about all of it.

Frank asked him not to send the letter to his mom until after the holidays. Ross agreed, saying that he would wait until after Christmas. But by the time we stopped for the night there was an email from Trina in Ross's inbox.

Frank had asked Ross to wait to send the letter, but he had taken it upon himself to repeat everything he and Ross had talked about over the phone. All Ross could do was switch to damage control mode, and address the conflict head-on.

It was done. Ross had shared his thoughts and feelings, and set specific boundaries for how things would proceed. I was free to enjoy the holidays without worrying about what Trina was going to dish out. In the end, Trina blamed me for writing the letter because it contained bullet points. She was convinced that her son didn't know how to use them.

We arrived at my parents' home, where we would stay through the holidays. As is our tradition, the next morning, we headed out as a family to cut down the Christmas tree. We were tying it to the top of the truck when Ross's cousins came snowshoeing up to us. It was an amazing impromptu meeting with extended family. The kids had a blast riding around on sleds and joining in a snowball fight.

Dusk set in as we drove back to my parents' house. We put up the tree and feasted on great food, good wine, and lots of love. We were able to kick back with my brothers and their families, with no deadline for us to be somewhere or do something. My oldest brother and his wife were expecting their first child in February, and Ryan gave them a good dose of what having a child really looked like.

44

Don't Look Back—You're Not Going That Way

April 2009
Twentynine Palms, California

*I*n April of 2009, Ross relinquished command of Fox Company and took over Weapons Company in 2/7. He was awarded a Bronze Star with Combat "V" for his efforts in Afghanistan. He didn't want a big deal to be made about—it didn't sit right with him that he got an award simply for doing his job, and that his guys were under-awarded. We held a quiet ceremony for him with our California family.

While he was still with the same unit, Ross would be training at Camp Pendleton—a two-and-a-half hour drive from Twentynine Palms—from May until September. It would mean that even though he was home, Ross would be hard-pressed to join in with our family's regular routines. I tried to focus on the positives.

Our preschool co-op was working well. We held school every

Fox Company change of command.

Tuesday through Friday. Since
we all lived in the neighborhood, we often gathered at
one other's homes, and col-
laborated on lesson plans. The
kids thrived in this educational
environment, and best of all, it
was free.

We started tae kwon do
classes and t-ball. Ryan loved
being active, and participat-
ing in sports. It kept him busy
four nights a week, so he didn't
focus on pining away, waiting
for Daddy.

But life in the military
meant constant change. Nancy
Osborne, my dinner-mate, fe-
male confidante, and surrogate spouse—one of the few friends with
whom I could just cut loose and laugh about the craziness of Two-
nine—was leaving. She and her husband both received orders to the
East Coast—hers to Bethesda and his to Quantico—and they moved
shortly thereafter.

I was determined to let change be a driving force for good in
my life, to not allow grief to derail my forward progress. I decided
this would be a good time for me to finish my master's degree. I had
started at Gonzaga University after giving birth to Ryan, but I took a
break from that when I gave birth to George. Going back to school
was exactly the kind of focus I needed to stave off potential—
even recurring—grief.

I was excited to stay with the battalion, happy about my move
to Weapons Company. First Sergeant Rummell moved over to
Headquarters and Services (H&S) Company. We had said a
heartfelt goodbye to the Halls, and welcomed in LtCol Reid. He
was what was known as a geographical bachelor, or a geobach.

He'd come to Twentynine Palms alone, leaving his wife and family back east. It was like being on a long deployment, except you could fly home occasionally.

It was a fairly common thing, but Twentynine Palms quartered an inordinately large number of geobach Marines, who'd left their families somewhere else because of the lack of employment or educational opportunity in the area. Kristine and I had never discussed the possibility, but I knew that if my career continued, it would be something we might need to think about in the future.

We continued our training until one day our battalion mission changed. We were going to be attached to the 31st MEU as a battalion landing team. I had been on that MEU during my time as an enlisted Marine. I wasn't crazy about it, but there were worse things. General Waldhauser, our former Regimental commander in Iraq and now the First Marine Division Commander, wanted to get 7th Marines involved in the MEUs. He thought it would be a good thing for us to expand our horizons and get involved with amphibious training.

On paper, that made great sense.

But practically speaking it made life . . . challenging. MEU-specific training only took place at Camp Pendleton. With this change, I would be gone far more often than I normally would have been. The battalion would spend anywhere from a couple of weeks to three months at a time away from home.

One of the first challenges we had to overcome with the new mission was the battery of qualifications required of us prior to training. For instance, only some of my guys were Fast Rope qualified (descending on a thick rope from a hovering helicopter in the same way a firefighter slides down a firehouse pole). Training and qualification for Fast Roping required rope towers, and the closest training facility with rope towers was, of course, Camp Pendleton.

It meant more time away from home, more of our unit's annual budget spent loading Marines onto buses, even money spent contracting civilian cargo trucks to move our gear, and all of it just to get pre-qualified to train for a MEU.

There were other courses we would be required to take as well, things like Helicopter Raid Force and Amphibious Tractor Raid training. On top of this, Division had "asked" us to participate in the rejuvenation of Division Schools. These were courses that had run fairly regularly before 9/11, working to create and reinforce standard operating procedures among the crew who served in weapons elements (such as my Weapons Company) across the 1st Marine Division.

Those Marines attending these courses who happened to be already stationed at Pendleton got to see their families in the evening. Since we weren't local to Pendleton, it added another two weeks away from home to our timeline. It was another example of how training for workups is sometimes harder on family life than a deployment is.

The whole idea of ordering a desert unit to be attached to a MEU was a logistical nightmare. The costs, both financial and personal, would be significant.

45

Create the Thing That
You Wish Existed

May 2009
Twentynine Palms, California

Charlotte lost her battle with cancer on May 14, 2009. It was very sad to see her go. She was caring; she embraced everyone around her. It was said of Charlotte that she "collected people," and it was true; she would truly be missed.

May also brought a wedding anniversary: seven years of marriage for Ross and me. We opted for a short cruise. We looked at it as a vacation with built-in childcare.

We invited Rick and my parents to join us; we wanted to spend time together as a family.

Our week together flew by. Ross and I had felt like we were finally free to spend time with each other, and we basked in the love and joy that can only come from spending time with family.

There were so many positives in my life, and even though things had much improved, I still wrestled for happiness. I felt mixed emotions when I heard the news that the key volunteer network program was being dismantled and replaced by family readiness officers.

The family readiness officers were basically a paid version of the full-time volunteer position I'd taken while Ross was in Fallujah. It was both a blessing and a curse, because while war is a terrible thing and having a paid professional on hand to help families was ostensibly a godsend, spouses—now relegated to the sidelines—would eventually disconnect from their units.

The years of experience and insight we had acquired through our service in the KVN were no longer being readily shared with new spouses and families. It was in the hands of the federal employees now; the professionals. There were times when all we heard about was how the KV program came with so much drama. There were issues, sure, but overall the program did way more good than bad for the military families it served.

I looked back on my own experiences, remembering how scared and confused I had been when I'd first married into the lifestyle of a military spouse. It was so difficult to dig in and get a foothold, find a connection, especially before and after moving.

I knew I wasn't alone.

I knew there were a ton of military spouses out there who needed help.

I wanted to tap into seasoned spouses' knowledge and experience, I wanted to provide families with an insider's guide to the Corps; something to help them navigate military life. I decided to start a website to inspire, connect, and educate other military families. My hope was to help them discover a happier military life by providing a little information and advice.

To that end, I created USMC Life, usmclife.com.

I continued work on my master's degree, and in my spare time I focused my energies on helping others through the development of my website. The effect took my focus off my own hurt and despair, enabling me to forge peace in regard to my circumstances.

Somewhere in all that busyness, I made the conscious decision to change how the world would see me. I didn't want to be known as the woman who had lost her child. If anything, I wanted to be remembered as a woman responsible for paving the way for others.

I leaned heavily on my sister-in-law Gail, an IT professional, who helped me create the forums on the website, and got it ready for real-world use. I was indebted to my brother, David, who graciously footed the bill for my website hosting expenses so that I could save those costs. He also provided me with invaluable advice when I needed it. I set a launch date for July 4, 2009.

During that time I also helped my friend Stephanie start a company: ECCO Tours. I built her website, wrote all the content for it, and did her marketing. It was a lot of fun, and it kept me busy.

Even after several months and several therapist visits, we hadn't made any progress in our relationship with Trina. She never took any responsibility for her actions, even when her therapist flat out told her she was in denial about events that took place. That's when I knew there was no hope for it. All we could do was insist on her respecting the boundaries we'd set.

46

Let the Wild Rumpus Begin

*I*t was no secret that Twentynine Palms was one of the worst duty stations for our kids' schools, especially in comparison to all the other Marine Corps bases. The local county ran the schools—even the one on base. The elementary schools weren't terrible, but the junior high hadn't met federal standards for years. According to the California School Accountability Report, it had a 68% suspension average during this time. Maybe a couple of kids got suspended more than once, and that affected the data a little bit, but anything anywhere near that number speaks volumes. There were obviously some major behavior problems at school. The high school wasn't much better.

School concerns are a major part of life for military families. Poor or failing school districts and the lack of educational continuity are just part of the issue. We often don't get to choose where we are stationed; and we can't always afford to live in better districts. Military kids sometimes pay a high price in the interest of Uncle Sam's directives for the military.

Ryan was due to start kindergarten at Twentynine Palms Elementary. Academically, he was ready to go. But emotionally? I wasn't sure if he was able to sit still in the classroom, and listen to the teacher. I was nervous about him riding the bus and that someone else would be responsible for him.

I tried to quell the misgivings that the mom of every kindergartner feels as I headed to the school to fill out enrollment paperwork. When I got there it was the middle of the day, but the school office was locked up. I headed back home and hopped online, looking to see if I could find more information about registration hours, but there was nothing. I ended up calling the school several days in a row until finally someone answered. They were open. Finally. I headed down to register Ryan.

I was met by a brusque older woman. She didn't seem happy with her job—or anything else, for that matter. I filled out all the necessary paperwork, hoping Ryan would be placed in a class with someone he knew. It would ease the transition from home to school.

Weeks later, I received a phone call from my friend, Karisa. She told me kindergarten roundup—orientation for parents—had been cancelled. This was the first I'd heard of it. For whatever reason, the school had never contacted us, even though we had registered. I was not taking this well. I had major trust issues already because of George's passing, and now the school had unilaterally decided that they weren't going to let us come to the facility to see where Ryan would be spending the whole next year? We weren't going to be given an opportunity to meet Ryan's teacher, to find out about what daily activities were being planned, to see the playgrounds and the facilities, or to learn about the class schedule.

I called the school, and guess who answered the phone—the gruff secretary. She informed me that my family was on the list to be called, and that she wasn't sure why we hadn't been. I asked if I could verify our phone numbers with her, to ensure it was correct in the system. She told me, "I don't have time to do that."

I was nervous. I wanted to make sure we were set up for success in the future. "I'd like to get this sorted out," I said. "I'm going to go pick up my husband. We'll be there together in about ten minutes, so please don't leave." I said this knowing that their working hours were extremely limited.

When Ross and I walked through the front door, the secretary was verbally combative. She stood there yelling and screaming at me, claiming I had threatened her by bringing my husband with me.

Gobsmacked, I replied, "I didn't threaten you. And I certainly didn't talk to you the way you're talking to me."

She continued to yell at me.

"You're being completely unprofessional," I said, calmly. "Who is your customer?"

Her reply was hesitant. "You are."

I managed to communicate with her that I was nervous already because I'd never enrolled my kids in grade school before. "You haven't given me any information. The school has been closed all week. I can't get any answers for anything online, nor can I get them in person or over the phone, because no one is ever here. I came down here to sort out why we hadn't been called about the cancellation of the kindergarten roundup. I need to know some basic information; like where's the bus stop, does my son need school supplies, and should I pack lunch for him or does he need lunch money?"

She provided little help, but she did confirm that my correct phone number was indeed listed in their registration. I was frustrated. I didn't want her talking this way to other military spouses, especially those who were younger or were afraid of confrontation.

We set up a meeting with the school liaison officer, a representative hired by the military to help military families, the principal, and the superintendent of the Twentynine Palms school district to discuss what had taken place. When the appointment came around, the superintendent didn't show up, sending someone else in his place.

In the end the school didn't have a problem with the secretary's behavior. They assumed we were a crazy Marine family. The liaison officer, however, was disgusted. She told us that she had dealt with case after case of military families who were given the runaround, and mistreated by the schools.

I reasoned that nobody cared about us because we would, like all the others, simply move on sooner or later. My family was made to feel as if we were a nuisance to the school administration. Obviously, some of them felt they didn't need to give us the time of day.

But they sure wanted our federal dollars. Every school district that includes military-connected children receives money from the federal government.

The first day of school arrived. I still didn't trust the school. I taped a sign to Ryan's back with his name, my phone number, and his bus stop.

I had become *that* mommy.

Then I got in my car and followed the bus to the school.

I left on my sixth deployment. The winter holidays had passed, and we made our way to Okinawa on commercial 747s from the States. My unit was assigned to float with the USS *Essex* (LH-2), the USS *Denver* (LPD-9), and the USS *Harpers Ferry* (LSD-49).

I wasn't crazy about the 31st MEU. It seemed to me that it was a waste of resources and money that could have been better spent. Why send Marines from Two-nine on float? Half my battalion had been to Afghanistan; we had a lot to offer, had we been selected to return to one of the theaters of combat.

Leaving my family was never easy. As the kids got older, it became exponentially harder. Ryan was now old enough to remember me being gone. Grace wasn't even two yet, but leaving either of them was all the harder when they didn't understand that Daddy was going to be leaving for a long time.

And I was leaving Kristine once again, too. She would be in charge of our two kids, of our entire house. I joked that at least she wouldn't have to worry about me being blown up by the Taliban this time around. I hoped that this one small fact would make things a little easier for her.

Six months.

That was our guaranteed deployment time. I felt it gave our family at least *some* stability, if there could be such a thing for Marines and our family members.

From: Ross
Date: January 9, 2010 4:19 AM
To: Kristine

We got here at 4:00 p.m. on Saturday (crossed the international date line) so that was 7:00 a.m. your time on the 9th. We're nine hours ahead of PST. Room isn't bad, very spartan. But it's not like I need much.

From: Kristine
Date: January 11, 2010 11:24 AM
To: Ross

Just left my doctor's office in Yucca Valley. I guess a homeless guy was stabbed behind the building—they'd cleared away the crime scene tape just before I got there. Gotta love Twentynine Palms.

Ryan had a hard time before going to bed. I sat with him for about 20 minutes, talking about stuff. We chatted about what it meant to be the man of the house, and he said, "I don't want to be in charge of anything."

:) Me neither.

He also said that he wished he were a daddy. I asked him why, and he said so that he could go with you. That melted my heart.

I thought getting him up for school was going to be difficult, but it wasn't bad at all. Seems like a good night's sleep was all that he needed. He went all week without getting put on the stoplight behavior chart at school (or so he says).

Graduate school starts again for me tomorrow, so I'll be pretty busy, too.

From: Ross
Date: January 12, 2010 11:32 PM
To: Kristine

I'm going to try to find a place where I can get on Facebook so that we can IM. Everywhere we go, we're set up for Wi-Fi. MWR has all these amenities tailored for that now.

A few of the Marines have even been able to Skype a couple times with their wives. I'll check it out around here.

I guess I should have thought about having that discussion with Ryan about being the man of the house. I miss the three of you a lot. 179 days left . . .

47

Let's Meet in Our Dreams

───── ★★★ ─────

January 2010
Okinawa, Japan
Twentynine Palms, California

We immediately began training. One of the first courses we took was Helicopter-crew Air Breathing Device training. If a helicopter ever crashed at sea, the HABD would provide about 15 minutes of air, so that we could find an escape hatch and slowly make our way to the surface. It consisted of a day in the classroom and a day at the pool.

After that, we set out to deal with the issuing of weapons. It required an update of the rosters, then each rifle had to be zeroed (by firing it at a range). It was a lot of busywork in addition to the almost overwhelming logistics of preparing two thousand five hundred people—and millions of tons of equipment—to go to sea. There was no time for libbo. Even regular downtime was scarce. Everyone in leadership worked 17-hour days.

MEUs that leave from the States don't have to do all this: just the Okinawa 31st MEU. The stateside MEUs use each unit's own equipment, so they don't have the myriad of logistical issues just before embarkation that rotational units have to deal with. Just one more reason the nickname "Thirty-worst MEU" stuck.

The 31st was constantly rolling in and out: it was three months back, three months out, three months back, three months out, and on and on. The cycle never really ended. After a while, the command element Marines became ambivalent and comfortable—sometimes too comfortable—with their routine. They tended towards an attitude of hearing but not listening, notching their belts with how many offloads they'd done because those notches were what they most cared about. Whenever we suggested a better or more tactical way of doing things, the MEU's permanent staff ignored us. They were interested in the maintenance of the status quo. Most MEUs exist on float in case the shit hits the fan. It's unlikely this MEU will ever see a fight, though; the 31st exists in a kind of perpetually-deployed limbo.

It didn't help that at least half the gear we received was either broken or unserviceable. If gear was broken, it was supposed to go into a maintenance cycle. Technically the MEU owned it all, but because it was regularly issued to battalions for short-term use and the turnover occurred in a never-ending cycle, the usual maintenance schedule had been completely ignored. Broken gear just continued to get issued to the next battalion that was rotating through.

It took every minute of the two weeks we had been given in Japan for us to get ready. And while I wasn't entirely happy with the state of our equipment, we'd done the best we could do.

We headed towards our first port of call—Thailand.

The annual Cobra Gold exercise, a large theater security cooperation exercise, took place every year in Thailand. It addressed a range of scenarios; everything from humanitarian assistance efforts to traditional warfare.

It was insanely hot. We couldn't dock pier side, as the water was too shallow, so small groups of Marines were ferried to shore. Many of us had to wait hours on end in 90° temperatures and 90% humidity.

When we finally made it ashore, the only water available was what we had brought with us, most of which we'd drunk while waiting for the ferrying to end. While we knew we'd have to wait for the local civilian-contracted trucks and buses to transport us to Thailand, we were not prepared for a four-hour stint on the beach. I ended up giving a street vendor $200 of my own cash to buy water for all my elements. A few of the other officers also bought water. By the time the trucks arrived, we already had two guys down with heat cramps.

We'd been promised secure trucks to transport all our gear. What arrived were canvas-covered trucks with padlocks on their tailgates. Canvas wouldn't stop someone with a knife from cutting a hole in the side and taking hundreds of thousands of dollars of equipment and weapons. We ended up stacking our weapons in the aisles of the buses, and throwing our packs into the trucks.

The trucks were just the beginning of the chaos. What should have been a strictly organized convoy descended into disorder as drivers split up and stopped for gas or food at will once we got outside the city.

We were also supposed to have secure satellite equipment and phones. There were supposed to be computers up and running at the training site.

None of that happened.

It took 18 hours for all the different units to finally arrive at the exercise's Rally Point.

I couldn't believe that the 31st MEU did business this way, but anytime I mentioned my dissatisfaction, I was met with a flat rebuke: "This is the way we always do it." It had been nearly 24 hours since we'd disembarked from the ship, and there had not yet been a single communication with command.

I was the senior man in Thailand for four days; I was responsible for more than six hundred personnel. Every element from the MEU was on the ground, but we had no representation from the command element to coordinate any part of the exercise. Somehow they expected us to show up and accomplish the mission with no comms. I held nightly meetings with all my elements in order to try to maintain some focus of effort, and ensure everyone was accounted for. The exercises themselves took place over the course of two weeks, across a half-dozen areas in Thailand. I hated the weather; it soared well above 90° during the day, in 90% humidity. It only slightly cooled in the evening. We slept on the ground under cammy netting and doused ourselves in DEET. No one slept all the way through the night. Even with the netting and bug repellent, there was always something crawling on us.

We cleared an area to set up our generators and tents. The Thais, however, went into the jungle and set up their hammocks. It was interesting to see the different approaches. The Thai way seemed much more practical, both from a tactical and from a comfort standpoint.

Even though our command operation center tent was air-conditioned, I spent as little time as possible in it. The coolness felt good, but it only made going back outside more miserable.

I accompanied a Thai colonel to inspect the range that we were going to use. He informed me that it wasn't a range they used often.

During those periods of nonuse, the local population moved in and began to farm it.

The Thais hadn't taken the time to clear the range for our live fire training, and furthermore, they refused to ask the local population to move. It was left to us to devise some kind of plan to move the civilians out of the area.

We made our way around the dispersed clusters of huts with our Thai interpreters to provide the dates and times of our scheduled training. The locals seemed to understand.

Our first day of training came. The Thai civilians showed up on the other side of the range to watch. We began working with a company of Thai marines and soldiers in a combined arms attack exercise with aircraft, light armored vehicles, artillery, and dismounted infantry. Things progressed well, but as soon as there was a break, the civilians rushed the field and began picking up the brass.

LtCol Reid ordered us into the clusters of homes near the range to inform the locals of the danger of their actions. We instructed them to wait until we had finished shooting and sounded the all-clear horn. We told them if they allowed us to complete the exercises, they could come and pick up our spent brass at the end of the day. If they interrupted us at any point in time the deal was off: we would police our own brass before we went home. Thankfully, that was enough to make them listen. The last thing any of us wanted was a hurt or killed civilian.

> From: Ross
> Date: February 2, 2010 7:55 PM
> To: Kristine
>
> I'm the lead guy for this entire portion of the operation, we have over six hundred guys from all over the MEU, and I'm responsible for setting up this training.
>
> This whole op has been a goatfuck.
>
> I just want this to be over. I don't know if I've ever looked forward to libbo more. Thanks for the video; it was awesome. I miss you guys so much. We're a month into it, and the time on ship went pretty quick, so hopefully the trend will continue.

From: Kristine
Date: February 2, 2010 11:47 PM
To: Ross

> Sounds like you've been crazy busy. I'm surprised they don't give
> you better communication tools. The 31st MEU sounds hor-
> rible . . . but there's only five more months to go.

> As for me, I'm just about halfway through my class. At least being
> in school will help keep me busy.

> Grace started this new trend of hugging my leg and not letting
> go. It's cute, but a little annoying at times—like when I'm trying to
> make breakfast or lunch or whatever. It's usually in the kitchen.
> She grabs hold and just smiles up at me. Her teeth look like they
> should be coming through in the next couple weeks. Her gums
> are really swollen, poor girl.

> Ryan is doing well. He hasn't spent as much time outside
> because the weather has been so crappy. It's really cold with the
> wind that's blowing through. Not fun. I tried going to the park
> with the kids yesterday, and we stayed for about ten minutes. I'm
> ready for spring.

From: Ross
Date: February 13, 2010 8:12 AM
To: Kristine

> Got back late on the 12th. Two shotguns that were not on the
> checkout list are now missing. Some Marine decided to take
> them on his own, then never took accountability for them. We
> took inventory every night, so I can't imagine how something like
> this happened. Nothing ever goes according to plan, but we did
> really well in the field. I'm really proud of our guys.

> It was hot—crazy hot. I'd hate to see what summers are like here.
> The bugs weren't fun either, but I'll take that over the stress I've
> had to endure on this ship. It was peaceful while we were out
> there.

> I had to bring a Marine back from the field because his wife
> didn't get the allotment he set up. It took a month to kick in, and
> now she's strapped for cash. They have two kids. As I'm lecturing

this kid about his finances, that he needs to access his account to transfer funds, he says his wife doesn't know his account number, nor does he know hers.

Then I realized that I have no idea how to access *our* account. But I guess as long as there's money in there, it doesn't matter much. It was just the irony of the situation.

From: Kristine
Date: February 13, 2010 9:40 AM
To: Ross

Ryan's doing okay. The other day I told him that he hurt my feelings. I asked him, "Do you care about Mommy's feelings?" He said, "No." I asked him again, and he said no again. So I sent him to his room. I'm sure it's all part of the territory that comes with having a five-year-old.

Last night I asked him to clean up his toys downstairs while I gave Grace her bath. He pushed everything under the couch. So I'm going to have to take away some smiley faces for that one . . .

Oh, and I forgot to mention that Ryan decided to cut his own hair yesterday. He didn't do too much damage, but he still managed to gouge a nice little trough at the front of his hairline.

How much longer until you're home again?

We were supposed to have three days of libbo in Thailand before we pulled out of port, but thanks to the missing shotguns, we spent all that time tied up in an investigation, trying to hunt them down. We sent the section leader (the one who signed out the shotguns), platoon commander, MEU intel officer, and force protection officer with the Thai interpreters to see if we could get the weapons back. LtCol Reid offered up $200 and I offered up $150 from our personal bank accounts as a reward, to see if we could entice the locals to give up the weapons. They're not that valuable, but in the Marine Corps it's a huge deal to lose a weapon.

Nothing came of it.

The SSgt who had taken the weapons from the armory without authorization was quickly relieved. Not only had he not recorded the name of the individual to whom he issued them, but also, for the entire time we were in country, he never reported the weapons as missing.

Investigators dug back as far as they could, even into my last deployment in Afghanistan. I had never lost one piece of serialized gear while in command. I had even written a policy letter about how important it was to maintain the accountability of gear and personnel while in Thailand. I had issued that so that we could institute accountability procedures in order to better monitor our serialized gear.

All of the Marines who were questioned about the missing weapons stated that they had seen and read the letter, that they knew it was our company's policy, and that no deviation had taken place at any point in time while we were in-country.

48

These Sweatpants Are the Only Thing That Fit Me Now

February 2010
Thailand
Twentynine Palms, California

*T*here were so many positives in my life, but with Ross gone and my days filled with the monotony of housework and raising kids, I was struggling. I needed a break. After having lost George, I wasn't comfortable with the idea of trusting my children with anyone but me. Play dates weren't easy because Grace was everywhere and into everything. I began to feel very isolated; I was in constant survival mode.

Some people turn to drugs or alcohol when they need to cope with stress. I chose to find comfort in the one thing we all have to have: food.

There were so many times when I just didn't give a crap about myself anymore. It was all too easy to exchange my frustration or self-loathing for a little something sweet. If it was cold and windy outside, I'd bake a pan of gooey sticky buns or some cookies, telling myself it was a great activity to do with the kids. A pastry and a fancy cup of coffee from Starbucks was an easy go-to fix.

I no longer cared about what I looked like because I felt empty inside. Over the holidays there had been plenty of happy times, but there were other times when I felt Ross detach from me. It was like he was just going through the motions, like he wasn't genuinely vested in the moment. I didn't know if it was from my weight, the stress of his mom, or the upcoming deployment, but sometimes it felt like we were just moving forward because we were married and nothing more. Some days we were just roommates.

I began to medicate with food. The more I ate, the less I cared, and the less I cared, the more I ate. I knew that the weight was just a symptom of heartache—loss and hollowness. It was an outward symbol of everything I had been through. It was a heavy, flabby, in-my-face testament to my struggles, my failures, and my coming to terms with everything awful that had happened.

From: Kristine
Date: February 20, 2010 12:10 PM
To: Ross

> I feel overwhelmed right now and just all-over blah. I haven't lost any more weight; I don't care about anything. Sometimes I feel resentful towards you, believing you won't love me or want to be with me if I don't change, then I feel like not trying to change. I know that the smart thing to do is to get healthy, and I know that I'm not happy with myself the way that I am . . . so I need to do something about it. It's a vicious cycle. I never got the baby weight off this go-around because I've been eating my feelings, dealing with George's loss, and not being able to diet while breastfeeding Grace because my milk was affected. It doesn't help that there are no gyms on base with childcare (or out in town either).

From: Ross
Date: February 28, 2010 3:19 PM
To: Kristine

> I wish I were there to help with the kids and give you a break to do your homework, or just have a glass of wine with the girls. I know it's a lot of stress on you to have to do everything with the kids.

> Babe, I'm always going to love you, no matter what. I want you to be healthy; I want you to be happy. I know you're not happy with the way things are. I'm hoping—now that you have your body back to yourself—you will be able to find some motivation. You're right; this is a vicious cycle.

> Does it ever worry you that we don't have as much to talk about on this deployment? I don't feel the same kind of connection with you that I've had on previous deployments. Do you think

it's because we just have too much going on? Something seems different this time. Is everything . . . with us . . . okay from your perspective?

My feelings haven't changed, but you don't seem the same. Is anything the matter? My mind begins to wander. I have had bad dreams about you finding the love that you want and need somewhere else.

Babe, I love you more than anything. Deployment helps to remind me what an incredible person you are and how lucky I am to have married such an incredible woman, wife, and mother. I miss you so much. I can't wait to move on to our next duty station together.

From: Kristine
Date: February 28, 2010 9:05 PM
To: Ross

I don't know what's the matter. I feel like I'm disconnecting from everyone. I'm just in a funk, I guess. I know my weight has become an issue in our marriage; eating is a coping mechanism that helps me get through my grief. I feel like I've become a big disappointment to you.

Right now I'm so busy with school and the kids that I'm tired and just blah . . . so . . . I guess it's obvious that you're seeing all these things, too.

You've been more than understanding about how I relate to your mom. But that issue has ground us down as a couple, and it compounds the stress between us. You keep telling me that I need to not give up on her. Well, right now, I do. I no longer want to go to therapy. I want peace in my life; I want happiness. I want to be in a positive place. I really hope that moving to another duty station might allow us a fresh start.

Know that I love you. I'm not purposely getting off the phone when we talk. Most of the time you don't say much, and you rarely ask questions. That means I routinely get to a point where I no longer feel I have anything to say that seems important to you. Plus you get interrupted all the time. That's fine, but it reiterates that you are busy. I feel like people are listening in on our phone conversations anyway.

I love you so much, really, because you are the only man I love and want to spend the rest of my life with.

From: Ross
Date: March 1, 2010 12:13 AM
To: Kristine

I'm so sorry you feel isolated. As I've said before, I want you to be happy with your body. I want you to lose weight, I want you to be healthy, but I can't make you do it. I want you to do it for all of us (the kids, too). If I'm distant, it's not because I'm just going through the motions. It's because things weigh on me. My job—that I'm really not enjoying much right now—George's death, my inability to get into the shape I want to be in.

I look forward so much to being with you in our later years, and think about it (and, I thought, I share it too) a lot. It doesn't take a deployment to make me feel good about you. I just really appreciate what I have, and you need to know that I know I'm lucky in that area.

I've never had a reason to worry about things between us since we've been married, except when George passed. I'm not asking you to become overly enthusiastic because that would be false. I love you so much. There just seems to be something wrong between us that I can't fix.

From: Kristine
Date: March 2, 2010 11:25 AM
To: Ross

I feel like I have the most boring, ordinary everyday life. I feel like I have nothing to say that's of any interest to anyone.

I'm tired of being the only one who takes the trash out, of being the only one who gets up with kids in the middle of the night, of having to explain to people where my husband is, and what he's doing (again), or dealing with this harsh desert landscape and this hostile town. I'm tired of never being able to plan vacations, tired of the missed holidays, missed birthdays, missed anniversaries, missed pregnancies and births. I'm tired of doing everything myself, basically acting as your personal assistant.

I have lived the same day continually, with miniscule differences. My life with an eighteen-month-old and five-year-old is completely exhausting.

I'm just tired of everything, and I miss you, my husband. This too shall pass.

It was incredibly difficult to have a discussion about the strength of our marriage via email. I needed to see his face, hear his voice. Marriage to my Marine was so much more difficult than I would have ever imagined.

Maybe it's because when kids are involved, our responsibilities are tied to something bigger than ourselves. No matter what, we're expected to figure it out along the way, and we've only got one shot to make it happen. We have to give our all, all the time—we're parents for life. It's exhausting, especially when your partner is constantly away training or deployed.

Marriage is different, in a way, because when it gets too difficult it can end in a divorce. We have to make a choice to work with our spouse over and over again, sometimes day by day. We have to want to be with the other person; we have to place their needs as a priority in life, sometimes above our own. There are so many factors that make for a successful marriage, but for Ross and me, the one thing keeping us together was forgiveness.

We were successful because we trusted each other, and we didn't keep score. We didn't bring up the past unless it was pertinent to the conversation. Love has seasons, and frankly, sometimes it's hard. We learned to accept flaws, to keep pushing through pain. We saw each other at our worst, our darkest selves, and instead of allowing that to fester into malcontent, we chose to use it to cultivate a deeper love for each other. We resisted the off-chance temptation to run away from problems, from each other; we resisted the lie that something else might be satisfying. We both knew that this fragile thing we had was worth saving.

We learned to say, "I'm sorry" and, "I still love you." We savored the small things. We made moments matter. We laughed, we quoted old movie lines; we tried to connect in a positive way physically, even when we were angry. There's something about skin caressing skin, embracing in tenderness together. It's healing in a marriage.

But we had been separated so much. Deployments and long training cycles took their toll. Even when he was home, he was tied to work, constantly preparing for the next deployment. Continued, lengthy, physical separation made it extremely difficult to repair things when they went wrong.

I'd lost track of the number of times my heart felt like it would break for the lack of his touch, or my need to feel his arms around me. How many of my own tears had I wiped away while I waited for him to come home? It was easy for me to feel abandoned in the chasm between us when it was filled with nothing but words. What could they mean without a touch? What could I do but read through his emails again and again, or sit and wait for one of our too-short conversations over the phone?

I had reached the point where I wanted to continue to be the strong, independent, supportive wife he needed and wanted, but I had needs, too. We were due to move again, and here I was arranging everything by myself . . . again. I knew the situation was out of Ross's hands. It's not like he wasn't willing to give me what I needed, it's just that the Marine Corps always came first.

I trusted his love for me, and I knew that I still loved him more than anything. I just hoped love would be enough to get us through.

Our next stop was the Philippines. We began our movement northward towards the ranges, traveling along the same route as the Bataan Death March in World War II. I can't imagine what it would have been like for the tens of thousands of Filipino and American prisoners of war who were injured, hungry, and tired, being forced to march that terrain in hot, nasty weather.

We arrived at a small training area where Philippine marines were standing by. During the exercise, they used our equipment instead of the Vietnam-era weapons they had on hand. The entire unit was a hodgepodge of experience and attitude. It was like they'd just grabbed anyone who was remotely available, then thrown them together to train with us.

I sat down to discuss the upcoming schedule with the Philippine marine LtCol who was responsible for the Philippine troops.

"Wow. Every day, huh?" He looked at me like I'd asked him to build a bridge out of toothpicks. Then he expressed his concern over the training I'd scheduled during the Manny Pacquiao fight—apparently the Republic of the Philippines shut down entirely whenever he fought.

It became clear that it was more of a strain on some of our Pacific allies than it was for others to support security cooperation ventures. Working with the Philippine forces was an entirely different experience than the exercises we'd done in Thailand. The Thais had sent a cohesive unit to participate, and their leadership had expressed interest not only in the training, but in the approach we'd used to conduct it. It seemed the Philippine forces, however, were just going through the motions.

We did the best we could under the circumstances. We managed to finish training early. Then it was back to Okinawa for the next phase. We were one step closer to going home.

49

The Girl Who Smiles When Her Heart Is Broken

★ ★ ★

March 2010
Philippines
Twentynine Palms, California

I still had major trust issues with the idea of leaving my kids in the care of a babysitter. I already had the worst thing in the world happen to me when I lost George, and I knew I couldn't go through that again.

I was invited to see a movie on base with my friend and neighbor Amy Young. I really wanted to see it, so I talked myself into going. Grace was eighteen months and Ryan was five, so I decided it was time to try stepping out into the waters. I hired a babysitter who was recommended by my girlfriends.

I was gone for one hour and forty minutes. When I got home I checked on the kids. They were both sleeping. I thought *maybe I can do this!*

The next morning Grace was more fussy than usual. She was upset, but I couldn't figure out what was wrong. She hadn't been walking for very long, yet her normal gait was off. She didn't want to put pressure on one of her legs. I gave her some Tylenol and kept an eye on it, but she wasn't getting better, so I took her in to the ER.

They took some X-rays, and told me she had a buckle fracture in her leg. *You've got to be kidding me. I leave the house for less than two hours and in that time she breaks a bone?*

They fit her with a full-leg cast, from her toes all the way up to her hips. I was beyond angry with the babysitter, but I couldn't be completely sure that she was responsible.

I called her from the hospital, and asked her what had happened that night. She said nothing out of the ordinary went down. I probed her with questions: did Grace fall off the couch? Did Ryan wrestle with Grace? Did she fall over funny? No, no, and no. I didn't know what to think. Was it a freak accident in her crib that morning?

My sweet, darling daughter.

I hated the idea that someone might have hurt her, yet I couldn't be 100% sure the babysitter had done anything wrong. The hospital knew about the situation, and had the authority to call the police if there was abuse. They couldn't pin it down to anything other than it had been an accident.

I hated that I'd left her and something had happened.

I hated that I felt I couldn't trust anyone.

I hated being stuck in Twentynine Palms.

Without my husband.

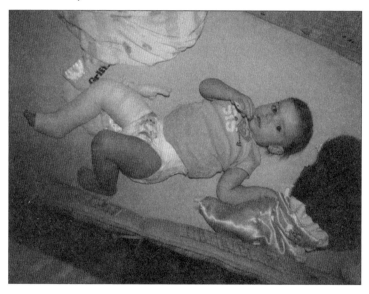

From: Ross
Date: March 16, 2010 8:51 PM
To: Kristine

> My poor little girl. We have no idea how she fractured it? That seems weird, babe. How does that happen and you don't notice? Don't leave Grace with that girl again. I'm sure that having to take care of the kids completely on your own is making this a harder deployment.

From: Kristine
Date: March 16, 2010 11:32 PM
To: Ross

Grace is doing well, all things considering. She has figured out how to crawl with the cast on, climb onto the couch, and ride her truck. She whined a lot in the beginning, but I just let her try to figure it out so that she could become more self-reliant. We spent a good part of the morning at the hospital getting her cast X-rayed to make sure everything was set properly. The official diagnosis is that there's a buckle in the bone. It can happen from a fall, getting stuck in the crib, etc. Needless to say, I won't be using anyone else's babysitting services.

I am so sick of things happening to our kids! Then you add George on top of it. It's really depressing to think about.

I. Just. Can't.

From: Ross
Date: March 17, 2010 10:42 AM
To: Kristine

Babe, you are an incredible mother. Nothing is worse than what we've experienced with George, but we are fortunate that our kids are healthy. There will be more broken bones, scrapes, stitches and minor surgeries. Her leg is going to be atrophied when they pull it out of the cast. She sure has had some challenges for being on this earth for such a short time.

The CO is going to make the switches to the company commanders in Oki and said he was going to MOST LIKELY send me home with the advance party. If that's the case, we'd only be looking at a month before I see you again.

From: Kristine
Date: April 5, 2010 11:10 PM
To: Ross

Thanks for the confidence. Sometimes I feel like I'm letting you and the kids down. It just gets so overwhelming, and I feel like I don't have the answers or the patience to figure things out.

Are you still online?

From: Ross
Date: April 5, 2010 11:17 PM
To: Kristine

   Yes, what are you wearing?

From: Kristine
Date: April 5, 2010 11:19 PM
To: Ross

   I'm sitting in lingerie with black high heels and a toy, hanging out
   and watching porn.

From: Ross
Date: April 5, 2010 11:20 PM
To: Kristine

   Are you really watching that?

From: Kristine
Date: April 5, 2010 11:21 PM
To: Ross

   No. I'm sitting in black sweat pants, no bra, gray T-shirt, and I'm
   surrounded in Kleenex from being sick.

From: Ross
Date: April 5, 2010 11:25 PM
To: Kristine

   Oh dang, you had me there for a minute.

From: Kristine
Date: April 05, 2010 11:23 PM
To: Ross

   You made me laugh out loud. I needed that after today! I'm
   taking a break from school and watching TV; nothing terribly
   exciting on.

From: Ross
Date: April 16, 2010 11:31 PM
To: Kristine

   I had a hard time last night thinking about George. I don't know

what hit me. I saw a couple of pictures of him and suddenly this
wave of grief hit me hard. It's hard to believe it's been a year and a
half since he's been gone.

From: Kristine
Date: April 17, 2010 12:02 AM
To: Ross

I'm sorry you're going through this alone. We both have hard
days, and it sucks that we can't be there to comfort each other.
Just know that I love you and that I wish you were here.

From: Kristine
Date: April 23, 2010 8:52 PM
To: Ross

Ryan went to school in tears from me trying to get him to do stuff
before he went to school (turn off the TV, finish his homework,
put his shoes on) . . . He wasn't listening, so I told him he wasn't
going to Jack's or Caleb's house after school today while I went to
get a haircut.

Then I found out that he'd lied to me about getting in trouble at
school. I found a yellow naughty note in his bag. There were lots
of tears and, "You're mean!" and so on. He said, "I don't love
you!" after I said I love *him*.

Not shaping up to be a good day. Grace wouldn't eat breakfast.
She tried escaping out the dog door again this morning . . .

From: Ross
Date: April 23, 2010 8:53 PM
To: Kristine

I'll be home in a little while. HOLD THE LINE!

From: Kristine
Date: April 25, 2010 5:20 PM
To: Ross

So a big milestone yesterday, sissy started walking flatfooted
again after her cast was removed! Her walking has improved

dramatically. She's starting to pick up speed. She did look pretty cute walking like a peg-leg pirate, though.

I took the kids to the new water park on base today. Grace had no fear of the water; she went right into the sprinklers. That didn't last long, though. She wanted to walk up and down the ramp to the pool . . . over and over and over and over again. I thought I would be able to put my chair in the shade and watch her as she ran in and out of sprinklers. That wasn't to be.

Another milestone: Ryan took off one of his training wheels by himself (only on one side). I guess it was a bit loose, and he figured why not take it off. So he's been riding around with one training wheel. He's convinced that he can ride without a training wheel, but I told him that he would have to wait for you to come home and do that (I just want you to get included in some stuff!). He says that he can do it now without waiting, but I told him too bad.

Just when I started to think we were in a better place, I got another email from my mom. Kristine had tried really hard, and I knew it was up to me to lay down the law again. I hated to do it, but even as I pressed send, I held out hope that one day my mom would finally understand where we were coming from.

From: Ross
Date: May 30, 2010 2:42 AM
To: Trina

Mom,

The emails you've sent over the past few weeks about the cabin were more than just you getting things off your chest. I can't help but feel like you're trying to discredit Kristine in my eyes. If you want to clear the air like that, please do it with Dad, your therapist Teresa, or a trusted confidant. Please remember: I share everything with Kristine. If you want to be upset with both of us or just me, that's fine. But for you to single out Kristine for decisions made or information you feel has not been passed correctly is inappropriate. It's like you're afraid to hold me accountable, that you place all the blame on Kristine. This can only make things worse.

Just look at your recent email correspondence about her (painting her as the bad guy to me). These are your words:

"Is she so rigid and intolerant"

". . . making your life miserable"

"I didn't even know whether the packages I sent reached her and Ryan" (Ryan has called you)

"Is she not teaching him manners?"

"She has issues with your cousins (she doesn't) so do you really believe that she would choose to include them in any of the decision-making? "

"So why would I expect her to be nice to my family"

". . . even if she would rise above everything"

"I resent her making me into the enemy"

". . . let alone a thank you, common courtesy?"

"I've apologized for everything she perceived I've done to her."

"She can apologize to me for her misjudgment at issue about my treatment of her and I will forgive her for all the hurt and exclusion from your family life. "

"rude, intolerant, or disrespectful"

When you perceive Kristine as being inconsiderate or rude, what's really happening is this: she's simply trying to protect herself from being hurt. You're unsafe for her, Mom. That she needs protection from you is the reason why she has refused to communicate with you any further.

If things are going to get better, you need to do something for me. Please do not send me emails that single out Kristine accusing her as a bad mother, or insinuating that she's inconsiderate or rude.

Kristine is none of those things, Mom. She's exhausted from your negativity. What we've been told by our therapist from day one is that she needs to distance herself from you. That is what she has done.

Many things, all of them of your own devising, hinder your relationship with Kristine. They are too numerous to mention in this email. When you say things like, "I've apologized for everything Kristine has perceived I've done to her," your own verbiage confesses that you've not given recognition to the hurt Kristine has felt, nor have you extended to her proper courtesy and respect. Kristine wants nothing more from you—or from anyone, for that matter—than to establish a relationship that is at least founded on mutual respect. I would like for you two to have more than that, but I find I need to be cautious and manage my expectations with you. We're a long way from that right now, as you must know.

50

A Rainbow of Chaos

Summer 2010
Okinawa, Japan
Twentynine Palms, California

*R*oss was finally home.

It was time to pack again: the eighth move since we'd been married. This time I made sure to ask the movers, "Please don't send any felons to pack our belongings this time. The last ones weren't able to get on base; one of them was actually apprehended at the gate."

Truthfully I only said it tongue-in–cheek, thinking it couldn't possibly happen again.

The man with whom I was talking said that they only hired reputable workers, and that we certainly shouldn't experience such a thing with *his* company.

But guess what? It happened again.

Usually a moving company would send three or four men to pack our belongings, but today the only one allowed on base was a woman. The other two men were felons. They couldn't get on to the base. Nothing could be done because all the company's other employees were assigned to other sites. Everyone else who was remotely available was in Riverside, a good hour and a half away.

I had to hire a local house cleaner to assist. After a very long day, we were packed. The following morning the truck came.

The driver was assisted by two 18-year-old-kids. They looked eager enough to get started. He began barking orders at them to move faster, to hold the items differently, to "hurry up and pick that up, you idiot!" His mannerisms were upsetting to me, to say the least, and I didn't like exposing Ryan to his words and actions. I asked Ross if he could pull him aside to discuss the situation, since I thought maybe he might take suggestions better coming from a man.

Later that afternoon, we discovered that the 18-year-olds had no experience; that he had literally picked them up a mile away from the base, near the California DMV off Adobe Road. Where were my *professional* movers? We never did figure out what had happened to the men supposedly assigned to our job. Maybe they too were felons; or maybe they didn't show up to work. I reminded myself to relax; it was just one more box checked before we headed back to the Pacific.

Eventually, we made our way out west to restart our lives again. We hoped for a fresh start with a new job, and hopefully new life in our relationship.

We left the desolation and remoteness of Twentynine Palms for more civilized country, driving a few hours to our new duty station: Camp Pendleton. We had rented a truck and loaded up the propane tank, lawn and automotive supplies, as well as the other items not normally sanctioned in a move.

I didn't cry when leaving the base for the last time, unless one considers tears of joy, in which case, hell yes, I cried.

Looking back, I fully acknowledge the fact that not everyone will have had the same experience with Twentynine Palms I did. It was a dark time in our lives. Coupled with those negative encounters at the two schools our son attended, our issues were compounded.

Counterintuitively, the lack of career opportunities at Twentynine Palms—plus the operational tempo for troops— created the perfect incubator for the formation of tight-knit friendships. This weird vacuum of opportunity opens pathways for the truly motivated to reach their personal goals. Many really do enjoy their time stationed there, the relationships formed, and the different pace of life at this relatively remote duty station.

That wasn't my experience overall, though I treasure the friendships made.

It was fall, Ross was home, and with a fresh change afoot, I was optimistic and hopeful for our family. Ross finally had an assignment that guaranteed he wouldn't deploy for at least a couple of years. My primary personal goal was to use my new master's degree, plus almost a decade of experience working at Fortune 500 companies throughout college and after, to find the perfect job.

I met with an employment specialist to review my resume, making sure to fill in the various gaps of employment with my stints of volunteer work. I began scouring dozens of websites and applying for job after job, spending week upon week applying for anything that sounded interesting.

I was sure I would get an interview.

Crickets.

I might as well have printed my resume on camouflage paper because it screamed *military spouse* through and through. The few interviews I managed to pull down ended in the hiring manager telling me I was overqualified for the position, or asking me questions in a way that, as I responded, unavoidably painted me as a military wife. Clearly no one wanted to take a chance on hiring someone who would eventually have to move. Maybe they saw it as a risky investment, but I was eager to dig in and prove myself. If I were given a chance, I knew they'd never have a more loyal employee. All they had to do was offer me a job.

In the meantime, Ryan started kindergarten again. We had him repeat the year. He was fine intellectually, but emotionally he was struggling. In the end he'd be the same age as the other kids when we moved home to Idaho. It was a difficult decision for us to make, but it proved to be the right one in the end.

We enrolled Grace in a part-time preschool for three hours a day, two days per week. True to her sassafras self, she preferred the company of others to good ol' M-O-M. She insisted on doing absolutely everything on her own, which of course made everything take four times as long. She was trying to spread her wings. I felt it was best if I let her.

I loved our new neighborhood on base. I made new friends, and ran into old ones. It was a place where impromptu hangouts and play dates were once again the norm. We'd often sit out front while the kids played in the yard, catching up and swapping stories with a half-dozen other families. I would miss the ladies of Twentynine Palms, but in the end, they too moved on to new duty stations.

It was good to be back at the School of Infantry. I was the Commander of Unit Leader Infantry Training Company, part of the Advanced Infantry Training Battalion.

My main responsibility included the training of squad leaders, platoon sergeants, machine gun leaders, assault men, anti-tank missilemen, mortarmen, and Marine Corps martial arts instructors.

I was part of a training team that was preparing small unit

leaders to deploy with their battalions; most of them were headed for Afghanistan.

Best of all, my fairly regular routine meant that I could spend more time with Kristine and the kids.

I had missed so much of everything while I was with a unit that was either deployed or preparing to deploy. Kristine worked really hard, and I knew that this was a time in which I could help her out, too. It was a good place to be.

51

Run Wild My Child

Fall 2011
Camp Pendleton, California

*F*ast forward. There was a year of changing diapers, giving baths, cleaning up, taking kids to sporting events, completing homework, making meals, doing laundry, and everything else under the sun that happens in the life of a normal family—Ross worked the normal nights (which would be considered late nights in the civilian world) and the occasional weekend, but we were still able to spend a significant amount of time together as a couple, and as a family.

It was the first time since George's passing that we enjoyed this kind of life. I lived in the dichotomy between my emotions and my expectations: hope versus experience. Part of me was in the honeymoon phase, welcoming home my husband and being grateful that the respite of his consistent presence gave me a break from the kids. The other part of me was still working on rebuilding our relationship and learning to trust him.

Like any couple with young children, we dealt with the regular challenges that came with parenthood, but in addition to that, we were still trying to come to grips with the fallout of losing our son.

Ross was a great dad, but he was an absentee husband. His priority was the kids, which I completely understood. I often felt his detachment from me. I wasn't sure if it was because he had endured such arduous combat in Afghanistan, or if it was from losing George, but Ross had changed. He became angry more quickly, and nothing would set him off quicker than having to interact with people who seemed more concerned with vapid Hollywood gossip than with the names and legacies of those fallen heroes who'd been killed fighting for the very freedom that allowed civilians to be able to take that sacrifice for granted.

We vowed to go on more date nights, and hire babysitters so that we could just focus on us, but more often than not, I felt like the Marine Corps made that impossible. Our usual routine included Ross falling asleep on the couch as soon as the kids went to bed.

Our marriage was strained, but at the end of the day, we still loved each other. We shared an easy comfort with each other, an unfaltering mutual respect; our physical connection to each other was always persistent. More importantly, we honestly still respected each other. It was going to take time, I knew that, but I was also worried. We didn't have time to sit down and work on our marriage together—we were too busy trying to work on life as a family.

To add to the strain, my relationship with Grace had turned into a daily contest of wills. Try as I might to let her do things for herself, it wasn't enough for her. She didn't even want me *watching* her do things.

It became problematic. We both needed a change in our relationship dynamic. At the beginning of the school year, she officially became a preschooler. I hoped that a little more time away from me would help ease the tension between us.

Now that both kids were in school, I took a deep cleansing breath and rededicated myself to finding a job. I spent a solid six weeks looking for work. Jobs were few and far between, but I was desperate for something, anything that would give me the mental stimulus I needed. I spotted an ad for a 30-day internship that promised potential to turn into a full-time position. It was at a fitness boot camp. I thought I *can do that*. The pay was crap (and even that kicked in after the internship), but at least I would be able to get my fitness on, plus pay for Grace's preschool. I knew if I were given the internship opportunity, I'd be hired.

I had spent the last six years at home, utterly separated from an identity as a professional. In place of this were the duties of a mother, and being known exclusively as my husband's last four. I wouldn't have traded those things for the world, but I needed adult interaction and an identity all my own. When I found out I got the job, I was so excited I almost came out of my skin.

The following spring, I decided to really start taking USMC Life more seriously. I was still volunteering on base and on the website, posting regular life events, news, and other stories to the site. I knew there was potential for more, though.

It was time to put my site, and myself, really out there. A military blogging conference was coming up, so I purchased a conference ticket, booked a hotel room, bought a plane ticket, and headed out into the wild blue yonder.

Everyone was extremely welcoming and kind. It was the perfect start to a new season of life, and I was excited to begin planting the seeds for things to come.

As summer grew closer, I knew I'd have to give up the job at the boot camp, a discussion I had with my boss before I became an employee: the pay wouldn't be enough to cover childcare for Ryan and Grace while they were out of school. The good news was that I was given the opportunity to come back in the fall.

Over the summer, I was going back to being Mom.

Part Five

Hold the Vision,
Trust the Process

*"Be Who You Are, Not What the World
Wants You to Be"*

—unknown

52

The Secret to Getting Ahead Is Getting Started

Fall 2011
Camp Pendleton, California

*T*he summer months flew by. As flip-flops flopped and watermelon seeds dropped, I realized that with USMC Life, I had the makings of my own perfect job. And I didn't even have to leave the house to do it.

I come from a family of entrepreneurs—both of my grandparents had owned their own companies. I wasn't sure, though, if I was cut out to be one, too. The timing was right, though, once the kids were back in school. *What do I have to lose?*

Grace began her morning preschool program once again. I used that time to work on USMC Life. I spent hours writing about life as a military spouse; I networked, built partnerships, taught myself about SEO, search engine optimization, learned how to build a website, and more.

There was much to learn, but I was incredibly motivated. My three precious hours of daily quiet time flew by. Before I knew it, my phone alarm would ring, reminding me that it was time to pick up Grace from preschool. Some afternoons, she and I would run errands, swing by a park or meet up with some friends for a play date. We'd make it home just in time to meet Ryan walking home from school.

Once home, I was back to my usual routine as a mom. There were after-school sports, household chores, dinner, and a whole laundry list of other normal mom tasks. But once the kids had bathed and eaten, it was time to get back to work.

And once they were in bed, I could really focus. I'd sit for hours on end, easily until 2:00 a.m.—it was my most productive time of the day. The amazing thing was that I didn't feel like I was working. I knew I was helping someone else on his or her journey in this life, and I loved that feeling. And slowly but surely, I was successfully building my very own brand. Unfortunately, that didn't necessarily translate into any income.

I treated every day as a workday, and I didn't take weekends off. If my husband was around and engaged with the kids, I was working. I easily clocked 70-hour weeks, but the most important and best thing about this was that I could pick and choose the hours that worked for me.

Working from home, I had the flexibility of taking care of our family while my husband provided financial security. I'd spent so much time under the frustration that I couldn't find a job. I should have realized that I was sitting in the middle of the perfect opportunity, if only I was willing to start a business. I was glad I'd finally realized what was right in front of me.

It wasn't all easy. Phone calls could be a nightmare. It was incredibly difficult to sound professional and polished when the kids were having some kind of meltdown in the background, or when the dog started barking. I did my best to schedule the important phone calls when I knew the kids would be away.

Ross completely supported me with the venture, though at times he would have liked me to take more time for myself, or even to find a paying job once again. Even though a few years had passed, there were moments, days even, when life was still very painful for me.

Still, working on my business allowed me once again to focus on something other than my grief. After a year of hard work, my site boasted about fourteen thousand monthly visitors. In my mind, this was a considerable achievement. That was more people than all the civilians and Marines stationed at Quantico put together.

But could I really make USMC Life into something more? Could I build a future doing something that came naturally to me?

A friend suggested that I apply for *Inc. Magazine's* 500/5000 Conference as a Military Entrepreneur Delegate. If I was going to take my business to the next level, I needed to get my head in the game, network more, and meet some new people. I applied and was accepted to the December conference in Phoenix, Arizona.

I met Courtney Walters McNeese, who opened Inc.'s doors to the military after watching an episode of *Oprah,* in which Oprah asked people to step up and do something to help out our veterans and military families. Courtney took up the challenge, and she has changed lives. She hired Natalie Thomas. Natalie was a fellow Boise State alumna. She managed the military entrepreneurs with finesse and charisma; later they would form a partnership: the McNeese-Thomas Group, for event and conference management.

The Inc. event was geared for the fastest-growing 5000 privately-owned companies in the US. It provided an opportunity for attendees to network and learn from one other. Among these were social media guru Guy Kawasaki, Bert Jacobs (the founder and CEO of the Life is Good company), astronaut Mark Kelly, and Simon Sinek, author of *Start with Why*.

Inc. rolled out the red carpet. They gave the military delegates VIP seating, special meet-and-greets, and more. I was paired with a mentor, Stephane Come, CEO of LCS Technologies. He sat with me, providing one-on-one advice on how to more effectively grow USMC Life with some hard-hitting business savvy. Stephane was generous with his time. He even surprised me with an iPad as a gift, just because! And all he got from me was a lousy T-shirt. But I was certainly grateful for his guidance and his insight.

The most invaluable experience was the ability to network with other military entrepreneurs. We began to collaborate and partner to help build one other's businesses.

I also brought on new writers at USMC Life, providing diverse points of view that augmented my own, and showcased them on the site. I even decided to kick off a podcast called *Semper Feisty Radio* with fellow military spouse Jackie Heatherman.

By January 2013, the time had come to render USMC Life an officially incorporated business. We weren't exactly planning on raking in huge profits at this point, but I needed to make things official so that I could deduct expenses from our taxes.

A few businesses had reached out, expressing their desire to advertise on the site in the past, but I hadn't been ready then. The number of inquiries kept on rising, so I finally took the plunge. I accepted my first advertising contract.

T-Mobile was my first sale. I began working with a number of other companies after that, too. It was awkward at first, trying to negotiate with these big companies on advertising agreements. I have never had an affinity for sales. But it was a way for the business to begin to recuperate costs, and maybe, just maybe—start to pay back my sweet husband's generous investments, as he had been footing the bill for my venture to help others.

I'd forged quite a lot of speaking experience before I'd married my Marine, so I set out to do more of that now. I booked my first event as the keynote speaker with Operation Homefront for an event in Honolulu. I was excited for the chance to talk to fellow military spouses. The entire event was designed so that military spouses could gather around and break bread, laugh, be inspired, share stories about life, and from that, gain new insight and perspective.

I stood in front of a room full of military spouses and, for the first time, spoke publically about losing George. There were tears. There were moments my voice faltered, but I delivered my address. My hope was to be able to share the idea that it's our perspective in life that defines us, not the bad things that happen to us. "I had a really big reason to leave my husband, but I had a million reasons to stay," I said. "I know that our lifestyle can be difficult at times, but it can also be amazing. We have to seek out those moments and live them up."

I had finally come to a good place.

These words resonated deep within me as I spoke them aloud before so many who, I was sure, could relate to what I was saying.

What happened next stunned me: The entire room stood to applaud at the conclusion of my presentation. So many came up to me after the event to thank me personally; it was an amazing experience. I was booked again for February in Las Vegas.

By April of 2013, USMC Life had reached a milestone of six thousand Facebook likes and approximately thirty-seven thousand monthly website visitors. I spoke to spouses on Marine Corps bases at my Live, Laugh, Learn events. I had so much fun interacting with military families.

Meanwhile, USMC Life was expanding on all fronts. I created a new position, hiring Ashley Strehl as my national advertising executive. She was integral to our moving forward, as advertisers kept knocking on the door to work with us. I also hired Kim Costello to manage the volunteers, and assist with social media.

I could no longer manage the business by myself: a good problem to have. The site had gained a tremendous amount of momentum, and I was excited to be a resource for helping so many people!

53

Courage, Dear Heart

★ ★ ★

Summer 2013
Quantico, Virginia

*I*t was time to move again: the ninth move of our marriage. Ross received orders to Marine Corps Command and Staff College. We relocated to Quantico, a Marine Corps base in Northern Virginia. I was looking forward to being close to our nation's capital, and for the opportunity to become more involved with the military community in the greater DC area.

At that time it was a shock to find out that my sweet dog Zazu had cancer. She wouldn't live another week. She was the source of so much love and happiness in my life; my constant. I guess somehow I'd imagined that she would navigate our military lifestyle along with us until the very end. But she wouldn't make it that far. It made the move all the more bittersweet.

While we waited for our household goods to arrive back east, we stayed with Ross's brothers on their farm in Virginia. The kids loved it there. They chased the guinea fowl and the chickens, were herded like sheep by their uncle's German Shepherds, and ran themselves to their hearts' content.

We celebrated George's birthday with a nice family dinner; something we could look forward to as our family grew throughout the years. The kids regularly talked about him, and Grace referred to him as her little brother, even though she was younger than he would have been. She always saw him as a baby, but she asked how old he would be if he were still here.

She never shied away from George's angel, the bronze casting by uncle Dean, which protected his ashes. Grace didn't understand that George's ashes were in that Lacewood box. She liked to place barrettes on the figure or wrap scarves around the angel's neck. She's still very connected to the idea of George, even though she never knew him.

I guess in the end, that's all we can hope for down here: to keep him alive in our hearts and minds.

Fall arrived; life kept moving forward. Grace started kindergarten and Ryan was in 3rd grade, his third school. Once again, while the kids were at school, I was working on the company.

Ross was able to carve out some time to coach baseball with a friend who had moved to Quantico the year before. We knew the Cohens from Camp Pendleton and were thrilled to reconnect with their family, to share meals and play dates.

While I was planning Ryan's birthday party, I re-membered how empty and alone I'd felt after the ma-jority of my friends left the Marine Corps at the end of their initial four years. But now just months into our new duty station, I discov-ered that two-thirds of the kids invited to his party were friends of Ryan's from our previous duty stations. I was thankful for our small Marine Corps, our tight-knit commu-nity. It was so cool that Ryan could stay connected with his buddies.

Earlier that month, I applied for and was accepted onto the Military Officer Association of America Military Spouse Advisory Council. The Council exists to serve MOAA programs and the military community. It was here that I began to get involved in legislation designed to protect our veterans and military families.

USMC Life continued to grow at a tremendous rate. At times it felt overwhelming, but there wasn't a day in which I didn't love what I was doing.

We were in a tumultuous time, and Congress was scrutinizing military budgets, but they wouldn't make any substantial cuts without some kind of process in place. They established and appointed the Military Compensation and Retirement Modernization Commission, MCRMC, to determine which benefits were important for military recruitment and retention; to identify which programs were successful and which needed to be retired.

The DOD, however, was pushing for budget cuts without waiting for the Commission's findings. It's funny how none of those budget cuts were inflicted on any of the massive corporations that lined their pockets with federal contracts.

The Friday before Christmas break, Congress slipped in a piece of legislation that took away retirees' Cost of Living Allowance, COLA, essentially taking away $100,000 or

USMC Life's booth at the Modern Day Marine Expo—Quantico, Virginia.
(from left) Ashley Strehl, Kari Cillo, me, Jackie Heatherman

more from retirees, depending on rank. It was a disgusting move for them to make, especially considering everything military families have been through.

I wasn't happy.

I knew others wouldn't be, either.

Our active duty military members did not have the right to speak out against what was happening to them. The day they signed on the dotted line, they had given all that away. As a military spouse, I knew I needed to do something, if only for the benefit of my own conscience. A small group of military spouses had floated the idea of holding an impromptu town hall meeting to discuss everything. I was on board. The first one was scheduled on December 12th.

After that first town hall, we formed a grassroots social media movement that we dubbed #KeepYourPromise. We eventually allied with several other organizations and individuals with sizable platforms, and we called Congress on the carpet through a big social media campaign with millions of people on Facebook, email, and 157 million Twitter timeline hits.

We wrote letters to our Senators and Representatives, and in the end we won by a landslide. The COLA amendment was repealed; it was a huge victory. We were able to connect nonprofits, for-profits, social media powerhouses, and grassroots initiatives together to fight for one purpose. That's what I call success.

54

Be the Voice for Those Who Cannot Speak

Spring 2014
Quantico, Virginia

We'd won a major victory, but military cuts were still coming. As it turned out, it wasn't just Congress we wrestled with. I could hardly believe the latest story from *The Marine Corps Times*. Sergeant Major Barrett, the Sergeant Major of the Marine Corps, had shared his thoughts about the pending pay and benefit cuts in a Congressional hearing. I was left frustrated and flabbergasted at his comments: "I truly believe it will raise discipline," he said of the proposed military pay cuts. "You'll have better spending habits. You won't be so wasteful . . . In my 33 years, we've never had a better quality of life," Barrett said. "We've never had it so good."

I had just returned from two days of storming Capitol Hill with other members of MOAA. Our primary focus had been on convincing Senators, Representatives, and their various staff members that a balanced budget shouldn't come on the backs of military service members. The Sergeant Major's words left me deflated. All the joy and enthusiasm from the past two days' events rushed right out of me. It was right there in black and white, but I couldn't believe it. Surely he had been taken out of context?

The next morning I tweeted the Sergeant Major, hoping for an answer.

I received a reply from someone else with a link to the video. I watched in disbelief. He hadn't been taken out of context. He testified to Congress in the Senate Armed Services Hearing on Personnel that service members actually needed to be paid *less*.

I couldn't stand by and do nothing as another ax came down on our military families. Unlike law enforcement and firefighters, we had no unions to represent us.

I wrote him an open letter, but unsure of any repercussions for Ross, I gave him a quick phone call. True to form, my Marine encouraged me to charge forward and not back down from the fight. As soon as I hung up the phone, my letter went live on the site.

By the following morning, my open letter had gone viral. *The Marine Corps Times* ran a feature article on both me and the letter, since it resonated with so many families. I received countless comments, emails, texts, and messages from people I knew and people I didn't know. Marines with whom my husband had served reached out with praise for the letter I'd written.

Marine Corps Times newspaper featuring the controversial statements made by SgtMaj Barrett and my open letter.

55

Purpose and a Plan

Spring 2014
Quantico, Virginia

Many people don't realize the kind of help military families need the most. Reconnecting as couples, not just after deployments, is integral to marriages. Most of us go home on leave to visit family, but these aren't vacations in any sense of the word. It's just more schedules and requirements piled into a shorter window of time, although it definitely comes with the bonus of being able to connect with our loved ones. It's not a break, though, and it's certainly not a vacation.

Ross and I needed to get away to spend some time together. The Marine Corps had been a harsh mistress in our marriage for over a decade. We needed to reconnect, to find a few moments to be together and just be us. No war. No kids to manage. No problems to solve.

Nothing on the agenda except each other.

And while our relationship was far from repaired, Ross asked if his mom could watch our kids over a long weekend so that he could take me to New York for my birthday.

It wasn't so much about New York as it was about taking an opportunity to see the nearby attractions at our short-lived duty station. We just wanted to spend some time together, to share some laughs, to explore together. It was one of the limited opportunities we'd get before we had to move again.

After all the bad blood, the arguments, the counseling—all Trina had to do was say yes; after all, she was retired. But she couldn't do that. But of course she wanted to visit, so she chose to fly in the weekend *prior*, in classic Trina style. Never mind the fact that she could have visited with us before or after our trip. That meant we were scrambling to find childcare so that we could get to New York the following holiday weekend.

I ended up asking our friend and former neighbor from Twentynine Palms, Amy Young, to see if she'd watch our children for the weekend. They were now stationed near Quantico. She and her husband happily agreed. I offered to watch their kids in exchange, hoping to provide them the opportunity to get away sometime, too. That's one thing I've learned in our military journey: military friends are there for you when your family just can't—or in this case —opted not to be.

With orders in hand for move number ten, it meant we were headed back to Camp Pendleton, and the warm Southern California sun. We had the most successful pack-out we'd ever had to date. This led me to believe something would go wrong, that maybe our furniture would catch fire as the truck made its way across the country, or that we'd run into another disaster.

That's when we crossed paths with the twin F-4 tornadoes as we drove from Chicago to Sioux Falls. We didn't know if we were driving into the storm, away from the storm, or where it was, exactly. It blew over semi-trucks and flooded roads. It was the disaster I'd been expecting and waiting for.

Spending the weekend with the Young family, former next door neighbors from 29 Palms, California

We eventually made it to Camp Pendleton, and settled into base housing, assigned just down the street from the house where we'd lived just a year earlier.

I was happy to be back in the fleet. I checked into 1st Light Armored Reconnaissance, 1st LAR, as the XO. I was the number two in command in the battalion. I synchronized the staff, administration, logistics, communications, and ensured operations were supported.

This position meant I was back to working long hours. I'd leave the house at 6:30 a.m., returning home just in time to give the kids a hug and kiss goodnight after 8 p.m. I'd help, trying to pitch in when I could, but I couldn't be counted on. Weekends were hit-and-miss, depending on the training calendar; I would get calls in the middle of the night whenever anything went nuts.

The burden of taking care of everything at home still rested on Kristine's shoulders: cleaning the house, doing the laundry, going to the grocery store, cooking meals, school lunches, helping the kids with their homework, driving them to and from their sports events and everything else in between, all while working a full-time job. I honestly don't know how she managed to do it. Even with all these responsibilities, Kristine had built USMC Life into something truly amazing. I had never been more proud of her.

October brought with it the official withdrawal of the Marine Corps from Afghanistan after the president declared that US major combat operations had ceased. The Marine Corps' Special Forces, MARSOC, known as the Marine Raiders, would continue to deploy to Afghanistan and Iraq despite this declaration. Alongside those Marines, a small contingent of infantry and other essential personnel would also be sent back to Iraq and Afghanistan in various advisory roles, but precisely how that would play out remained to be seen.

After everything I had been through, after all the deployments and challenges that came with building USMC Life, I didn't think anything could surprise me anymore. Funny: it took one little email to throw that idea out the window.

> "Hi, I'm with Bright Mountain. Can you put me in contact with the right person to talk about a possible partnership, or outright purchase of usmclife.com?

I reread the email a couple of times, letting the idea sink in. *Sell USMC Life?*

It was an interesting idea, for sure.

My gut reaction was *no way,* but I knew the conversation was worth having.

The truth was that I had absolutely poured myself into the website and its extension on social media, taking it about as far as I possibly could. The website had averaged over 2 million page views in the past couple of years. The Facebook page had grown to over 208,000 likes—we reached 2.5 million people a month. All this had been accomplished with organic traffic, only a few hundred dollars of sponsored ads, and one hell of a lot of blood, sweat, and tears over five years.

It was difficult to keep tabs on everything that was on my plate: I was the SEO expert, social media guru, content creator, and posts curator extraordinaire. I compiled data analytics, created and up-dated the media kit, oversaw advertising, and was responsible for my two staff members, Ashley and Kim. We managed 15-plus private Facebook groups that helped people dig into their respective com-munities, with ten amazing volunteers managing them.

But I knew that the website landscape always changed fast, and without warning. I had been maxed out for several months; I needed help taking the site to the next level.

The more I talked with Bright Mountain, the more it seemed like we were a good fit, both at the business and at the mission levels. Bright Mountain was interested in gaining a larger foothold in the military marketplace, and I was interested in having the support of a team of experts.

I was still hesitant. I had built this thing from the ground up. They wanted complete ownership of the endeavor, but they also wanted me to stay on for a number of years to manage the site.

I contacted two other large companies that I worked with

regularly, informing them that I was engaged in talks with a buyer. But then they suddenly began talking about buying me out, as well.

In an instant I was negotiating with three businesses about the acquisition of my company—it was exciting and nerve-racking to say the least. My new mission was to find the best fit, both for me and for USMC Life.

I'd spent years of my life building something purposefully designed to help others. I needed to know that if I sold, the mission I'd established would hold true. I spent several weeks going back and forth on my decision and second-guessing myself.

I received my first offer, following up with Bright Mountain the day before Thanksgiving. I took time to consider their offer, and followed up with the other companies to weigh their offers, and craft a strategy moving forward.

In the end, I decided Bright Mountain was the best fit for the company—and for me. I would still be able to carve out content according to my interests moving forward, and I still had flexible hours working from home, so that I could still support our family. They, in turn, would give USMC Life what it needed to transition into its next phase, while maintaining the site's integrity alongside their other properties; military, fire, and police websites. It was a win-win.

The acquisition officially closed on January 2, 2015.

56

There's No Education like Adversity

(Benjamin Disraeli)

Spring 2015
Camp Pendleton, California

Nothing teaches us more about life than the simple act of living through each day. The education I've been afforded as a military spouse, through 15 years of war, has brought its share of tough and surprising lessons.

There was a time when I felt my identity, my goals, and my dreams had been shunted by the ever-evolving mission of the United States Marine Corps. Looking back, I realize that I should have been more open to creating a new path instead of being so determined to follow one that was no longer realistic.

I've come to learn that the definition of who I am and the evaluation of my self-worth comes solely from me. I don't need the approval of others, or a label, to know that I've made a difference in the world.

Some people may think that losing my child has left me with a cold, intolerant heart. I think it simply gave me a low tolerance for bullshit. I refuse to let negativity take away any of my focus, time, or effort any longer.

I've learned that there are both givers and takers in this world. I made the choice to spend more of my time with the givers, with those who inspire me to do more, to be more. Takers are draining, and those relationships are worth letting go. I believe in fifth and fifteenth chances, but there comes a time when enough is enough. Distance can often be the first step in providing the peace necessary for discovering hope and fulfillment.

Some time has passed between the life we live now and all the therapy sessions we undertook with my mother-in-law. She has respected the boundaries we've set, but I still don't allow her to contact me through social media, email, or by telephone. When I'm around her, I try to be pleasant and kind. Anyone looking in from the outside would never notice the underlying scars.

It took me years to realize that a viable relationship with her wasn't possible. No matter what I did or said, she wouldn't be capable of understanding my perspective. To her I was just a worthless, second-rate actor, incapable of following her script.

My heart was bitter for a long time. She had inflicted immeasurable pain on me over the years. In a way, it was easier to forgive my husband, father-in-law, and step mother-in-law for the loss of my child than it was to even consider forgiving Trina for the things she had done. The others had made one mistake— one awful mistake—but they didn't have a longtime pattern of hurtful behavior like she did.

I see now that I was hypersensitive to her behavior. I whined too much to my husband about her. Truthfully, I was so hurt and confused by the pain she caused that I wasn't in a place to step back and view her through the lens of a woman with a disorder. All I could see were the problems she caused in our lives.

I have finally come to a point where I can honestly say that I have forgiven Trina. But forgiveness doesn't mean that I have to pretend things didn't happen. I learned this: it's more important to let go of the emotions that tie me to those wrongs.

It has been nine years since we lost George.

I think about our son daily. The truth is, I will never heal from losing him. I've covered my heart with whatever I could find to keep me functional. These Band-Aids help me get through life. None of us deserve tragedy, but I've learned that it's how we respond to life's adversity that shows us who we really are.

I made a conscious decision many years ago to try to be more than just the woman who had lost her child. I aimed to be someone who paved the way for others. That single focus gave me more than I could have imagined—an amazing project that has had a positive impact on millions of people's lives.

All I can do now is encourage others to dare greatly, to do the things my son never got a chance to do—to live for George. That's why I've started The Happiness Challenge. I'm encouraging others to join me in a weekly challenge, where simple tasks are completed that don't take up a lot of time. Each week is different, and with it, I hope others will find joy in the *pursuit of perspective* with me and live a fuller, happier life.

I'll never forget the good memories we forged with our son. I'm thankful for the too-short opportunity I had to be his momma and love on him. Even though the event of his loss has forced upon me the greatest pain I have ever known, it has also birthed an incredible gratefulness inside of me.

It has transformed how I perceive and live my own life. I find myself trying to be mindful and present each and every day. I relish the quiet moments with Ross, and I celebrate the small victories with the kids: my *pursuit of perspective*.

I've learned that sometimes, it's the simplest things we take for granted. I have the ability to touch, see, hear, smell, and taste. I'm alive. Many of our veterans have paid the ultimate price, and too many of them have returned home forever changed by the effects of war. What wouldn't they give to be able to see, or hear, or gain back a lost limb?

There will always be a special place in my heart for our military kids, who get drafted into this life by virtue of their parents. They love hard; they are the strongest, most resilient human beings I know. They have seen and endured more of this world than most adults, they've faced hardships few will comprehend, and all because someone—their someone—needed to stop the bad guys.

I count my blessings regularly.

Along with those blessings, I have received the most unexpected gift from the Marine Corps: my military spouse sisters. They are the ones with whom I shared meals, wine, stories, and extraordinary times. We raised our kids together, we became a village. We will be friends for life, and our community stretches across every branch in the military, every state, and several parts of the world.

And of course I'm grateful for my Ross, my loving husband. He gives his all to this country and for our family. He has supported me through all my crazy, harebrained ideas. He fully backed me when I decided to dig in and be a voice for military families, even when it was unpopular.

Now it's almost time for him to hang up his uniform for the last time. I know many see military retirement as something that's easily earned, done simply by pulling a trigger and putting in the time. He has missed easily half our marriage. He missed most of two pregnancies, and the birth of one child. He has missed his kids growing up, and countless milestones. His body is worn, and he has to live with the daily physical and psychological reminders of war.

He and his Marines have lived through the kind of hell many people wouldn't even be able to imagine, and they've done it not for awards, money, or fame, but for the guy on their left and on their right. It's a camaraderie that cannot be understood unless you've lived it.

As much as we want to dictate the events of our lives as they transpire, we're all navigating on the same sea, waiting for the storms in our lives to pass. I am confident that I can weather the future storms that cloud our horizon, holding tightly to my husband's hand. Together, we can navigate through the dark and celebrate the shining moments of life on the other side.

Today, I am exceptionally blessed to find myself in a peaceful place, both mentally and physically. It was easy to be swept up with the daily struggles of raising young kids, or even to allow the challenge of building my business get in the way of becoming a better me. Now it's Kristine, party of one, making reservations for the rest of my life.

And for the first time in a long time, I have hope that the future me will be better than I have ever been.

Ross received orders transferring him as an individual augment to Marine Forces Central Command with Task Force Al Asad.

He headed back to Iraq in April, 2015.

Once again, the Marines needed a few good men.

Once again, we would send ours.

And pray that he would come home to us.

Author's Note

After spending six months in Iraq, Ross returned safely in late September, 2015. Months later, he was selected for Lieutenant Colonel. While the Marine Corps sees great potential in him as a future leader, workups, training, and war have left him weary. Instead of accepting the promotion, he has made the decision to retire, and to spend time with his family before his kids leave home.

I started this book more than five years ago, after considering my grandparents' war and how the generations before us had wartime keepsakes of correspondence, stories, and mementos. Our generation's wartime correspondence has been almost completely digital, and I realized in considering the differences that our individual histories could easily become forever lost. I therefore set out to locate the emails from the past, and piece together my family's wartime communications to create a tangible memento we could share with our children and grandchildren.

Then suddenly the unthinkable happened: my computer crashed.

My hopes of synthesizing a written history of our family, of everything that had unfolded in our marriage during the longest war in US history, was in danger of vanishing in an electronic poof.

Thank God for good habits. I might have been a little naïve about the durability of my digital footprint, but I had always been pretty consistent about backing up my data. I dug through all the old files, painstakingly stitching together thousands and thousands of emails. Reading through them took me back through some of the best and worst moments of Ross's deployments.

With my plans for a book back on track, I began to fill in any gaps with my own memories. As I wrote, I found myself wondering what Ross had been doing in those moments and days (and sometimes weeks) in between our emails. I knew he was a Marine and an infantryman, but even after all the years we had spent together, I didn't really know what that meant.

I set out to interview him, but there never seemed to be a good time. There I was, trying to capture our journey, and there he was, constantly busy being a Marine and a father. But then fate, or rather the Marine Corps, stepped in with orders to Quantico. We left San Diego, Ross at the wheel, and me camped out in the front seat with my laptop.

For more than a week as we drove across the country, I interviewed my husband (he would say interrogated). I asked a million questions and took dictation as Ross recounted experiences he'd never told me about before. There were times when he grew frustrated with me. He just wanted to drive in peace, but I was on a mission. I'd joke with him, "Honey, we've got nowhere else to be." He literally could not get away from me!

In the end, it took another change of duty station and a cross-country move to get all the content for his sections in this book. He is a quiet man, particularly when it comes to his experiences as a Marine in combat. I'm indebted to my husband for his willingness to share his thoughts and stories about everything he has been through. Without him, this book would only tell half the story.

While I am under no illusion that our story is unique—many military families have endured countless deployments and dealt with loss on numerous levels—my hope is that this book will spark conversations. To my fellow military spouses: I hope this book will inspire you to talk to your service member and seek to really understand what it is they do every day when they button or zip up their uniforms, and head out to answer the call of duty. To service members: I hope you've received a glimpse at the sometimes-monotonous obligations and career pitfalls that face military spouses at home. This is a different kind of trial. To those outside the military community: I hope this book gives you a glimpse into military family life, and fully inspires every one of you to take the time and trouble to get out there to meet those in your community who serve and protect every day without fail. If you can do nothing else, strive to hire veterans and military spouses, and support legislation efforts that fight to keep the benefits and pay promised for retirees, veterans, active duty, and their immediate family members. Remember: #KeepYourPromise.

Finally, you may have noticed a lack of reference to female Marines who served alongside my husband. During the time in which these events took place, women were barred from serving in the infantry. That ban was lifted on December 3, 2015. You may also have noticed that the word Marine wasn't consistently capitalized throughout the book. That is because while American Marines are regarded as a proper noun, our foreign counterparts are not. Blame 240 years of tradition. And my editor.

Acknowledgments

There are many people to whom I am indebted to on this journey. First, I'd like to thank my amazing husband, the love of my life and my better half: there's no one with whom I'd rather share this journey than you. Thank you for loving and accepting me as I am, for making me a better person, and providing encouragement when I had given up. I appreciate your fantastic sense of humor, loyalty, and love. You're still the best man I know.

To my children: you have given me unfathomable joy. I'm blessed and proud to be your momma. Remember that I love you more than all the words—in all the books—in all the world. You make life worth living.

To the 1% who provide the blanket of freedom under which our families safely sleep, to our wounded warriors, and those who paid the ultimate price with their lives: "Thank you" is never enough. We live life fully because of you. Your sacrifices will not be wasted.

To my military spouse sisters: I feel as if I have monumentally failed in trying to convey the connection and friendship we have as a community; failed to describe the special village in which we've raised our families; failed to describe the volunteerism that the Department of Defense relies so heavily upon; for without it, I know without a doubt that the military would not be as successful as it is today. Know that your sisterhood and friendship is indescribable and has provided an abundance of happiness in my life. There are too many of you ladies to name individually, but your friendships mean so much to me—you know who you are.

To my military spouse brothers: thank you for building a special community and letting others know that you're out there, too. Thank you for your friendship, perspective, and advocacy work.

To my parents: thank you for raising me to believe that I can achieve anything I set my mind to do. Thank you for supporting our family and swooping in to watch the kids for military functions and business trips. I couldn't have done this without you! To my family: David and Cindy, Michael and Jen, thank you for embracing the crazy and making family get-togethers so fun and so memorable. I'm looking forward to raising our kids together in this next chapter of our lives. To my extended family: Thank you for making my childhood and life so memorable. GG Pat, I am blessed to have you in my life.

To my father-in-law, Rick: thank you for your loving heart and for marrying Charlotte. Ross truly did receive the greatest gift by getting fantastic new siblings in his 30s. To David, David, Ricardo, Jeanie, Tom, Gail, Ron, Kristin, Robin and family: thank you for all the laughs, amazing food, wine, and memories with your family. We will cherish these years for a lifetime.

To Chad and Trevor Estes: thank you for providing a compass and laying the groundwork to save our marriage. Your advice and love has truly been life altering.

To my Boise friends: thank you for making coming home so wonderful. I treasure the relationships we have, as well as those that our children share—here's to making new memories. To Christie, Christy, and Carina; thank you for all the support through twenty years.

To Stephanie Finnegan: thanks for giving me a home when I didn't have one. You'll always be like a sister to me.

To Mia Saling, my first military friend: I'm thankful for your support and friendship through the years. I'm pretty sure I'll never meet a classically-trained chef and attorney in the same package again; thanks for your professional help as an attorney to dot my i's and cross my t's.

To my mentor Jackie Franks: thank you for the twenty-five-plus years of encouragement and advice. You helped shape me into the person I am today.

To my dear friend Mollie Gross: thank you for all the laughs, encouragement, and the meetings of the minds over coffee. I treasure your friendship. Thank you for introducing me to Savas Beatie publishers.

To Karen Pavlicin-Fragnito: thank you for publishing me in *Stories Around the Table* and continuing to encourage my work alongside your expert advice. I'm grateful.

To my USMC Life staff and volunteers who helped pave the way for others: I'm grateful for your time and support. USMC Life would not be where it is today without you: Kim Costello, Ashley Strehl, Jenni Balbier, Abbey Bertolone, Charlotte Berry, Kari Cillo, Sarah D'Urso, Mandy Deines, Heather Elgie, Caroline Elizabeth, Carly Ford, Kristina Hammock, Jaclyn Heatherman, Theresa Laux, Brittany Marchetti, Rebecca Meyer, Kella Price, Rachel Martinez, Kristy Rose, Robyn Rimkus, Shannon T., Holly Vega, and Kristina Whitfield.

To my editor Chris White (C.P. White Media), to whom I handed a mountain of words consisting of emails, narrative, and anecdotes: You painstakingly read through every single email that passed between Ross and I over the course of four deployments, and so much more. I daresay you know our marriage more intimately than anyone else. You crafted me a beautiful boulder to refine and hone. Then you lovingly accepted it back after I reworked it. I'm indebted and grateful for your expertise and knowledge utilized in the final pass to complete the project. You helped me polish this gem into what I have today.

I rewrote, rewrote, and rewrote again. Thank you to Veronica Jorden (First Page, Last Page) who helped cut and refine my story into the gem I have today. I'm grateful for your patience, expertise, and the ability to harness the best in this project.

To Terri Barnes, thank you for inviting me to participate in *Stories Around the Table*, and giving my book the final look before it hit the presses.

To my cover designer, print and e-book formatters, Colleen, Chris, and Kella: thank you for your patience, and working with me to make this the best work possible.

To my Beta Readers, who provided feedback with notes and advice to help shape this book for future readers: I cannot thank you enough for your time and providing such invaluable insight.

To Andrew DeGrandpre: thank you for answering my email when I was just another reader. You gave me the encouragement to keep writing.

To fellow authors Angela Rickets, Karen Pavlicin-Fragnito, Mollie Gross, and Bob Hamer: thank you for taking the time to discuss your journey with me.

To my publisher Savas Beatie, and everyone there for helping me get my book into print. Thank you.

Finally, thank you to all the civilians and veterans fighting on behalf of this special community. Your advocacy work is not going unnoticed. In particular, I'd like to thank the leaders and writers in our community who help enrich and uplift others, who believe in the philosophy that there's room for everyone, and who connect and assist others.

Honor the Fallen

Pfc Nolen R. Hutchings, 3/23/03

Battalion Landing Team 2/1 Iraq
Operation Iraqi Freedom

Pfc Leroy Sandoval, Jr. – 3/26/04
Cpl Tyler R. Fey – 4/4/04
LCpl Phillip E. Frank – 4/8/04
Cpl Matthew E. Matula – 4/9/04
LCpl Brad S. Shuder – 4/12/04
LCpl Robert P. Zurheide Jr. – 4/12/04
Pfc Brandon C. Sturdy – 5/13/04
LCpl Scott E. Dougherty – 7/6/04
LCpl Justin T. Hunt – 7/6/04
LCpl Nicholas D. Larson – 7/6/04
Cpl Jeffrey D. Lawrence – 7/6/04
Pfc Rodricka A. Youmans – 7/6/04
LCpl James B. Huston – 7/2/04
Cpl Dean P. Pratt – 8/2/04
LCpl Seth Huston – 8/21/04
LCpl Michael J. Allred – 9/6/04
Pfc David P. Burridge – 9/6/04
LCpl Quinn A. Keith – 9/6/04
Cpl Joseph C. McCarthy – 9/6/04
Cpl Mick R. Nygard-Bekowsky – 9/6/04
LCpl Lamont N. Wilson – 9/6/04
LCpl Derek L. Gardner – 9/6/04
Cpl Christopher S. Ebert – 9/17/04
Mr. Abdel Noor Mohammed Sayyed Ali "Sammy"
– 9/17/04

Honor the Fallen

Task Force 2/7 Afghanistan
Operation Enduring Freedom

LCpl Layton B. Crass – 6/14/08
Pfc Michael R. Patton – 6/14/08
Pfc Dawid Pietrek – 6/14/08
Sgt Michael T. Washington – 6/14/08
LCpl Andrew F. Whitacre – 6/19/08
Capt Eric D. Terhune – 6/19/08
Hn Dustin K. Burnett – 6/20/08
Sgt Matthew E. Mendoza – 6/20/08
Mr. Mohammed Abaid Dawary – 6/20/08
SSgt Christopher D. Strickland – 6/25/08
LCpl Ivan I. Wilson – 7/21/08
Cpl Anthony G. Mihalo – 8/14/08
LCpl Jacob J. Toves – 8/14/08
LCpl Juan Lopez-Castaneda – 8/14/08
Sgt Jerome C. Bell Jr. – 9/19/08
Cpl Jason A Karella – 10/9/08
Cpl Adrian Robles – 10/22/08
LCpl San Sim – 10/22/08
Spc Deon L. Taylor – 10/22/08
Capt Trevor J. Yurista – 10/27/08

About the Author

Kristine Schellhaas's success as an entrepreneur and nationally known advocate for military families is the result of her unwavering passion, fearless commitment, and unique authenticity. Kristine has spent nearly two decades with her Marine, and has dedicated thousands of volunteer hours helping military families through five wartime deployments.

She and her recently retired Marine reside in the Pacific Northwest with their two children and their dogs. Kristine enjoys reading, good red wine with friends, and celebrating life.

To book Kristine for speaking or to discover more about her, please visit KristineSpeaks.com, or connect with her on social media.